D0898992

SIGHT, SOUND, AND SENSE

ADVANCES IN SEMIOTICS

General Editor, THOMAS A. SEBEOK

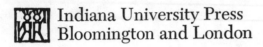 Indiana University Press
Bloomington and London

SIGHT, SOUND, and SENSE

Edited by
Thomas A. Sebeok

Published in Canada by Fitzhenry & Whiteside Limited, Don Mills, Ontario

Manufactured in the United States of America

Library of Congress Cataloging in Publication Data

Main entry under title:
Sight, sound, and sense.
(Advances in semiotics)
Includes index.
1. Semiotics—Addresses, essays, lectures.
I. Sebeok, Thomas Albert, 1920–   II. Series.
P99.S47   001.5   77–21520
ISBN 0–253–35230–4
1 2 3 4 5 82 81 80 79 78

Contents

PREFACE

Throughout the 1975–76 academic year, a pilot program in Semiotics in the Humanities, unprecedented in the nation, was undertaken at Indiana University with the aid of a generous grant from the National Endowment for the Humanities (EP 22467–75–375). The intent of the project was to inaugurate and facilitate the integration of semiotics into the curriculum of the Bloomington campus of Indiana University (with the cooperation of the Indianapolis campus).

The pilot program consisted of: (1) a year's lecture course, Signaling Behavior in Man and Animals, conducted by the undersigned under the sponsorship of the Honors Division, and open to qualified undergraduates and interested graduate students from any department of the university; (2) a series of lectures and seminars in connection with the course, offered by outstanding visiting semioticians, who also advised on the shaping of the eventual semiotics curriculum; and (3) a thorough survey of the Indiana University Library holdings in semiotics, with recommendations for relevant acquisitions of books and serials. This three-pronged development undoubtedly succeeded in increasing awareness among members of the faculty and in the university community at large of the usefulness and importance of semiotics as a general method of analysis, and in opening the way to the accommodation of semiotic studies into already existing curricula. We found that student interest was so widespread to begin with that our efforts were greeted in those quarters with animation and much more ready acceptance than by their conservative elders in the ranks of the administration and teaching staff.

On June 1, 1976, I submitted a lengthy narrative report to the National Endowment for the Humanities summarizing the results of the experiment. This statement was based, in part, on a very careful and exhaustive prior assessment of the overall impact of the program by a distinguished outside evaluating committee, which, in turn, reported to the Visiting Committee of our Research Center for Language and Semiotic Studies. Since curricula in semiotic studies are now also unfolding in other universities throughout the country, notably, Brown, Colorado (Boulder), and Vanderbilt, even in the Public School System of Brookline, Massachusetts, it may be worth mentioning that a limited number of copies of the final report, with extensive supporting documentation, including copies of the video-taped television interviews with six of the visiting speakers, can be made available through the facilities of the Research Center, which administered the pilot program.

Eighteen visiting speakers participated in this enterprise, some of whom gave several lectures. Thirteen of the papers, most of them revised, were then selected for inclusion in this volume. Some of the others have appeared, or will appear, elsewhere, in more or less modified form; they include:

Raymond Bellour (Centre National de la Recherche Scientifique), "Hitchcock's *The Birds*: Analysis of a Fragment," previously published (in French) in *Cahiers du cinéma*, no.219 (September 1968).

Erving Goffman (University of Pennsylvania), "Picture Frames," now incorporated in his monograph *Gender Advertisements*, in *Studies in the Anthropology of Visual Communication*, vol.3, no.2 (1976).

Henry Hiż (University of Pennsylvania), "What Do Stones and Bricks Have to Say: Meaning in Architecture," partially incorporated into his 1976 presidential address to the Semiotic Society of America.

Roman Jakobson (Harvard University and MIT), "Science of Sounds as Signs," to be incorporated in his forthcoming book (with Linda Waugh), *The Ultimate Constituents of Language* (Indiana University Press).

Sebastian K. Shaumyan (Yale University), "Linguistics as a Part of Semiotics," *Forum Linguisticum*, vol.1, no.1, but also to appear, in substantially enlarged form, in the Studies in Semiotics series (Peter de Ridder Press).

The choice of topic was left to each of our guests to determine, the only constraint being, of course, the overall theme of the program. Variety was desirable because we wanted to appeal to the largest possible segment of the university community, and, in fact, audiences ranged from about fifty to a thousand or more.

Semiotics can be informally defined as a science that studies all possible varieties of signs, the rules governing their generation and production, transmission and exchange, reception and interpretation. Concisely put, semiotics has two complementary, interdependent aspects: communication and signification. As I have delineated in a number of recent publications, semiotics is an ancient discipline, stemming from pre-Socratic clinical roots, which then led to the development of three fundamental semiotic traditions—the medical, the philosophical, and the linguistic—that have thoroughly intermingled at various periods in Western intellectual history, although there were times when they strove for autonomy. In the middle of the last decade, semiotics underwent a spontaneous and rapid international development that led to the emergence of semiotic workshops in Eastern and Western Europe, North and South America, Australia, Israel, and Japan. The influence of the semiotic method has variously encompassed or influenced all subjects commonly called "the humanities," most of the social sciences, some of the behavioral sciences, and even some natural sciences such as genetics, physiology, and, most notably, ethology. Although most often involving the "sciences of man" (especially the nomothetic sciences), semiotics has also become a powerful tool in animal communication studies. Further, one may speak of the semiotic behavior of machines such as computers.

This explosive development no doubt partially derives from the pressure and technological improvement of the mass media, in consequence of which the problem of communication has proved to be one of the most pivotal ones of our civilization. It is readily understandable, therefore, why so many disciplines were reoriented and have converged upon the study of the general laws of cultural and natural signification. Another pertinent factor here has been the emergence of a few charismatic figures at the turn of the century (e.g., Ferdinand de Saussure in linguistics, Charles S. Peirce in philosophy), followed by such creative contemporary synthesizers of their major traditions as Roman Jakobson.

No single collection, such as this one, can possibly claim to present a complete panoramic vista of so complex an area of human concern, with its venerable history and with so many disciplinary ramifications, as the doctrine of signs. Nonetheless, when read in conjunction with *A Perfusion of Signs* (Indiana University Press, 1977), one can gain a fairly comprehensive overview of current semiotic theory and practice, for these two compendia were meant to complement one another. The ordering of the contents was imposed by the editor after the fact. It is arbitrary. The essays can be sampled, at the reader's pleasure, and enjoyed according to any arrangement.

Now for some concluding words about the title of the present volume, *Sight, Sound, and Sense*. Since the Greeks proposed that the sign is constituted of two indispensable moieties, one *aisthēton*, "perceptible" or "sensible," the other *noēton*, "intelligible" or "rational," almost every semiotic model put forward since has retained this dual conception, labeled with one pair of terms or another. Accordingly, the last noun in the title alliteratively renders *sēmai-nomenon* and its successive transformations. The first two nouns split the Stoic *sēmainon* with a view to the two main channels upon which semioticians have lavished the bulk of their attention: the optical and the acoustical. It is important, however, to be mindful that these are but two out of the much vaster range of media of communication at the disposal of organisms, including particularly man. Some of them are discussed in a very recent book, *How Animals Communicate* (Indiana University Press, 1977); in much larger part, however, they constitute an endlessly fascinating area of research still on the threshold of man's scientific grasp.

The pilot program owed much to the help of Theresa de Magalhaes Calvet, Research Associate (now at the University of Paraiba, Brazil), and Margot D. Lenhart, Administrative Assistant in the Research Center. May Lee assisted, with her customary skill, in the transmogrification of the manuscript into print.

Bloomington, Thomas A. Sebeok
February 7, 1977

I. Historiography

Toward the Origin
of Semiotic

John N. Deely

I. THE PROBLEM

The "semiotic web" Professor Sebeok envisions takes its origin in the reality of public life—what Kendon (1972:443) calls "communication, a system of behavior patterns by which people are related to one another," or, as Sebeok himself (1975a:10) more precisely puts it, avoiding even the hint of a priori anthropocentrism: "the subject of the holistic field of interaction ethology (alias semiotics)."

Well, communication is not behavior, for not all behavior is communicative, and indeed behavior can be significant and yet fail to be perceived as such (cf. Eco, 1976:9, 23, 32). Not even signals, the most 'automatic' of all the semiotic *moyens*, perhaps, can infallibly guarantee their being significantly perceived in all cases.

The fact is that there is no *one invariant line* by means of which behavior can be separated into "a kind that communicates and a kind that does not communicate," for the irrecusable reason that one and the same event can fail and not fail to have significance at the same time in the here and now perceptions and sense impressions of any two distinct organisms of same or different species.

Nevertheless, of course, this random possibility, always present in a proximate way particularly in situations of possible gain by deception, is not at all incompatible with and in many ways presupposed to the historical development of distinct forms of behavior—distinct, that is, not only in function of conspicuous biological differences (e.g., the humanesque perception of the contrast between "animal" and "insect" life, despite the fact that insects are themselves animals), but also, as in the primate species, in *idiosyncratic, semiotically induced* differences such as Hockett (1965:36) once described as "evidence for culture of a rather thin sort among the hominoid apes," as also among waterfowl.

The attribution of culture in such cases, even of a "thin" sort, is a bit too much for some very well informed anthropologists to swallow[1] (and even Hockett [1965:36] admits "it is not clear in either case that it is the *communicative* systems of the species that are so transmitted"), but all are prepared to admit at least this much: that there is an *empirical ambiguity* that recurs in careful studies of the semiotic behavior of men and other highly developed mammalian and especially anthropoid species, an ambiguity sufficiently profound to occasion repeated claims by comparative psychologists and other students of animal lore to the effect that there are, at bottom, no essential traits of human sign-using behavior that cannot be illustrated in the behavior of non-human animals.[2]

How are we to account for this empirical ambiguity? That is the question I want us to consider in this essay. Is there something about the nature and being proper to signs that makes their function in social life ambiguous, or are such ambiguities as surround sign-using behavior merely the result of subjective deficiencies in perception?

If the former is the case, as the terms of the theory I will shortly expound will show, then, just as there is no one, invariant line separating communicative from non-communicative behavior, so will there be no empirically unambiguous example of sign-using behavior that will effectively and always contrast members of our own species with members of other related species on the evolutionary tree, or even with members of species from other galaxies or other parts of this galaxy. And yet, by grasping the reason in the nature of signs for their ambiguity in public life, we will still have a way of defining semiotically the line between men and animals.

II. BACKGROUND TO A SEMIOTIC APPROACH

Sixteen thirty-two is a year of great importance to semioticians. It marks the birth of John Locke, the man, as is well known, to whose work

Peirce principally owed the inspiration for his conception of semiotic as "the doctrine of the essential nature and fundamental varieties" of signifying (*Collected Papers* 5.488). It is also the year, as is not (yet) so well known, of the publication in Iberia of a work virtually lost heretofore, which has so far proved to be the earliest full-scale realization of exactly the doctrine Peirce envisaged (cf. Herculano de Carvalho, 1969: 131–32). I refer to the *Tractatus de Signis* of John Poinsot,[3] a treatise introduced by its author as being aimed at "explaining the nature and divisions of signs"—"ad explicandam naturam et divisiones signorum" (a formula amounting to a translation into seventeenth-century European school Latin of Peirce's definition of semiotic); or, as he puts it in slightly expanded form a few lines later, aimed at expounding "the two principal points concerning signs that must be considered, *first*, the nature and general definition of a sign, and, *second*, the classification of signs and the contents of each class in particular" ("circa ipsam rationem signorum duo principalia occurrunt disputanda: *Primum* de natura et definitione signi in communi, *secundum* de divisione eius et de quolibet in particulari").[4]

Now this distinction between the definition and the division or classification of signs, adverted to by both Peirce in his definition of semiotic and Poinsot in explaining the internal structure or scope of his *Tractatus*, is altogether fundamental and, I am inclined to believe, more important than has until now been generally perceived. I would go so far as to suggest restricting the term *semiotic* to the investigation of what a sign is as such, employing the term *semiotics* for the critical working out and comparative evaluation of divisions or 'classifications' of signs made now on this basis and now on that, in hopes of obstructing the common tendency (well noted by Greenlee, 1973:14) to bypass thorough consideration of what a sign *is* in favor of detailed analyses of this and that kind of sign—secondary concerns, of a certainty, inasmuch as such analyses always presuppose a range of implications, more or less consistent, in the notions of sign they deploy, which range demands explicitation all the more to the extent it is left unexamined (at least from the point of view of principle, theoretical elegance, and transparency).

But, without relying overmuch on this suggested piece of linguistic legislation (because of the huge improbability of its becoming generally adopted), we can see that while there is no *one* way of rightly dividing and classifying signs, but many ways, each legitimate from a critically aware point of view and superior or inferior in different respects,[5] there is *one* way (not, of course, *verbally* and empirically but indeed *conceptually* and, as it were, "ontologically") of rightly defining and setting forth *what a sign is, in the sense that* no definition of signs that excludes any one or part of the many possible classifications of signs can be considered fully valid.

Yet these tasks, though distinct, are by no means entirely separable. For how could one approach the task of defining what a sign is, unless one were already familiar with examples of signifying? And who can be familiar with examples of signifying without being aware of fundamentally different examples and varieties of signifying? Thus a critical classification of signs, though in principle never the only possible one, is nevertheless necessary as a preliminary to any attempt to define signs, which definition in turn (as we saw above) will serve to ground any classifications and measure their justice. Classification and explanation in this field (semiotics and semiotic, if you like) are related as provisional and (in possibility and principle, at least) definitive phases in the statement of a doctrine of signs.

Poinsot's *Tractatus* shows the original genius of its author in both these phases of investigation, it seems, though more crucially, of course, in the latter, foundational aspect. When I was invited to develop an essay on the origin of semiotic, I first thought of Poinsot's unique historical position and the innovative elements of his work retrospectively and prospectively viewed. I saw in the invitation an opportunity to deepen and extend the attempt to situate historically the thrust of Poinsot's *Treatise* (Deely, 1974b:876–905). However, when the invitation was followed by newsletters limning the scope of the program proposal out of which this volume developed and its theme of signaling behavior in man and animals, the philosophical side of me quickly bested the inclinations to pursue academic historical considerations in my presentation. My long-standing interest in evolutionary matters prompted me to re-interpret the phrase *origin of* in my title along, as it were, Darwinian lines; and I began to think of the *origin* of semiotics not in the sense of textual and authorship priorities (see note 9, below) but rather in the sense of the *semiotic behavior* that gave rise to the possibility of semiotic treatises in the first place. That is, I began to think in terms of the essential structure of the semiosis of mankind as it differs from that of the anthropoids and other animals generally, so far as this difference might be clarified by a consideration of the theoretical framework of Poinsot's work—the "doctrina" of signs.

Why is the sign, empirically considered, an ambiguous reality, susceptible of myriad classifications and transformations in the course of public life? More particularly, how do the terms of Poinsot's theory of signs, his semiotic and semiotics, assimilate this irrecusable fact of experience?

III. HISTORICAL EXCURSUS: SEMIOTIC AND SEMIOTICS IN JOHN POINSOT

Let me begin by summarizing briefly the terms of Poinsot's semiotic and his classification of signs, in order to show where they intersect with the problem of ambiguity posed above for present consideration. Then, with the intersections marked, we can explore the problem in detail in the light of Poinsot's theory.

Poinsot's work belongs to the period of Latin scholasticism, a milieu that had its origin in the sixth-century translations by Boethius of Aristotle's categories and its demise in the seventeenth-century stirrings of the national language traditions that roughly marked the end of medieval and the beginnings of modern times. Poinsot comes at the very end, then, of a linguistically unified and internally rich tradition that covers approximately eleven hundred years of our intellectual biography.

Throughout the medieval period, the dominant focus of semiotic concern was neither linguistic nor philosophical—though the currents were there—but theological (the sacraments of the Church as *signs*). The definition of signs that gave precision to this focus was the one essayed by Augustine in the fifth century and incorporated by Peter Lombard in Book IV of his *Sentences*, the universal medieval textbook after its completion c. 1150–1152. Augustine defined a sign as "something that, besides the impressions it conveys to sense, makes something else come into cognition."[6] Translating more freely, we can say that Augustine defines the sign as anything that, on being perceived, brings something besides itself into awareness. Thus Sebeok's observation (1974:240) that, historically, signs tend to be conceived of as sensible phenomena first of all, is certainly warranted in the period from which Poinsot's work comes.

In this context, the originality of Poinsot's semiotic first manifests itself in his taking exception to this all but universal way of characterizing signs as, not invalid *tout court*, but *restrictive* of our understanding of signs in an a priori way, i.e., in a way not warranted by sufficiently thorough attention to what is most central to our experience of the action of signs (semiosis).[7] For what is experimentally central and primary in our use of signs is not their being *sensible* but their being *relative*. Wherever there is in awareness "a representation of one thing not only for itself, but for another thing distinct from itself," there is the use of a sign.[8] What is essential to the sign, truly by *all* accounts this side of sophistry, is that it be *relative ad alterum;* but from this it does not follow that the sign, as such, must itself be something in the order of sensible phenomena—and, moreover, sufficient attention to our experiences reveals that the sensible signs of our perception, as something present in our awareness, *already depend* for that presence on something besides themselves, namely, on an *intraorganismic factor* (Deely, 1972a, 1975a: 90–94, 1975b:277–92), the perceptions and conceptions of things formed by the work of a cognizing organism. This work thus *already* produces something relative to *its* objects in just the way that some among perceived objects are relative to other objects as their signs—that is, as serving in awareness to make present something that they themselves are not. The idea that has horses for its object, for example: *horses* are not ideas, but *ideas* of horses cannot exist without making *horses* present in our awareness. The idea of a horse, in short, is entirely relative to its object; and so it is for all the products of mentation as such—imaginations, estimations, memories, concepts, percepts: they are not the objects that we cognize directly, but that on the basis of which the objects or whatever else that we cognize are present in our awareness. They are a source of the objective being of occurrences, without themselves being perceived preliminarily as "objective" phenomena in their own right.

These remarks, pregnant with not a few subtleties, contain the whole semiotic of Poinsot. Moreover, they open doors in epistemology—the philosophy of mind and knowledge—closed since the time of Descartes's identification of objective with ideal being, a move in which, unfortunately, even Locke as much as followed Descartes's lead. That, however, is another story; but it hardly seems too much to say that we have, in the confrontation at last between the account of ideas as pure signs of objects and the account of ideas as the first of all our objects of experience, an entirely new chapter in philosophical thought and the way out of the proclivity toward solipsism that has characterized modern thought since its origins in the seventeenth century.[9]

Sticking to our immediate concern, we may outline Poinsot's definition and division of signs on the basis of the above remarks, as follows. If we shrive the traditional, Augustinian definition of signs of its element restrictive a priori, and define signs strictly in terms of what is central to our experience of signifying, we shall not say that a sign as such makes an impression on the senses, but simply that it *makes present in cognition something other than itself.* Since a sign is something relative to another for a cognizing organism, Poinsot continues, signs may well be *divided* either from the point of view of their relativity to *what* they signify, or from the point of view of their relativity to the one *for whom* they signify. From the first point of view, they divide according to the foundation or *causes* of their relativity (understanding "cause" in the fundamental sense of dependency in being—in this case, as that on which the significant relativity proximately depends for its exercise) into signs based upon stipulation, nature, or custom: *signa ad placitum, naturalia,* and *ex consuetudine.* From the second point of view, they divide according as the foundation of their relativity is not or is itself an object of sense perception into what Poinsot calls formal signs (because they form and structure objects directly apprehended, constituting them as known, while remaining distinct from those objects) and instrumental signs: *signa formalia* and *instrumentalia.*

First a few more words on what is innovative about Poinsot's classifications of signs, before discussing his account of the relativity constitutive and definitive of all signs as such—his semiotic proper, the account of what it is for anything to be a sign.

The division of signs into formal and instrumental—the explicit thematization and appellation of this contrast—may well have been original with Poinsot. Certainly the aspects of experience brought together in this designation had already begun to be discussed in what appears to us as a generally semiotic context at least as early as William of Ockham (d. 1350), and probably much earlier. Whether Poinsot's actual terminology here is to be found in some other and earlier authors is an historical question that cannot be answered decisively at this time. Preliminary researches of my own have turned up no traces of such usage, and certainly, once one sees how directly the classification of formal signs follows from Poinsot's criticism of the a priori element in Augustine's definition, which was accepted as standard throughout the milieu of the Latin scholastics, it would not be surprising to find that we have here a neologism, so to speak, of Poinsot's own coining.[10]

For present concerns, however, it is his other division of signs into

natural, customary, and stipulated that holds the greatest interest, because it is this division that takes us straight into the empirical ambiguity of semiotic networks. In our experience, the contrast between what
Poinsot calls stipulated and natural signs *arises out of* and *passes back
into* the reality of customary signs. As we shall see, it is just this *experi-
mentum* that Poinsot's semiotic enables us to explain. Customary signs
are the particular sort of signs that provide, in function of the sort of relative being proper to all signs as such, the interface between nature and
history, the structure and cement of cultural traditions as something
added to the social life of anthropoids.

The distinction between *signa ad placita* and *signa naturalia*, nom-
inally considered, is not by any means original with Poinsot. It comes
to him from a long tradition of medieval semiotics and was already
present in the semiotics of Roman stoicism, the *Cratylus* of Plato, and
throughout Aristotle. In our own American-English heritage it has
come down to us most commonly as the distinction between "conventional" signs, on the one hand, and "natural" signs (clouds–rain; smoke–
fire) on the other. This usage, in turn, goes back principally to the social
contract theories of seventeenth- and eighteenth-century philosophers
in England and France, taking deep root in our own political and social
heritage from those philosophers.

Yet the long history and widespread usage of this distinction is,
when it comes to Poinsot, almost sure to be misleading. Here, as at all
points in his treatment of signs, superficially traditional and common
terminology has had its sense transformed by employment in the wake
of his account of the relativity constituting the being proper to signs in
cognition. Few terms (perhaps only one—the traditional term *ens
rationis*) better illustrate this than the present example. Poinsot would
find the conventional–natural dichotomy of modern languages simply
insufficient to support a minimum critical understanding of either the
common ground or the dividing boundary between human and animal
semiosis. For this, a trichotomy at least of sensible signs is required; for,
while several animals emphatically do use signs that are *conventional*
(Maritain, 1957:90–91; Sebeok, 1975b:90–91; von Frisch, 1954, 1967;
and many others), they do not use signs that are, in Poinsot's sense,
ad placitum.

Thus, in Poinsot's semiotic, any simple dichotomy between the *signum ad placitum* and the *signum naturale* is misleading, bound to ob-
fuscate and probably miss what is distinctive in the semiotic contrast

between men and animals; for it is in the twilight zone of the *signa ex consuetudine*, whence natural, "conventional," and stipulated signs alike arise and return, that anthropo- and zoosemiotics merge and define a common ground.[11] The signaling behavior of the higher animals has its origin here.

Leaving the extended consideration of Poinsot's *signum ex consuetudine* to the following theoretical and main section, therefore, let me conclude this historical excursus with a brief statement of Poinsot's explanation of the being common to signs as something relative, for it is this in the end that governs all the other elements of his theory, including, as I have said, his twofold classification of signs.

The discussion of relative being in the Latin West goes back to the seventh chapter of Aristotle's book of *Categories*, translated and commented upon by Boethius in the sixth century A.D. (Krempel, 1952). The gist of that discussion, as it culminates in Poinsot, may be summarized as follows.

A being can be relative in two distinct and exhaustive senses. When something is said to be "relative," the thing referred to may be either (1) an individual that requires for its full intelligibility the bringing into account of other things besides itself—e.g., a dent in a previously undented garbage can "refers" to something besides the garbage can, even though the dent is in and is not at all distinct from the can itself ("non est forma adveniens subiecto seu rei absolutae, sed illi imbibita, connotans tamen aliquid extrinsecum, a quo pendet vel circa quod versatur," Poinsot would say); or (2) a relation considered precisely as a supra- and intersubjective reality existing between though quite dependently upon at least one of two or more individual existents. Anything that is relative must be such in at least one of these ways;[12] and so the problem of signs' relativity as signs comes down to the question of which of these two conceptions circumscribes the relative being constitutive of the sign as such.[13] Taking over the terminology current in the Latin tradition from Boethius' day, Poinsot designates the former relativity as *relativum secundum dici*, or (synonymously) *transcendental relation*;[14] the latter relativity he designates as *relativum secundum esse*, which I translate as "ontological relation."

Ontological relation, as Poinsot understands it and makes of it the ground of signifying, is closely related to the notion of "external relation" as it has come to be familiar in recent times, particularly through the work of Bertrand Russell. That is, by identifying the relative being proper to signs as ontological rather than transcendental, Poinsot makes of signifying an intersubjective reality that overcomes and unites the otherwise isolated individuals making use of signs ("in whom those signs are founded"). But for Poinsot what is decisive about ontological relation is its indifference to being caused by or caused independently of the activities of perception and conception—what I have elsewhere characterized as "the functional equivalence of real and unreal relations in perception" (1975a:96–97) and "indifference to subjective ground" (1974b:870, 1975c:486). It is this fact, true only of pure relations, that explains the empirical ambiguity of signs, as well as (or what is perhaps the same as) their relative indifference to the physical reality of what they signify (Deely, 1971b, 1972a,b, 1975b:276–92): a given relation, formed once by nature, another time by mind, is equivalent for signifying precisely because the relation is in either case an intersubjective mode of being, having its proper reality in the union of two (or more) otherwise distinct objects.

When one realizes that, for two hundred years before Poinsot (Ockham to Suarez) and for another two hundred years after him (e.g., unanimously in the works of Hobbes, Locke, Berkeley, Hume, Descartes, Spinoza, Leibniz, Kant), the reality—i.e., the possible mind-independent character—of external relations was flatly denied in the mainstreams of modern thought (Weinberg, 1965: esp. 112–16), one begins to suspect something of the revolutionary potential of his account of signs. But that again is another story.[15]

To see in detail how Poinsot's identification of ontological relation as the being proper to signs accounts both for their empirical ambiguity and for their differential (as well as for their common) function in human and animal semiosis, it suffices to concentrate on his account of customary or "behavioral" signs (*signa ex consuetudine*) as they merge and contrast with natural and stipulated signifyings.

IV. THE AMBIGUITY OF SEMIOSIS AND THE *SIGNA EX CONSUETUDINE*

Signaling behavior in men and animals, the theme of these reflections, takes one straight to the center of semiotic concern. Taking signaling in what I believe to be the most ordinary, or at least paradigmatic, sense—the sort of information passed by semaphore, between

merchant marine vessels during World War II—at once brings us into
the realm of what Poinsot terms *signa ex consuetudine*, habitual signs,
the signs by which one anthropoid population develops a sign-system
which, while not impenetrable to outside interpretation and understanding, is easily recognizable as an "in-group" or even "ethno-centric"
sign-system. It is a "private language" in the only real sense of "private"
—something that, while not immediately available in interpreted terms
from A to B, could of course become so *if* sufficient critical control were
exercised by B (or A, for that matter) over its objectification—the sort
of thing demonstrated, e.g., in the work of Altmann (1968), Carpenter
(1969), and countless other careful students of animal behavior.[16]

The operation of these signs defines or roughly circumscribes the
animal populations—such as dolphins, some dogs, certainly men and
apes—that are most interesting in the contrasts they provide to the in-
nate, or genetically endowed and determined, perception–pattern–response mechanisms found in numerous (far more numerous) other
species of animals, ranging from ducklings to the astounding array of
the insect (or "exo-skeletoned") animals.

Yet, as the naturalist thinks more and more about the semaphore
example, it illustrates certainly a *form* of behavior that is by no means
confined to the historically more versatile species and forms of biological
life. Many are the gene-dominated systems of display that function in
exactly semaphoric ways, from the sexual display of the peacock to the
million other "trigger mechanisms" that define populations all the way
up, down, and across the scale of sexually compatible, cross-fertile biological populations.

This brings out the first decisive ambiguity in the category of customary signs: the need for distinguishing them from *signa naturalia*, the
signs that seem connected to what they signify in ways that, while no
doubt historically conditioned (since the world, as distinguished from
what could have been the world, *is* history), yet fall fully outside the
social control of the group perhaps even genetically determined to use
them in reflex or "semaphoric" ways.

For higher animals, for the anthropoid and many mammalian populations, let us say, clouds and rain, smoke and fire, the favorite examples
of semioticians throughout the New and Old World periods of philosophical semiosis, serve perfectly well to illustrate the sort of natural
relation constitutive of the *signa naturalia* involved even in trigger or
releasor mechanisms of sexual and predatory animal behavior.

How is this so? While the display of peacocks, let us say, may serve immediately as a trigger from organism A to B, it is not at all in this way that, from Jones to Hati, clouds are signs of rain. Here experience intervenes, there it does not: how can the two be put on a par?[17]

Because, Poinsot demonstrates, if one is sufficiently patient in the analysis of *the way* experience intervenes in the constitution of behavioral, or customary, signs (*signa ex consuetudine*, the signs based on experienced associations of X and Y as constant relative to Q), one will be able to see how they differ from *all* objectively natural signs, regardless of whether or not experience intervenes in the apprehension of what is natural about the signification. For what is "natural" about the designation of a sign as "natural" in the experience of its difference from a *merely* consuetudinal sign is this: among the signs that have a relation to what they signify dependently more upon experience than upon the genetic constitutions of the organisms for which they signify, some turn out, upon sufficiently controlled observation, to be connected with what they signify *entirely due to the social action* whereby they became signs (became assimilated as relative within cognition) in the first place; while others, in addition to being conjoined to something signified through experience, also turn out—or so give every reason to believe—to be conjoined *antecedently to and partly independently of* our experience of their conjunction. Thus they are natural signs—*signa naturalia*—in precisely the sense that releasors, as we observe their function, signify something as related in but on a ground antecedent to (independently of in this sense) our or any other organism's awareness of the connection.

This clears the way for recognizing, within the class of consuetudinal signs common to the populations of higher anthropoids, i.e., defined by the acquisition of significance largely as the product of the experience of social interaction, the inevitability of a *natural overlap* or *mutual penetration* of the semiotic fields defined by "natural" (gene-dominated) and "social" (experience-structured) semiotic behavior: for, as elements of experience become assimilated through cognition to other elements of experience, it will not necessarily be apparent whether the source of associations and sequences is at bottom society alone, organic disposition ('heredity') alone, or society and nature "in collusion" (as Poinsot describes the naturally determined interactions that lead to objectification in cognitive life[18]).

Even when it is due to society alone, the process of assimilation of

X through experienced behaviors to the status of *sign* of Y may take place so unobtrusively and on the fringes of thematic consciousness that it transpires entirely 'naturally', i.e., *as if* independently of conscious awareness: for so it is indeed relative to the consciousness of *any particular one*, and to that of the many (*"das Man"*) who have "better ways" (or at least more commonly absorbing ones) to occupy their attentions than reflexion upon socialization processes as such (hence the "cultural unconscious" [White, 1973:163–78]).

Thus we see that the ambiguity in the type of signs circumscriptive of higher primate behavior is not something that can be entirely remedied or defined away: to signify consuetudinally is to signify naturally, not of itself, but in respect of those for whom the connection is established; nor is it unusual for two modes of signifying to attach to the same thing under different aspects of its objectification.[19]

Here we arrive at the semiotic boundary between what Poinsot calls, in the quaint term of the old scholastics, "brute" and human animals. It is here that Poinsot's semiotic defines an interface between the activities and attainments of perception as such, and the peculiar work of human understanding in the spinning of semiotic webs.[20]

Consider the sort of creative activity whereby laws are enacted, or that whereby conquering neologisms are introduced. A neologism—such as was Aristotle's sense of "substance" added to the consuetudinal force already attached (by earlier Greek society)to οὐσία, or such as seems to have been Poinsot's *signum formale* category in the usage of European society both before and after 1632 (the year of the publication of his *Treatise*), or Teilhard de Chardin's "biosphere" (or indeed Locke's "semiotic")—is precisely a new classification, a new shaping, of things, and it is obviously bound up with the free initiatives, the "stipulations," of its originator, just as laws re-define and order things according to authoritative stipulations. To illustrate: Before Aristotle, there may have been what Aristotle stipulated "substance" to refer to (yet it was not there as an object of thematic awareness before Aristotle). But "substance" in Aristotle's sense, or the term *substantia* that came from οὐσία in the cultural traditions of the Latin West uniquely as a result—so far as critical control of sources is able to maintain—of Aristotle's work: this is considerably more than a *signum ad placitum*.[21] It carries a freight of history and functions in the traditions of Latin Aristotelianism as a *signum ex consuetudine* as well as *ad placitum* (with the further ambiguities that implies).

The same remarks extend, *mutatis mutandis*, to each of the above examples, or to whatever others.

We have here the second of the two ambiguities in the class of signs we experience *ex consuetudine*: the need for distinguishing among them as now *ad placitum* and now relatively *naturale*, or functioning in this segment of the population predominantly one way and in that segment of the population the other, now at this time, now at that time.[22]

What is the basic contrast between a *signum* as *ad placitum* and a *signum*—rooted perhaps in one and the same objectified physical thing —as *ex consuetudine*, on the way to becoming or already established, within a given population, on a par with clouds as signs of rain and even with releasors and trigger mechanisms?

A *signum ex consuetudine* acquires or retains (as the case may be) the dimension or status of *ad placitum*, we may say as a first approximation, to the extent that an individual or a group exercises conscious critical control over its objectivity and mind-dependent status *as such*; while that same *signum*, to the extent in its *ex consuetudine* functioning that it falls outside the critical control of our society or group *precisely as including ourselves*—be we pumas, arboreal apes, lemurs, dinosaurs, or "men"—that same sign *ex consuetudine* is a *signum naturale*.[23]

Critical control of objectivity, then—a notion our remaining paragraphs will put in sharper relief—is the key to the *human* world of names for things. (I choose the case of names specifically only in view of the texts from Poinsot that will be cited and developed just below. The specific case of descriptions would do equally well [Deely, 1972a: 41, 42–43, 1975b:278]; for, generically, what is at stake here is any use of *signa ad placitum* or *ex consuetudine*, of which namings happen to be but the simplest instance, depending more principally on what is stipulated than on what is conventional about their significance.) For *a thing's name*, as an element of human language *ad placitum*, is what Poinsot calls an *impositio*, while that same thing's *name*, as an element of human language *ex consuetudine*, need be no more than what he calls a *comparatio* (an employment of a term or terms that can be made, for practical purposes, "sine discernendo relationem fictam a reali"[24]).

Here is Poinsot's description of the difficulty. As a matter of daily experience,

> we see non-human animals moved by signs, as well by natural signs, such as a groan, bleating, call, etc., as by customary signs, as a dog customarily responds when called by name, yet without understanding an imposition, but moved by custom.[25]

The functioning and use of customary signs among animals is guaranteed by the fact that some non-human animals are capable of learning by experience, and do not initially perceive some things that

> afterward, when a customary connexion has been established, they do perceive—for example, a dog is not automatically livened when he is first called by this or that name, though afterwards the name does come to elicit a regular response. Therefore non-human animals make use of signs based on custom; for they are not moved on the basis of the imposition itself of the name, because they are not aware of that imposition which is dependent upon the stipulation of the one doing the imposing.[26]

To this a behaviorist would be inclined to say: So what? Frequently a human animal fails to understand a word on first hearing, and then afterwards is conditioned to understand it. There is no ground here for distinguishing between animals that grasp relations between signs and signata also as based on stipulation (human animals) and animals that grasp those same relations only on the basis of some other form of reinforced association (brute animals). For children, too, do not learn their names from a first hearing, but must be accustomed (conditioned) to them.

But, for Poinsot, the elevation of a customary sign to a stipulated status is not a question of *when* the relation of sign A to significate B is grasped—from the first or only after repeated efforts—but of *how* it is grasped: "discernendo inter ens verum et fictum," vel non.[27] (One could also approach this conclusion by an analysis from the side rather of the sort of cognitive ability at play in the circumstance, in terms of how objects, including sign-objects, are *graspable* by an organism of a given type [Deely, 1971a:55–83, 1973:134–36].) When a customary sign in the strictest sense, a sign wholly dependent for its being on social interaction, is seen *precisely* by a given organism as a *mind-dependent* being in some *pure* respect, set off against nature as what is as against what is not dependent upon our perceptual and conceptual activities—the work of our minds—then, and only by that act of insight, does the *signum naturale ex consuetudine* acquire the added and distinct dimension of a sign *ad placitum*, i.e., a *signum* expressive of the way things are more dependently upon than independently of self-conscious awareness.

Thus, the clarification of Poinsot's notion of *signa ex consuetudine* as something common to the semiotic behavior of higher anthropoid populations uncovers two fundamental differences underlying the variety of signs present in the experience of those populations. On the one hand, there are signs related to what they signify in our experience, only some of which seem entirely dependent thereon: and this is the difference between *signa ex consuetudine* simply speaking and *signa naturalia*. On the other hand, among the signs that result from experience alone, some are recognized as so resulting, while others are not discriminated at all in their contrast with natural signs: and this is the difference between *signa ad placita* and *signa ex consuetudine*.

Here, then, we have the difference introduced earlier between a given sign known now owing to an imposition, now owing to a comparison. When a sign is known according to an imposition, that sign is a mind-dependent being recognized as such. But when a sign, though perhaps a mind-dependent being, is known solely because of a comparative perception of environmental features (acoustical, visual, etc.), its mind-dependent status need not be recognized as such in order for it to elicit quite determinate and 'satisfactory' practical responses. Thus, says Poinsot, we do not deny to non-human animals the grasp of stipulated signs on the grounds that they are unable to relate names to objects named, since this they unquestionably do, but "for want of their grasp of universality, because they do not cognize the more universal reasons by discriminating between true and fictive beings,"[28] though they do indeed grasp less universal reasons by discriminating between what is to be sought and what avoided (what the scholastics called 'accidental universals'—*universale quod pertinet ad accidentia alicuius rei existentis*, or *universale quod est accidens* [Deely, 1971a:55–83, esp. 72–76]), and materially employ in this light fictive beings as *means to ends* of vital preservation and well-being, not only in the pretenses and deceits of animal 'lying' (Sebeok, 1974:243, text and fn.82), but in the many forms of adaptive camouflage (Huxley, 1942: chapter 8) and problem-solving (e.g., Harlow, 1959: esp. 44–45), and even in the use of wholly arbitrary or "conventional" symbols (Maritain, 1957:90–91; Sebeok, 1975b:90–91): "quod est cognoscere non formaliter id, quod in ratione entis fingitur, sed materialiter id, ad cuius instar fingitur, quod in se non est."[29]

Yet the human animals, through their senses and by their habits, remain animals; and the order of stipulated signs as a semiotic region or zone restricted (so far as presently known biological forms go) to *homo sapiens*, is also, by custom, extended beyond man to whatever brute animals are brought into sufficient contact with us that they take comparative note of our conduct and adapt accordingly. In this way, the creative intrusions of individual genius, such as neologisms witness, just as the decisions of legal authorities, become established as part of the historical consciousness of a group rooted in its own customs and lifeways. Individual discovery is assimilated and socialized in the patterns of this or that society and civilization; what has its origin in the mind becomes through custom relatively independent of the mind and "naturalized."

> Essentially, the sounds of human language only signify through stipulation, though incidentally they signify from custom, which is to signify naturally not of itself, but only in respect of those among whom the custom is established. Nor is it contradictory for two ways of signifying to attach to the same thing according to distinct formalities. Whence when the one is removed the other remains, so that the same sign is never formally natural and stipulated, although they are the same materially.[30]

Thus we speak of English and German as "natural languages" (*ex consuetudine?*), in contrast to the "artificial languages" (*ad placitum?*) of the symbolic logicians. Yet what is artificial to the non-logician is a system of constructs the logician feels at ease in; and English in the hands of Shakespeare abounds in artifice. Yet *Hund* to the German is as natural a sign for *chien*, as *dog* is to the Englishman; while clouds are signs of rain for all anthropoids:

> For when it is said that a natural sign signifies the same for all, this is understood of something that is a natural sign simply. . . . Custom, however, is as another nature, yet it is not itself nature, and so it signifies for all those among whom the custom prevails, not for all without qualification. In this way a customary sign is something imperfect in the order of natural signs, just as is custom itself something imperfect in the order of nature.[31]

V. CONCLUSION

These insights drawn from the semiotic of John Poinsot cast, I believe, an unusually clarifying light upon such standard remarks of contemporary anthropology as these by Harlow (1959:44):

> The existence of a human-type culture is dependent upon learning capability and the capacity to transmit this learning to subsequent generations. Without language the capacity to transmit previous learning is dependent upon either such forms of imitative learning as we have described, or a simpler type of learning in which the infant follows the

group, and the movement and behavior of the group are such as to place the infant repetitively in the situations where the infant learns by direct experience the danger responses or affectional responses essential to individual and group survival.

The terms of Poinsot's theory enable us to grasp the origin of the human world in a semiotic act—the act of insight into the mind-dependent status of certain signs as such (Deely, 1975a:94–96, 98–99; Maritain, 1943:191–95, esp. 194 fn. 2, 1957:88–91; Poinsot, 1632)—that is in itself not empirically observable but is rather *that on the basis of which* the empirically observable is apprehended, here as it derives from the workings of nature, there from the workings of mind.

The effects of such insight—response to and the further development of truly *linguistic* signs—of course, are not unobservable empirically, and are so closely connected with the unobservable act of insight with its formal signs (being the *expression* and fullness thereof) that we are, at one level, almost inevitably inclined to mistake the two (e.g., Brown, 1958:82–83, 102–103)—a procedure that becomes a veritable matter of principle in the "pure" versions of behaviorist semiotic (e.g., Osgood, 1953:410, 681).

This original potential for semiotic ambiguity—the origins of semiosis in formal signs inaccessible to external sense—is further compounded by the process of assimilating *ad placitum* usage to the world of customs, which begins just as soon as insight expressed in sensible signs begins to enjoy the least measure of social success. Through this assimilation the achievements of one or a few become the heritage of many, available in subtly transmogrified forms not only to men, but to animals that perceive with interest the behavior of men.

It is in terms such as these, I believe, that semiotics insofar as it is influenced by Poinsot's account will advance in decisive ways our understanding of the human mind, its relations to nature, and its dependence upon history and cultural traditions.

NOTES

1. Leslie White (1959:74), in his "Summary Review" at the end of the volume containing Hockett's essay, takes exception to such assertions.

2. It is not a question here of whether such claims are or have ever been valid from a sufficiently sophisticated critical standpoint. (The answer to that

question is no: see, *inter alia,* Deely, 1975a: esp. 94–95, 98–99; Sebeok, 1975b: esp. 88–89.) What is of interest rather is the *depth of the ambiguity* attested by the fact that such claims are dissoluble only by the most refined critical techniques, and are no sooner rebutted in one formulation than they are reasserted in another.

The general character of this complex and troublesome source of ambiguity has been well limned recently by Sebeok (1975b:90): "A fair sample of the most commonly acknowledged and utilized signs—including signal, symptom and syndrome, icon, index, symbol, and name—were subjected to detailed scrutiny, particularly in the light of recently accumulated data on non-verbal communication, with the unexpected result that every type of sign thus analyzed has been found to occur in the animal kingdom as well as in human affairs."

3. The description of Poinsot's *Tractatus* as a "virtually lost work" is not excessive, despite the fact that certain secondary elements from his account of signs, as I will describe in note 10 below, have come in very recent times to attract some interest. For, in the very limited circle of those aware of the existence of Poinsot's account, none that I have been able to find have drawn upon it in such a way as to exhibit its systematic origins in and the dependence of its various elements upon the prior account of relative being (from which also hangs the notion of *ens rationis*). This is a somewhat surprising fact in view of Poinsot's quite explicit insistence upon this point both in his Foreword to the *Treatise* at 642a24–37, esp. 642a30–37, and in his opening paragraphs and most formal statement of the thrust of the *Treatise* in Book I, Question 1, 646b16–45, esp. 646b16–25 and b22–25. Yet, this fact is well calculated to illustrate the contrast I shall shortly suggest and insist upon (not terminologically, to be sure, but conceptually) between *semiotic* as the general doctrine of what a sign is and *semiotics* as the classification of signs into specific types. (The manner of referring to the text of the *Treatise* in terms of page, column, and line is set forth in the note immediately following.) Indeed, only in Maritain (1943:192) is there so much as a passing reference to this doctrinal origin, and that in but a single sentence.

If we look to the wider context of the semiotics movement proper, moreover, despite the Poinsot-based essay of Maritain (1943) and the systematic exposé with texts of Herculano de Carvalho (1969) covering about two-thirds of the *Treatise*, not even the most limited awareness or trace of Poinsot's pioneering doctrine is to be found as late as Jakobson's celebrated "Coup d'Oeil sur le Développement de la Semiotique," delivered at the opening of the First Congress of the International Semiotic Association in June of 1974, and published the following year.

This general ignorance of Poinsot's work, coupled with specific unawareness of its proper foundations as mentioned above, will explain the somewhat awkward circumstances of my having to rely on references to my own published articles as the principal research background for the ideas developed in the present essay so far as they derive from the *doctrina* rather than merely from the *divisio* of signs Poinsot proposes.

4. Both these formulae are from the Foreword to John Poinsot's *Treatise on Signs*, trans. by John Deely (Bloomington: Indiana University Press, forthcoming), 642a20–21 and 642a38–b43, respectively. Page, column, and line references are to the 1930 Reiser edition of Poinsot's *Ars Logica* (Turin: Marietti), in which the Latin text of the 1632 *Treatise* is incorporated, as I have explained more fully elsewhere (Deely, 1974b:858ff.). These "Reiser numbers" will appear in the margin of the published English translation (as, for example, the Bekker numbers appear in good translations of Aristotle), with the English text set alongside the original Latin of Poinsot on the subject of *signum* in the *Cursus Philosophicus* completed finally in 1635.

The reader may note that what in my earlier articles (1974b and 1975c) are referred to as Appendix A and Appendix B of Poinsot's *Treatise*, are here referred to as the Second and First Preamble, respectively, to that same *Treatise*. The material referred to as Appendix C in earlier writings has also been relocated under the literary-form heading of *Summulae* texts (as will be explained when the work appears), leaving what was formerly called Appendix D as the sole Appendix to the work as it will finally appear in published form. This reorganization has been made to reflect better and more directly Poinsot's historically conditioned reasons for treating signs at the point where he does in the larger context of his *Cursus Philosophicus* (of which the *Ars Logica* comprises only the first two of the original five parts), and should little, if at all, hamper those going to Poinsot from the article literature, inasmuch as all references to the *Treatise*, in earlier publications—Maritain (1943), Herculano de Carvalho (1969), Deely (1971–1975), and Oesterle (1944)— as in this publication, conclude with an identification of Reiser page, column, and line, irrespective of the names assigned the various internal parts of the work. Thus the Latin original remains, so far as presently possible, the fixed base equally for the initially proposed and the finally adopted organization of the forthcoming first independent edition of the *Treatise*. Further editings may result as the grounds of the original divisions progressively clarify, both historically and in themselves.

5. Poinsot was expressly aware of this circumstance: see the *Summulae* (or beginners') texts preliminary to the *Treatise on Signs*, 7a6–20, and the "Transition to Book III" in the *Treatise* proper, 722a45–b14.

6. "Signum est, quod praeter species, quas ingerit sensui, aliquid facit in cognitionem venire." Augustine, *De Doctrina Christiana*, Book II, chap.1, n.1, as cited by Poinsot in the *Treatise on Signs*, Book I, Question 1, 646a24–28. Both the Migne *Patrologia Latina* XXXIV. 35 and the *édition Bénédictine* of 1949 (Paris: Desclée, *Oeuvres de Saint Augustin*, vol.11, p.238), however, agree in wording Augustine's definition as follows: "Signum est enim res, quod praeter speciem quam ingerit sensibus, aliud ex se faciens in cogitationem venire." These differences in wording are not important theoretically, as can be seen from careful study of the texts identified in note 7, following.

7. *Summulae* text preliminary to the *Treatise on Signs*, 10a6–12, and note thereon; also Book I of the *Treatise* proper, Question 1, 646a14–28.

8. ". . . plane est uti signo, scilicet repraesentatione unius non solum pro

se, sed pro altero distincto a se." *Treatise on Signs,* Book I, Question 6, 685b41–44.

9. I say "the confrontation at last . . ." because, even though the doctrine of ideas as the known objects *representing* mind-independent things and the doctrine of ideas as *signs* were both spoken of in the writings of the seventeenth-century founders of modern philosophy (e.g., in Locke's *Essay,* Book II, chap.8, pars.12–16, chap.30, par.1; Book IV, chap.4, par.4; *et alibi*), these two formulations or 'doctrines' were treated as basically equivalent. Poinsot alone—who died without influence on the post–seventeenth-century developments of English and Continental thought—grasped and gave systematic expression to the essential *difference* between representation and signification (see the *Treatise on Signs,* Book I, Question 1, 646a39–b15, 649a11–b28, and the "Sequel" to Book I, 693a9–31), whereby he was able to show why ideas, though necessary for our awareness of things and representative of them, as *signs,* are not themselves the *objects* of which we are aware. Representation, when it occurs in signification, serves to *found* the "relation to another" constitutive of the signifying, but it *is not itself* that relation. In Poinsot's terms, an *idea as representation* is a sign *fundamentally but not formally* (e.g., see the *Treatise on Signs,* Book I, Question 3, 669a34–b12, Question 5, 684b10–14). Formally, i.e., as a sign, the "idea" is the relation to another—to the object signified—that is directly cognized or known. (See note 10 following.) It is this other—which may or may not, and sometimes does and sometimes does not, involve elements of mind-independent being (see Deely, 1974b: esp. 277–92)—which is the *direct* object of our experience and awareness of things, *not* our ideas, which serve (as iconic or "representations") only to *found relations* to what they themselves are not, namely, the objects of which we are directly aware. Cf. Oesterle, 1944:241–46.

This situation brims with irony. Given the distinction between representing and signifying as Poinsot construes it, we can see that the conclusion of Locke's famous *Essay,* where he marks out the domain of semiotic and identifies ideas as signs (Book IV, chap.XXI, esp. par.4), is in principle at variance with the doctrine of ideas as objects with which he introduces the *Essay* (Introduction, par.8) and on which he grounded the body of its expositions (e.g., Book II, chap.1, pars.1–6, chap.8, par.8). Thus, when Locke conjectured in the same breath with which he proposed *semiotic* as a distinct domain, that perhaps if "*ideas* and *words* [formal and instrumental signs, in the language of Poinsot] as the great instruments of knowledge . . . were distinctly weighed, and duly considered [precisely *as* signs], they would afford us another sort of logic and critic, than what we have been hitherto acquainted with," he spoke truly indeed, and as a prophet; but a prophet whose vision had in substance been realized by an earlier contemporary of another land, in a work that would wait some three hundred years to be heard outside the Latin world, when the project of semiotics, thanks to Peirce, Saussure, and a hundred others, would at last in our own time be ventured in earnest in the national languages.

For, if semiotic is before all else the doctrine of signs, and centrally the account of what it is for anything to be a sign; and if the first systematic investigator of this matter is to be titled, as it would seem he must be titled, the "real founder" (as Sebeok [1968:6] puts it) of semiotic, then this historical encomium must in one sense go to Poinsot even over Peirce, who nevertheless "founded"—or re-founded—semiotic in modern times insofar as it was destined to become an intellectual movement of international scope. In this other sense of "founding," Poinsot's work, coming as it did 58 years before Locke's *Essay* and provisional designation of semiotic as a distinct province of knowledge, truly fell "deadborn from the press," and passed without prospective trace into history. Thus Poinsot, as Sebeok remarks (1975a:3), "appears, in retrospect, to have forged the most solid, lasting link between the Scholastic semioticians—an intellectual milieu [extending in this area, as we have remarked above, over eleven hundred years of Western civilization] in which this keen thinker was still profoundly at home—and the emergent doctrine of signs envisaged, labelled, and foreshadowed by John Locke half a century later, in 1690."

10. The discovery that a fully consistent account of ideas as signs is inconsistent with an account of ideas as the objects of which we are directly aware, is what comes to expression in Poinsot's distinction of formal signs from instrumental signs, i.e., in his division of signs into those whose whole being consists in the giving of objective presence to—the founding of cognitive relations to—what they themselves are not (formal signs, "concepts" or "ideas") and those that depend in their fundamental signifying on being themselves objectively apprehended (instrumental signs). In secondary literature, the relation between these two kinds of signs, especially the relatively dependent status of the latter on the former (a point perhaps so evident for Poinsot—but perhaps not: read the "Transition to Bk. III," 722a45–b14—that he makes it expressly only *en passant* in Book II of the *Treatise,* in Question 1 at 701a17–23, and in Question 5 at 716a27–45), is well treated by Oesterle (1944: esp. 259–260). If this relationship is well understood, for example, a question can be raised as to whether the extensive debate in recent philosophy over the so-called identity hypothesis or thesis is rendered nugatory (Deely, 1975a: 92–93, 1975b:291–92). In general, according to the first systematic *semiotic* account of ideas and consciousness—Poinsot's theory of formal signs, essayed in the first four of the six Questions making up Book II of his *Treatise*—the theoretical impasse in philosophy since Descartes's enclosure of awareness within its own workings (the "casket" or "closet" of individual consciousness —a "monad without windows," in Leibniz's immortal expression) is overcome with a stroke, and the contemporary conviction that communication is real and objects are public is theoretically justified in the simple terms of two (or more) things being related to the same third thing, by the realization that ideas as *formal* signs, are not and *cannot* be that which we directly apprehend, experience, or know, but that rather on the basis of which ("id *in* quo") we are related to whatever we know, be it sensible or abstract.

Given the novelty of the perspectives opened up by Poinsot's notion of formal signs, it is not surprising that this is the one element of his semiotics that was fastened upon in the polemical climate of the last quarter century or so, by philosophers interested primarily in a "realist" epistemology and logic

—e.g., Maritain (1924, 1943, 1957, 1963), Adler (1967), Simon (1961), Veatch (1952), Parker and Veatch (1959), Wild (1947). The strictly limited success met with by these attempts to appropriate Poinsot's conception, I venture, traces directly to the fact that each of these authors to a greater or lesser degree (least by far in the case of Maritain) attempts to employ the distinction of formal signs as if it were independent of Poinsot's prior account of relative being—on which prior account in truth the formal/instrumental distinction depends for its proper force (Deely, 1974b: fn.26 pp.875–76). Indeed, in the case of Wild and Adler, so "independent" is the use made of Poinsot's notion in terms of its semiotic origin, that it is deployed against the background of a view of the reality of relation that is the contrary opposite of the one Poinsot regards as indispensably propaedeutic to the possibility of any finally coherent theory of signs (Wild, 1956:558; Adler, 1968:582)! In either case, if the notion of formal signs is detached from Poinsot's account of the relative being constitutive of *all* signs and treated, not as a particular instance (the intraorganismically founded instance) of *this* being, but as something posited independently, as it were, and cut out of whole cloth, it is bound to appear as an extremely interesting but essentially arbitrary and *ad hoc* construct, devoid of proper philosophical justification and hence finally unconvincing in its own right—a point Poinsot gave a great deal of thought to, as Herculano de Carvalho (1969:139) points out well.

With the semiotic foundation of this division of signs at last brought to light, this veneer of arbitrariness can be fully stripped away, and we may expect the distinction of formal signs to play the central role it is capable of playing in the entire re-assessment of the history of post–seventeenth-century thought that is long overdue, especially in all that concerns the theories of mind, knowledge, and truth.

11. J. Rey-Debove (1973:8) acutely notes that, in the semiotic movement, "deux courants de pensée se dessinent nettement: l'un pour lequel la signifiance est un phénomène humain dont la connaissance positive seule ne peut rendre compte, dans l'étude duquel le chercheur est lui-même impliqué, et qui fait de la sémiotique le fondement même de l'épistémologie des sciences dites 'humaines'; l'autre pour lequel les problèmes de communication et d'information sont fondamentaux, dépassent le fait proprement humain, et constituent un objet d'étude dont les données relèvent du mesurable."

There is no doubt of the direction in which Poinsot's semiotic resolves this "question actuellement controversée." The contemporary perspective most congenial to the theoretical requirements of Poinsot's doctrine of signs is the one Sebeok describes (1975b:95) as "a semiotics that eschews anthropocentrism, coupled with an ethology that shuns parochialism." As he explains more fully elsewhere (Sebeok, 1974:213): "*Anthroposemiotics*, that is, the totality of man's species-specific signaling systems, was the first domain concretely envisaged and delineated, under the designation *semiotic*. For most investigators, from 1960 to this day, both notions still remain synonymous. The second domain, *zoosemiotics*, which encompasses the study of animal communications in the broadest sense, was named and comprehensively outlined only in 1963. It would now seem more accurate to consider anthroposemiotics and zoosemiotics, separately and conjointly, as two principal divisions of semiotics, having in common certain essential features but differing especially as to the fundamental and pervasive role that language plays in the former in contradistinction to the latter."

12. The analysis establishing the distinction and exhaustiveness of these two modes of relative being—which is not to deny the possibility of many subdivisions under each of the headings—is just below the surface and between the lines of the first two of the three Articles making up the Second Preamble to the *Treatise on Signs*, 573b8–583a50. Much of the material from the Translator's Introduction to the *Treatise* covering the context and ground of this distinction as it provides the adequate foundation, pure and simple, of Poinsot's semiotics has been published in article form (Deely, 1974b:858–75). I have also essayed an independent philosophical explication of the essential notions at play here, by fleshing out the cursory rationale or *modus procedendi* indicated by Poinsot in his Foreword to the *Treatise*, 642a24–41 (Deely, 1975c: esp. 476–87). A satisfactory statement in English of that attempt has just become available (Deely, 1977).

13. Here accordingly is exactly where Poinsot's semiotic formally begins. See the *Treatise on Signs*, Book I, Question 1, "Whether a Sign Is in the Order of Relation," esp. 646b16–21: "Quaerimus ergo, an formalis ista ratio signi consistat in relatione secundum esse primo et per se, an in relatione secundum dici seu in aliquo absoluto, quod fundet talem relationem."

14. *Treatise on Signs*, "Second Preamble," Article 2, 578b19–25: ". . . relatio transcendentalis, quae non est alia a relatione secundum dici, non importat ex principali significato relationem, sed aliquid absolutum, ad quod sequitur vel sequi potest aliqua relatio."

15. It is in terms of the universal denial of the reality (the "mind-independence") of relations in the currents that formed distinctively modern philosophy—both in its early Latin phase (Ockham to Suarez) and in its transition to the national languages (Descartes to Kant)—that the uniqueness and revolutionary power of Poinsot's semiotic becomes most readily visible, as I have tried to indicate (Deely, 1974b:876–905).

16. "Ethologists refer to the behavioral dossier of a species as its *ethogram*," comments Sebeok (1975b:88). "In semiotic terms, this concept encompasses an animal's species-specific communicative code, in confrontation with which the human observer's role necessarily becomes that of a cryptanalyst, of someone who receives messages not destined for him and is initially ignorant of the applicable transformation rules."

17. Here we skirt a crucial point that is reduced by Poinsot to its ground in sensation as such only in Book III of his *Treatise*, long after the discussion of perceptual ambiguities in the notion of *ex consuetudine*: the distinction between cognitive life in its intuitive (restricted to the here and now) and abstract (structured by experience-borne, sometimes reflected modifications) phases, or, as we should more recently say, between the semiotic behavior of the higher anthropoid populations and that of the more common genetically dominated animal forms.

18. Poinsot, *Naturalis Philosophiae IV. Pars: De Ente Mobili Animato,*

Quaestio 6, Article 2: ". . . potentia quantumcumque habeat virtutem efficiendi vitaliter actum cognitionis, dependet ab obiecto, ut simul cum ipso cognitionem eliciat. Et hoc ideo est, quia potentia per cognitionem debet esse assimilativa vitaliter, non solum ea communi ratione, quo omne agens intendit assimilare sibi effectum eo modo, quo potest, sed speciali ratione, quatenus tendit ad uniendum et coniungendum sibi obiectum et trahendum ad se. In qua cognitione seu operatione non fit assimilatio per hoc, quod potentia operans faciat aliam potentiam sibi similem, sed solum facit simile seu assimilationem ex parte obiecti. Circa hoc enim operatur et negotiatur potentia, nec intendit in hac assimilatione propagationem et multiplicationem sui, sed solum manifestationem aut expressionem aut unionem actualiter exercitam erga obiectum. Non potest autem potentia emittere ex se vitaliter hanc assimilationem et unionem seu tendentiam erga obiectum nisi cum concursu ipsius obiecti. Et non sufficit terminari ad obiectum, quia ut terminetur ad obiectum, debet egredi a potentia ut determinate tendens ad illud obiectum, ad quod terminatur, siquidem notitia est partus quidam potentiae determinatus circa hoc obiectum eique potentiam assimilans. Ergo necesse est, quod non a sola potentia procedat, quae indifferens est ad multa obiecta, sed etiam ab obiecto, ut illi assimilatio fiat. Imo etiamsi virtus potentiae sit determinata erga tale obiectum in ratione viventis, non tamen est determinata in ratione foecunditatis, nisi ab obiecto perficiatur et determinetur, sicut virtus feminae licet sit determinata ad generandum dependenter tamen a foecunditate viri. Non potest autem exire cognitio ab obiecto ut extra, sed ut est intra ipsam eamque actuat et afficit media specie sui, eo quod ille actus seu cognitio vitaliter exit a potentia. Et quando exit ab ipsa, exit ut determinatus et specificatus circa tale obiectum, et non potest exire seorsum ab obiecto et seorsum a potentia, quia ab obiecto ut est extra non potest exire vitaliter, nec ut entitas unica et indivisibilis, cum multum distet aliquando obiectum a sensu. Opportet ergo, quod aliquid loco sui et repraesentativum sui ponat in potentia, ut exeat cognitio ab ipsa cum sua determinatione et specificatione et dependentia, quam habet ab obiecto per unicum et indivisibilem partum et vitalem processionem potentiae." (Original edition: Alcalá, Spain, 1635; citation is from the 3rd volume [1947] of the Reiser edition of Poinsot's complete *Cursus Philosophicus*, 182a29–b47.)

19. Significare "ex consuetudine . . . est significare naturaliter non ex se, sed solum respectu illorum apud quos est nota consuetudo. Nec est inconveniens, quod eidem rei conveniant duo modi significandi secundum distinctas formalitates": Poinsot, *Treatise on Signs*, Book II, Question 6, 722a13–19.

20. Cf. the "First Preamble" to the *Treatise on Signs*, Article 3, "By What Powers and Through Which Acts Do Mind-Dependent Beings Come About?" 301a1–306b45, esp. 301b33–304b7; and, in the *Treatise* proper, Book I, Question 6, 685a36–691a20, esp. 688a18–28, and Book II, Question 6, 719a18–722a37.

21. This, I should think, is why Poinsot indicates in the very first definition of the *signum ad placitum* (*Summulae* text 10a16–19) that the aspect of "ad placitum" that connotes an arbitrary or whimsical element in a stipulation is (as Herculano de Carvalho [1969:141–52] develops well) what is least important and least interesting for an understanding of this class of signs. On the

contrary, a stipulation will become interesting and "conventional" only to the extent that it expresses a *socially structured* human intention: "Signum ad placitum est, quod repraesentat aliquid ex impositione voluntatis *per publicam auctoritatem*" (emphasis supplied; see also Book II, Question 6).

Compare the discussion in Oesterle, 1944:247–49.

22. "Voces per se solum significant ad placitum, per accidens autem ex consuetudine, quod est significare naturaliter non ex se, sed solum respectu illorum, apud quos est nota consuetudo. Nec est inconveniens, quod eidem rei conveniant duo modi significandi secundum distinctas formalitates. Unde una sublata altera manet, et sic numquam est idem signum naturale et ad placitum formaliter, licet materialiter sint idem, id est conveniant eidem subiecto.

"Quod autem dicitur illud esse signum naturale, quod significat idem apud omnes, intelligitur de eo, quod est signum naturale simpliciter, quia natura est eadem apud omnes. Consuetudo autem est quasi altera natura, sed non natura ipsa, et ita significat omnibus, apud quos est consuetudo, non omnibus simpliciter, et sic est aliquid imperfectius in genere signi naturalis, sicut ipsa consuetudo est aliquid imperfectum in genere naturae" (*Treatise on Signs*, Book II, Question 6, 722a10–37).

23. This is the main thrust of Question 6, Book II, of the *Treatise*, which has been so frequently referred to in developing this section: "Sit ergo unica conclusio: Si consuetudo respiciat aliquod signum, destinando illud et proponendo pro signo, tale signum fundatum in consuetudine erit ad placitum. Si vero consuetudo non proponat aliquid vel instituat pro signo, sed dicat simplicem usum alicuius rei et ratione illius assumatur aliquid in signum, tale signum reducitur ad naturale" (719a35–44).

24. "Sensus internus ita comparat unum alteri formando propositionem et discursum, quod ipsa ordinationem praedicati et subiecti, et antecedentis ad consequens formaliter non cognoscit discernendo relationem fictam a reali. Et similiter montem aureum cognoscit quantum ad id, quod sensibile est in illis partibus repraesentatis auri et montis, non quantum ad rationem fictionis, ut distinguitur a realitate. Quod est cognoscere non formaliter id, quod in ratione entis fingitur, sed materialiter id, ad cuius instar fingitur, quod in se non est" (from the "First Preamble" to the *Treatise on Signs*, Article 3, 305a14–29).

25. In quotidiana experientia "videmus bruta moveri signis, tum naturalibus, ut gemitu, balatu, cantu, etc., tum ex consuetudine, ut canis vocatus nomine consueto movetur, qui tamen impositionem non intelligit, sed consuetudine ducitur" (*Treatise on Signs*, Book I, Question 6, 685b26–32). (Explication in the text above of this and the following citations from Poinsot in light of his doctrine concerning the relative being of signs is well calculated to illustrate further how, as was said above, this doctrine—his *semiotic* strictly speaking—transfuses superficially commonplace, quite "traditional," examples and usages of words with an entirely new depth of life.)

26. "Cum aliqua bruta sint disciplinae capacia, non statim a principio aliqua percipiunt, quae postea consuetudine procedente cognoscunt, ut canis non statim a principio movetur, cum vocatur tali vel tali nomine, et postea movetur habita consuetudine. Ergo utuntur aliqua bruta signis ex consuetu-

dine; nam ex impositione ipsa nominis non movetur, quia non innotescit illis
impositio ipsa, quae ex voluntate imponentis dependet" (*Treatise on Signs,*
Book I, Question 6, 686a1–12).

27. Jacques Maritain (1957:90), who himself learned this point from
Poinsot, expresses the matter thus: "what defines language is not precisely
the use of words, or even of conventional signs; it is the use of any sign whatever *as involving the knowledge or awareness of the relation of signification,*
and therefore a potential infinity; it is the use of signs *in so far as it manifests
that the mind has grasped and brought out the relation of signification* [italics
Maritain's].

". . . the invention of those particular conventional signs which are words,
the creation of a system of signs made up of 'phonemes' and 'morphemes' was
in itself . . . a further discovery of human intelligence, no less characteristic
of man, but less essential than, and by nature not prior to, the discovery of the
relation of signification.

". . . the word 'language,' when referring to animals, is equivocal."

Cf. Sebeok (1975:88–89), who concludes: "It is therefore scientifically
inaccurate, as well as, even metaphorically, highly misleading, to speak of a
'language' of animals."

28. "Sensui autem interiori non negamus formationem entis rationis ex
defectu comparationis, sed ex defectu universalitatis cognoscendi, quia non
cognoscit universaliores rationes discernendo inter ens verum et fictum, quod
tamen facit simplex apprehensio; discernit enim praedicamenta ab iis, quae
in praedicamento non sunt" (from the "First Preamble" to the *Treatise on
Signs,* 305b19–28).

29. "First Preamble," 305a25–29. I wish to stress here and make as clear
as possible that Poinsot's distinction between *ens verum* and *ens fictum,* as
the difference between what depends upon and what is independent of cognition, is not isomorphic with the difference between *what will and will not
work* in the accomplishment of vital purposes. It is this latter difference *as
encompassing mind-dependent and mind-independent beings indifferently,*
that is at stake in the pretenses, camouflages, and deceits deployed in animal
'lying'. The analysis of *signa ex consuetudine* as absorptive of *signa ad placita*
and overlapping the conduct of human and animal affairs, thus, easily encompasses, in Poinsot's semiotic, this ingenious variety of animal communications.

30. *Treatise on Signs,* Book II, Question 6, 722a11–23 (lines included in
the Latin citation for note 22 above).

31. Ibid., 722a25–37 (also included in note 22 above).

REFERENCES WITH SOME ANNOTATIONS

Adler, Mortimer J. 1967. *The Difference of Man.* New York: Holt, Rinehart,
& Winston, esp. p. 320n8, p.327n10, p.331n11. In this work, Adler uses "the
ideas without the terminology" of Poinsot, or so he would have it.

———. 1968. "Sense Cognition: Aristotle vs. Aquinas." *The New Scholasticism* XLII (Autumn):578–91.

Altmann, Stuart A. 1968. "Primates." In *Animal Communication*, Thomas A. Sebeok, ed. Bloomington: Indiana University Press, pp.466–522.

Augustine. c. 427. *De Doctrina Christiana*. Both The Migne text of 1865 and the *édition Bénédictine* of 1949 (Paris: Desclée), *Oeuvres de Saint Augustin*, vol. 11, were used in preparing this essay.

Brown, Roger. 1958. *Words and Things*. New York: Free Press.

Carpenter, C. R. 1969. "Approaches to Studies of the Naturalistic Communicative Behavior in Nonhuman Primates." In *Approaches to Animal Communication*, Thomas A. Sebeok and Alexandra Ramsay, eds. The Hague: Mouton, pp.40–70.

Deely, John N. 1971a. "Animal Intelligence and Concept-Formation." *The Thomist* XXXV (January):43–93.

———. 1971b. "The Myth as Integral Objectivity." ACPA *Proceedings* XLV: 67–76.

———. 1972a. "How Language Refers." *Studi Internazionali di Filosofia*, A. Guzzo and G. Tonelli, eds. IV (autunno):41–50.

———. 1972b. "The Ontological Status of Intentionality." *The New Scholasticism* XLVI (Spring):220–33.

———. 1973. "The Emergence of Man." In *The Problem of Evolution*, John N. Deely and Raymond J. Nogar, eds. New York: Appleton-Century-Crofts, pp.119–45.

———. 1974a. "Il riferimento del linguaggio al non-esistente." *Renovatio* IX, nos. 2 and 3 (April-September):155–75, 283–310.

———. 1974b. "The Two Approaches to Language." *The Thomist* XXXVIII (October):856–907.

———. 1975a. "Modern Logic, Animal Psychology, and Human Discourse." *Revue de l'Université d'Ottawa* 45 (janvier-mars):80–100.

———. 1975b. "Reference to the Non-Existent." *The Thomist* XXXIX (April):253–308.

———. 1975c. " 'Semeiotica': Dottrina dei Segni." *Renovatio* X, no.4 (ottobre-dicembre):472–90. The translator of this essay, originally titled " 'Semiotic' as the Doctrine of Signs," unfortunately chose the variant spelling of "semeiotic," which has mainly medical connotations in the Italian. There are some imperfections in the printed text—e.g., note (33) on p.487 should be note (34) on p.488, end of first paragraph, following present note (34), which should be (33), etc.; and the concluding paragraphs with "Postscript" are omitted. The complete and corrected text, updated, is now available in English.

———. 1977. " 'Semiotic' as the Doctrine of Signs." *Ars Semeiotica* 1/3 (Fall), 41–68.

Eco, Umberto. 1976. *A Theory of Semiotics*. Bloomington: Indiana University Press.

Greenlee, Douglas. 1973. *Peirce's Concept of Sign*. The Hague: Mouton.

Harlow, Harry F. 1959. "Basic Social Capacity of Primates." In *The Evolution of Man's Capacity for Culture*, arranged by James N. Spuhler. Detroit: Wayne State University Press, pp.40–53.

Herculano de Carvalho, José G. 1969. "Segno e Significazione in João de São Tomás." In *Estudos Linguisticos*, vol.2, Coimbra: Atlântida Editora. Pp. 129–53 are exposition; pp.154–68 reproduce selected passages of the Latin text. This careful essay, a most important piece of work, along with the essay of Maritain (1943), stands as a first-hand presentation of Poinsot's Latin texts.

Hockett, Charles F. 1959. "Animal 'Languages' and Human Language." In *The Evolution of Man's Capacity for Culture*, arranged by James N. Spuhler. Detroit: Wayne State University Press, pp.32–39.

Huxley, Julian S. 1942. *Evolution: The Modern Synthesis*. New York: Harper.

Jakobson, Roman. 1975. *Coup d'oeil sur le développement de la sémiotique*. Studies in Semiotics 3. Bloomington: Research Center for Language and Semiotic Studies.

John of St. Thomas: under Poinsot, for the reasons set forth in Deely (1975c: 474n9; 1977:59n8).

Kendon, Adam. 1972. Review of Ray L. Birdwhistell's *Kinesics and Context: Essays on Body Motion Communication* (Philadelphia: University of Pennsylvania Press, 1970). *American Journal of Psychology* 85:441–55.

Krempel, A. 1952. *La doctrine de la relation chez St. Thomas: exposé historique et systématique*. Paris: Vrin.

Locke, John. 1690. *An Essay Concerning Human Understanding*. A. C. Fraser edition. New York: Dover Publications, 1959.

Maritain, Jacques. 1924. *Réflexions sur l'intelligence et sur sa vie propre*. Paris: Nouvelle Librairie Nationale.

———. 1943. "Sign and Symbol." In *Redeeming the Time*. London: Geoffrey Bles, text pp.191–224, notes citing Latin text pp.268–76. This is the Binsse translation of "Signe et Symbol," originally published in *Quatre essais sur l'ésprit dans sa condition charnel* (Paris, 1939). The notes comprise "extracts in Latin from John of Saint Thomas," mainly from the *Ars Logica*'s text of the *tractatus de signis* of 1632, but also from Poinsot's last posthumous volume (1662) of the later *Cursus theologicus*. Further divisions of signs into *practicum* and *speculativum* are made by Poinsot there.

———. 1957. "Language and the Theory of Sign." In *Language: An Enquiry into Its Meaning and Function*, Ruth Nanda Anshen, ed. New York: Harper, pp.86–101.

———. 1963. *Les degrés du savoir*, 7e ed., rev. et aug. Paris: Desclée, esp. Annexe I. "A propos du concept," pp.769–819.

Oesterle, John A. 1944. "Another Approach to the Problem of Meaning." *The Thomist* VII (April):233–63. In this essay Oesterle attempts a detailed comparison of Poinsot's theory with that of Ogden and Richards in *The Meaning of Meaning*.

Osgood, Charles E. 1953. *Method and Theory in Experimental Psychology*. New York: Oxford University Press.

Parker, F. H., and Veatch, Henry. 1959. *Logic as a Human Instrument*. New York: Harper.

Peirce, Charles Sanders. 1931–1938. *Collected Papers*, vols. I–VI, Charles

Hartshorne and Paul Weiss, eds. Cambridge: Harvard University Press.

――――. 1958. *Collected Papers*, vols. VII–VIII, Arthur W. Burks, ed. Cambridge: Harvard University Press.

Poinsot, John. 1631–1632. *Ars Logica* (Alcalá), containing the *Treatise on Signs*. The Reiser edition of the *Ars Logica* (Turin: Marietti, 1930) was used in preparing this essay.

――――. 1635. *Naturalis Philosophiae IV. Pars: De Ente Mobili Animato* (Alcalá). Reiser's edition of this work (Turin: Marietti, 1947) was used in preparing this article.

Rey-Debove, J. 1973. "Introduction" to *Recherches sur les Systèmes Signifiants*, J. Rey-Debove, ed. The Hague: Mouton, pp.5–8.

Sebeok, Thomas A. 1968. "Goals and Limitations of the Study of Animal Behavior." In *Animal Communication*, T. A. Sebeok, ed. Bloomington: Indiana University Press, pp.3–14.

――――. 1974. "Semiotics: A Survey of the State of the Art." In *Current Trends in Linguistics*, vol. 12, T. A. Sebeok, ed. The Hague: Mouton, pp.211–64.

――――. 1975a. "The Semiotic Web: A Chronicle of Prejudices." *Bulletin of Literary Semiotics* 2:1–65.

――――. 1975b. "Zoosemiotics: At the Intersection of Nature and Culture." In *The Tell-Tale Sign*, T. A. Sebeok, ed. Lisse, The Netherlands: Peter de Ridder Press.

Simon, Yves R. 1961. "To Be and To Know." In *Chicago Review* 14, no.4 (Spring):83–100.

Veatch, Henry. 1952. *Intentional Logic*. New Haven: Yale University Press, esp. pp.11–15, 29–31, 39–41, 81–115.

Veatch, Henry, and Parker, F. H.: See under Parker.

von Frisch, Karl. 1954. *The Dancing Bees*. London: Methuen.

――――. 1967. "Honeybees: Do They Use Direction and Distance Information Provided by Their Dancers?" *Science* 158:1072–76.

Weinberg, Julius R. 1965. "The Concept of Relation: Some Observations on Its History." In *Abstraction, Relation, and Induction*. Madison: University of Wisconsin Press, pp.61–119.

White, Leslie A. 1959. "Summary Review." In *The Evolution of Man's Capacity for Culture*, arranged by James N. Spuhler. Detroit: Wayne State University Press, pp.74–79.

――――. 1973. "Cultural Determinants of Mind." In *The Problem of Evolution*, John N. Deely and Raymond J. Nogar, eds. New York: Appleton-Century-Crofts, pp.163–78.

Wild, John. 1947. "An Introduction to the Phenomenology of Signs." *Philosophy and Phenomenological Research* VIII (December):217–44.

――――. 1956. Review of *The Material Logic of John of St. Thomas*, Y. R. Simon, J. J. Glanville, and G. Donald Hollenhorst, trans. (Chicago: University of Chicago Press, 1955). *Philosophy and Phenomenological Research* XVII (June):556–59.

Peirce's General Theory of Signs

Max H. Fisch

Both the general theory of signs and certain specialized branches of it, such as symptomatology and grammar, may be traced back to the ancient Greeks. But when today's semioticians speak of the founders of their science, they seldom mention anyone earlier than Charles Sanders Peirce (1839–1914), and they mention him oftener than any later founder.

If Peirce was one of the founders, perhaps even the founder, of modern semiotic, when and how did the founding take place? What are his relevant published writings? What did he take the business of the science to be? What importance did he attach to it? How did he conceive its relations to other sciences? To logic, say; or psychology, or linguistics? And by what steps did he come to be recognized as such a founder? Has all his relevant published work been either assimilated or superseded, or are there things still to be learned from it? Is any important part of his relevant work still unpublished? In what follows I suggest approaches toward answering such questions as these.

1. A PRELIMINARY NOTE ON SPELLING AND PRONUNCIATION

Most of the vocabulary of Peirce's doctrine of signs—for examples, *representation, sign, object,* and *interpretant*—is derived from Latin, and poses no difficulty of spelling or pronunciation. But for the science itself and for what it studies, he uses English forms of two Greek terms that are more troublesome in both these respects. Now Peirce was, among other things, linguist, philologist, lexicographer, and exponent of the ethics of terminology. So if we count him a founder of our science, we shall wish to know what these terms were, and how he spelled and pronounced their English forms.

For σημείωσις—sign-action, the operation or functioning of a sign, sign-interpretation, or the act of inferring from signs—he uses two English forms, *semiosis* and *semeiosy*. The former he tells us to pronounce with the *e* and the first *i* long and with the accent on the *o* (5.484*).[1] He does not tell us where to place the accent in semeiosy (5.473), but I think he put it on the second syllable, pronouncing it "my."[2] For the plural of semiosis, he uses semioses (5.489).[3]

For σημειωτική—the art or science or doctrine or general theory of semioses—he uses *semeiotic*; much less often, *semeiotics* or *semiotic*; very rarely, *semeotic*; never *semiotics*. To tell us how to pronounce his preferred form, he marks it sēmeio'tic (Ms 318 p.15).[4]

His rationale for that spelling and pronunciation was probably two-fold. (1) There is no more reason for *semeiotics* or *semiotics* than for *logics* or *rhetorics*. (2) Both the spelling and the pronunciation should (in this case, at least) be signs of etymology; that is, should make it evident that the derivation is from Greek σημεῖον, sign, not from Latin *semi-* ("half-"). There is nothing halfway about semeiotic; it is all about signs, and it is about all signs. And the *o* in semeiotic should be long because it has behind it a Greek omega, not an omicron.

In the remainder of this paper, I shall use in quotations whatever spellings Peirce there uses, but outside of quotations I shall use only semeiosis and semeiotic, and I invite the reader to pronounce them with

---

* References in the form 5.484 are to the *Collected Papers of Charles Sanders Peirce* by volume and paragraph number. (Cambridge: Harvard University Press, vols. 1–6 edited by Hartshorne and Weiss, 1931–1935; vols. 7–8 edited by Burks, 1958.) References in the form "Ms 318 p.15" are to the Charles S. Peirce Papers in the Houghton Library at Harvard University, quoted by permission of the Department of Philosophy. References in the form NE 3:886 are to *The New Elements of Mathematics by Charles S. Peirce*, edited by Carolyn Eisele (4 vols. in 5, The Hague: Mouton; Atlantic Highlands, N. J.: Humanities Press, 1976), by volume and page. References in the form W75 are to the pages of *Semiotic and Significs: The Correspondence between Charles S. Peirce and Victoria Lady Welby*, edited by Charles S. Hardwick (Bloomington: Indiana University Press, 1977). Christian J. W. Kloesel has helped me by calling my attention to manuscript passages I might otherwise have missed, by criticizing drafts of this essay, and in numerous other ways.

me "See my o, sis" and "See my o tick." I cannot believe that Peirce
ever pronounced the latter "semmy-AHT-ick."

2. THE FIRST FOUNDING
(1865–1869)

Peirce's training was in chemistry. His career was in the service of
the United States Coast Survey, 1859–1860, 1861–1891. His work for the
Survey was primarily astronomical and geodetic, but it involved metrol-
ogy, spectroscopy, optics, color theory, map projections, the four-color
problem, and the history of astronomy and of science in general. His
contributions to the annual reports of the Survey included one on the
theory of errors of observations in the *Report* for 1873 and one on the
economy of research in that for 1876. He deliberately diversified his
researches beyond the requirements of his work for the Survey, not
from ambition to contribute to as many sciences as possible, but with a
view to advancing the logic of science; that is, of hypothesis and induction. His first professional publication was on the chemical theory
of interpenetration, his second on the pronunciation of Shakespearian
English. He was a mathematician also, but with a view to advancing the
logic of mathematics, that is, of deduction.

In the spring of 1877, when he was being considered for election to
the National Academy of Sciences, he submitted a list of four of his published papers in logic and asked that his eligibility be judged by these
rather than by his contributions to the special sciences.[5] He was elected,
and in his letter of acceptance he expressed his "gratification at the recognition by the Academy of Logic as entitled to a place among the real
sciences."[6] Many of the papers he later presented to the Academy were
in logic, and at least one in semeiotic.

For five years, 1879–1884, he was part-time Lecturer in Logic at the
Johns Hopkins University, while continuing his work for the Coast
Survey.[7]

From time to time he gave single courses of lectures at Harvard
University, at the Lowell Institute in Boston, and elsewhere. These were
usually in logic, in the history of logic, or in the history of science considered from the viewpoint of the logic of science.

His first such course was given at Harvard University in the spring
of 1865, under the title "The Logic of Science." In the first half of the
first lecture he reviewed various definitions and conceptions of logic,

psychological and nonpsychological. In the second half he approached his own nonpsychological definition by way of Locke's identification of logic with semeiotic, "the doctrine of signs," in the last chapter of his *Essay Concerning Human Understanding* (1690). The resulting definition of logic, Peirce said, would serve as a first approximation; but it was too broad, since, of the three kinds of representations, logic treats only of symbols. (Locke had used "representation" as a synonym of "sign," and Peirce at this time was using "representations" as his technical term for signs in general.[8])

> A second approximation to a definition of it then will be, the science of symbols in general and as such. But this definition is still too broad; this might, indeed, form the definition of a certain science, which would be a branch of Semiotic or the general science of representations, which might be called Symbolistic, and of this logic would be a species. But logic only considers symbols from a particular point of view. . . .
>
> A symbol in general and as such has three relations. . . . I define logic therefore as the science of the conditions which enable symbols in general to refer to objects.
>
> At the same time symbolistic in general gives a trivium consisting of Universal Grammar, Logic, and Universal Rhetoric, using this last term to signify the science of the formal conditions of intelligibility of symbols. [Ms 340]

On May 14, 1865, Peirce began a book called *Teleological Logic* with a chapter of definitions, in which, like Locke, he makes semeiotic one of the three most general kinds of science. With no further help from Locke, he then makes symbolistic one of the three divisions of semeiotic, as he had done in his lecture; and he makes General Grammar, General Rhetoric, and General Logic the three divisions of Symbolistic (Ms 802).

In Boston in the fall of 1866 he gave a course of twelve Lowell Lectures on "The Logic of Science; or, Induction and Hypothesis," in which the doctrine of signs was carried into somewhat greater detail (Mss 351–59, esp. 357, 359).

The first published sketch of his semeiotic was in a paper "On a New List of Categories," which he presented to the American Academy of Arts and Sciences on May 14, 1867. Forty years later he described this paper as the outcome of "the hardest two years' mental work that I have ever done in my life" (1.561). He first establishes, in place of Aristotle's ten categories and Kant's twelve, a new list of three: Quality, Relation,

Representation. He then uses these categories to distinguish: (1) three kinds of representations—likenesses (which he will later call icons), indices, and symbols; (2) a trivium of conceivable sciences—formal grammar, logic, and formal rhetoric; (3) a general division of symbols, common to all three of these sciences—terms, propositions, and arguments; and (4) three kinds of argument, distinguished by their three relations between premisses and conclusion—deduction (symbol), hypothesis (likeness), induction (index) (1.545–59).[9]

It is evident that Peirce is still using *representation* in the general sense in which he will later use *sign*. In effect, therefore, he is making of *sign* an ultimate and irreducible category. It would seem to follow, though he does not press the point, that we need an autonomous science or doctrine of signs. Other sciences—perhaps *any* other science—may supply indispensable data, but no synthesis of these will suffice to constitute the science.

Nevertheless, it might plausibly be objected, Peirce is a logician, and he concerns himself with semeiotic only so far as is necessary to place logic within the larger framework of that one of the three most general kinds of science that Locke, following the ancient Greeks, had distinguished. To that objection, however, it may fairly be replied that at no time of his life did Peirce set any limit to the intensity of cultivation of the larger field of semeiotic that would be advantageous for purposes of logic, even if the cultivating had to be done by logicians themselves because, for the time being, they were the only semeioticians.

In any case, it was not enough in Peirce's eyes for semeiotic to provide a pigeonhole for logic in the classification of the sciences. This became fully apparent in 1868–69 in a series of three articles in the *Journal of Speculative Philosophy*: "Questions Concerning Certain Faculties Claimed for Man," "Some Consequences of Four Incapacities," and "Grounds of Validity of the Laws of Logic: Further Consequences of Four Incapacities" (5.213–357).

The first two papers are there for the sake of the third. The upshot of the series is a theory of the validity of the laws of logic, including those of the logic of science (that is, of hypothesis and induction) as well as those of the logic of mathematics (that is, of deduction). Yet the first paper is in the form of a medieval *quaestio*, a disputed question, and the second begins with a four-point statement of "the spirit of Cartesianism," followed by an opposed four-point statement of the spirit of the scholasticism that it displaced. In respect of these four antitheses, "modern science and modern logic" are closer to the spirit of scholasticism. The first paper was "written in this spirit of opposition to Cartesianism." It was meant to illustrate as well as to commend the "multiform argumentation of the Middle Ages." It resulted in four denials.

> 1. We have no power of Introspection, but all knowledge of the internal world is derived by hypothetical reasoning from our knowledge of external facts.
> 2. We have no power of Intuition, but every cognition is determined logically by previous cognitions.
> 3. We have no power of thinking without signs.
> 4. We have no conception of the absolutely incognizable. [5.265]

These propositions cannot be regarded as certain, Peirce says; and the second paper puts them to the further test of tracing out some of their consequences. The third paper then constructs a theory of the validity of the laws of logic in the form of "further consequences" of these "four incapacities."

The central positive doctrine of the whole series is that "all thought is in signs" (5.253). Every thought continues another and is continued by still another. There are no uninferred premisses and no inference-terminating conclusions. Inferring is the sole act of cognitive mind. No cognition is adequately or accurately described as a two-term or dyadic relation between a knowing mind and an object known, whether that be an intuited first principle or a sense-datum, a "first impression of sense" (5.291). Cognition is a minimally three-termed or triadic relation (5.283). The sign-theory of cognition thus entails rejection not only of Cartesian rationalism but also of British empiricism.

The sign-theory of cognition leads into a semeiotic theory of the human self, "the man-sign" (5.313), and thence into a social theory of logic. "When we think, then, we ourselves, as we are at that moment, appear as a sign" (5.383); "the word or sign which man uses *is* the man himself" (5.314). "Finally, no present actual thought (which is a mere feeling) has any meaning, any intellectual value; for this lies not in what is actually thought, but in what this thought may be connected with in representation by subsequent thoughts; so that the meaning of a thought is altogether something virtual" (5.289). "Accordingly, just as we say that a body is in motion, and not that motion is in a body, we ought to say that we are in thought and not that thoughts are in us" (5.289n1).

"The real, then, is that which, sooner or later, information and reasoning would finally result in, and which is therefore independent of the vagaries of me and you. Thus, the very origin of the conception of reality shows that this conception essentially involves the notion of a COMMUNITY, without definite limits, and capable of an indefinite increase of knowledge" (5.311).[10] "So the social principle is rooted intrinsically in logic" (5.354).

Along the way, with the help of his three categories, Peirce's doctrine of signs is worked out in greater detail in these three papers, and especially in the second of them.

As a first approximation, then, we may say that, if Peirce was a founder—perhaps *the* founder—of modern semeiotic, the first founding took place in the years 1865–1869. The most relevant publications were "On a New List of Categories" (1867) and the three papers developing the sign-theory of cognition (1868–1869). The chief occasions for the founding were that Peirce was invited to give lecture courses in "the logic of science" at Harvard in 1865 and at the Lowell Institute in 1866; that he presented five papers on logic to the American Academy of Arts and Sciences in 1867; and that the editor of the *Journal of Speculative Philosophy* challenged him in 1868 to show how, on his principles, the validity of the laws of logic could be "other than inexplicable" (5.318).

The semeiotic thus founded was semeiotic as viewed from the standpoint of logic and studied for the purposes of logic, and more particularly for those of the logic of science rather than for those of the logic of mathematics. But it was a semeiotic that *included* logic.

3. THE FIRST NON-PEIRCEAN ERECTION ON THIS FIRST FOUNDATION (1913)

So far as I am aware, nobody but Peirce himself deliberately built on this first foundation until forty-five years later. Then, in 1913, Josiah Royce, though acquainted with much of Peirce's later work, discovered in the doctrine of signs contained in these four early published papers just the foundation he needed for solving "the problem of Christianity." In a two-volume work under that title he moves toward the solution in the following four chapters:

The very first step toward the solution was to abandon the dyadic models of perception and conception and to adopt in their stead Peirce's triadic semeiotic model of interpretation.[11]

4. PRAGMATISM A SECOND FOUNDING? (1877–1879)

As we shall see, when modern semeioticians began in the 1920s and 1930s to recognize Peirce as a founder of their science, the Peirce they had in mind was the founder of pragmatism. Pragmatism was, at least in the first place, a theory of meaning, and therefore a contribution to the doctrine of signs. Peirce's first published exposition of pragmatism was in a series of six "Illustrations of the Logic of Science" in the *Popular Science Monthly* in 1877–78.[12] A book under the same title was announced as in preparation for the International Scientific Series but never appeared. The "Illustrations" bore the following titles:

ILLUSTRATIONS OF THE LOGIC OF SCIENCE

First Paper.—The Fixation of Belief.
Second Paper.—How to Make Our Ideas Clear.
Third Paper.—The Doctrine of Chances.
Fourth Paper.—The Probability of Induction.
Fifth Paper.—The Order of Nature.
Sixth Paper.—Deduction, Induction, and Hypothesis.[13]

A reader coming to these papers directly from that "On a New List of Categories" and those on the sign-theory of cognition and the validity of the laws of logic would soon make the following observations. (a) Peirce is having another go at the validity of the laws of logic, and more particularly those of the logic of science; that is, of hypothesis and induction. (b) The upshot is not radically different; we reach the social theory of logic at the same stage (2.654); but the pragmatism that is only implicit in the earlier papers, if present there at all, is now unfolded as the lesson in logic taught by Darwin's *Origin of Species* (5.364).[14]

(c) Though there is no mention of the categories or of the doctrine of signs, they are omnipresent, and the "Illustrations" become fully intelligible only in the light of the four papers of a decade earlier. (d) The categories are the key to the analysis of belief, doubt, and inquiry in the first paper, and to the distinction of the three grades of clarity in the second paper. (e) The sign-object-interpretant triad is the key to the maxim for attaining the third grade of clarity: "Consider what effects, which might conceivably have practical bearings, we conceive the object of our conception to have. Then, our conception of these effects is the whole of our conception of the object." (f) The whole series is thought out within the framework of the doctrine of signs. (g) Peirce has presumably suppressed the terminology and the technicalities of semeiotic so as not to put too great a strain on the readers of the *Popular Science Monthly*. (h) Perhaps the book never appeared because he decided that this suppression had been a mistake, but he did not find time for the rewriting that would have been needed to save the book from the same mistake. (i) Even so, the "Illustrations," just as they appeared in the *Monthly*, constitute an anti-Cartesian *Discourse on the Method of Rightly Conducting the Reason and Searching for the Truth in the Sciences*.

Take observation (e). In the second paper Peirce applies the maxim to the scientific conceptions of hardness, weight, and force, and to the logical and metaphysical conceptions of truth and reality; and in the third and following papers he applies it to the most difficult conception of the logic of science, that of probability. Take hardness, for example. The object is the physical property designated by the sign *hard* as used both by laymen and by mineralogists. The three grades of clarity are exemplified by three kinds of interpretants of this sign. The second presupposes the first, and the third presupposes the first and the second. The first is that of familiar feel, ready use, and easy recognition; the second is that of abstract genus-and-differentia or synonym-and-antonym definition. At the very least, what is hard is not soft, and what is harder than x is less soft than x. Suppose that the second kind of interpretant, and thereby the second grade of clarity, that of distinctness, is already attained; then the rule for reaching the third involves two further steps. In the first further step we specify, in this case, the sensible effects of one thing's being harder than another; say, of a diamond's being harder than glass. Sensible effects are not effects upon our senses, but perceivable public effects. For example, diamond will scratch glass but glass will not scratch diamond. In the second further step we specify practical bearings of these effects. Practical bearings are bearings on practice or conduct; that is, on habits of action. A sensible effect has a practical bearing if it is such that to conceive ourselves as being in a certain situation and having a certain desire is to be ready to act in a certain way if such a situation should ever arise. For example, we can conceive ourselves as desiring to divide a sheet of glass, and as having no regular glass-cutting tool available, but only a diamond ring. So to conceive is already to have formed the habit of using the diamond to cut the glass in such situations. On the other hand, we can conceive ourselves as having a sheet of glass we do not want scratched; say, a mirror. The habit of action determined by the belief that diamond is harder than glass will in that case be the habit of keeping the diamond ring away from the mirror. In each of these cases, the third and final interpretant, which marks the third level of clarity, consists of conceived sensible effect, conceived desire, and habit of action *together*. At that level of clarity, interpretants such as these constitute the whole of our conception of the object represented by the sign *hard*. The mineralogists' scale of hardness is arrived at by interpreting *hard* in this way, and the scale itself is so interpreted.

Much of this, however, would have escaped a reader unacquainted with Peirce's earlier papers. If the pragmatism of 1877–79 was indeed a second founding of semeiotic, this would have been evident at the time only to a reader who had the first founding very much in mind. In both foundings, the semeiotic is one that includes logic and that serves logic.

5. PHILODEMUS AND SEMEIOSIS
(1879–1883)

In 1865, the first year of the first founding, Theodor Gomperz published an edition of the Herculaneum papyrus remains of a Greek treatise on inductive logic by the Epicurean philosopher Philodemus. The papyrus lacked the title, but the one most often given it is the Latin *De signis* ("On Signs").

Peirce seems not to have made the acquaintance of this work immediately, but at the Johns Hopkins University he had a student named Allan Marquand, with whom he made an intensive study of it in 1879–80. To meet the thesis requirement for his Ph.D. degree, Marquand

translated the treatise under the title "On Inductive Signs and Inferences" and wrote an introduction to it. The introduction, or an abridg-
ment of it, was published under the title "The Logic of the Epicureans"
as the first essay in a volume of *Studies in Logic* edited by Peirce in
1883.[15]

One of the most striking features of the treatise is the frequency of
the term *semeiosis*. The Greek suffix -*sis* means the act, action, activity,
or process of. Peirce was prepared to understand semeiosis in either of
two ways: (1) from the side of the sign, as sign-action, the functioning
of a sign, or (2) from the side of the interpretant, as sign-interpreting or
inferring from signs. Philodemus used it primarily in the latter sense,
and even more narrowly as drawing inductive inferences from inductive
signs. But for Peirce sign-action and sign-interpretation were not two
different kinds of semeiosis but one and the same semeiosis considered
from two points of view. To act as a sign is to determine an interpretant.

Furthermore, a sign is not a kind of thing. The world does not consist of two mutually exclusive kinds of things, signs and non-signs, each
with its subdivisions, yet with no subdivision of the one overlapping
any subdivision of the other. There is nothing that may not be a sign;
perhaps, in a sufficiently generalized sense, everything *is* a sign: "all this
universe is perfused with signs, if it is not composed exclusively of signs"
(5.448n1). The fundamental distinction is not between things that are
signs and things that are not, but between triadic or sign-*action* and
dyadic or dynamical *action* (5.473). So the fundamental conception of
semeiotic is not that of sign but that of semeiosis; and semeiotic should
be defined in terms of semeiosis rather than of sign, unless sign has antecedently been defined in terms of semeiosis. A quarter of a century
later, in 1907, Peirce could still describe himself as "a pioneer, or rather
a backwoodsman, in the work of clearing and opening up what I call
semeiotic, that is, the doctrine of the essential nature and fundamental
varieties of possible semiosis" (5.488).

6. SEMEIOTIC AND THE LOGIC OF MATHEMATICS (1866–1911)

Peirce wrote in 1903: "It has taken two generations to work out the
explanation of mathematical reasoning" (NE 3:1119; cf. 1:256). What
were the essential steps that he himself took or observed others taking?
A list of some of them follows.

But first a prefatory note. It all started in 1854 with *The Laws of Thought* by George Boole, the Copernicus of modern logic (Ms 475 p.6).[16] After an introductory chapter on the nature and design of the work, Boole began the work itself with a chapter entitled "Of Signs in General, and of the Signs Appropriate to the Science of Logic in Particular; also of the Laws to which that Class of Signs are Subject." Of Peirce's five papers on logic in 1867, the first was "On an Improvement in Boole's Calculus of Logic," the fourth took off from Boole, and Peirce later showed how study of Boole led him to the "natural classification of arguments" in the second (Ms 475 pp.2–28). Now for the steps:

(1) In a privately printed paper of 1866 (at 2.801–804) and in his second and third papers of 1867 (at 2.470, 474 and 1.559) Peirce showed, as he later put it, that "all logical thought" is "an operation upon symbols consisting in substitution" but did *not* claim or assume that such substitution is "an indecomposable operation."[17]

(2) In 1870 Peirce published his "Description of a Notation for the Logic of Relatives" (3.45–149), with sections on the various signs (for examples, of inclusion, equality, addition, multiplication, involution). The logic of relatives became the key to the inexhaustible richness of mathematical reasoning, its ability to draw indefinitely numerous necessary conclusions from a single hypothesis, a single premiss or conjunction of premisses (NE 4:58–59).

(3) In the same year his father, Benjamin Peirce, began his *Linear Associative Algebra* with the sentence: "Mathematics is the science which draws necessary conclusions." He went on to discuss "the language of algebra"—its letters and signs and rules of composition. The first principle he states is that of "the substitution of letters," which "is radically important, and is a leading element of originality in the present investigation."

(4) During the period in which son and father were working on (2) and (3), they had frequent conversations. The son later remembered two things: (a) The father at one point seemed inclined toward the view, later embraced by Dedekind, that mathematics is a branch of logic; but the son "argued strenuously against it," and thus the father "came to take the middle ground of his definition" (NE 3:526). (b) The father as mathematician and the son as logician were both struck by the contrary nature of their interests in the same propositions and

in the systems of notation in which they were represented. Take the algebra of logic for example.

> The mathematician asks what value this algebra has as a calculus. . . .
> The logician . . . demands that the algebra shall analyze a reasoning into
> its last elementary steps. Thus, that which is a merit in a logical algebra
> for one of these students is a demerit in the eyes of the other. The one
> studies the science of drawing conclusions, the other the science which
> draws necessary conclusions. [4.239]

(5) In the 1870s, the British mathematicians Cayley, Sylvester, and Clifford made two-way connections between mathematics and chemistry. Cayley applied his mathematical theory of "trees" to a problem in chemistry. Sylvester and Clifford shortened to *graph* the "graphic formula" of the chemists, and, starting with the theory of invariants, they began adapting such graphs to mathematical uses.

(6) Sylvester became professor of mathematics at the Johns Hopkins University in 1876, founded the *American Journal of Mathematics* there in 1878, introduced the new term *graph* in the first issue, and said that Clifford had found "the universal pass key to the quantification of graphs."[18]

(7) Peirce joined the Hopkins faculty in 1879. As chemist, mathematician, friend of Clifford (who had died in the spring), and now younger colleague of Sylvester, he welcomed the adapting of chemical graphs to mathematical uses. To the *Journal's* first seven volumes (1878–1885) he contributed a review and four articles, as well as a new edition of his father's *Linear Associative Algebra*, with many notes and two addenda by himself.[19]

(8) Cayley was visiting lecturer at Hopkins from January to June 1882. Peirce, as usual, was attending meetings of the Mathematical Society, presenting papers to it, and taking part in discussions of papers presented by others. At its January meeting, for example, papers were presented by Cayley, Sylvester, and Peirce.[20] In the spring Peirce gave a short course of three lectures on the logic of relatives for students of mathematics.

(9) In 1883 George Chrystal gave an account of mathematics in the ninth edition of the *Encyclopaedia Britannica*, which Peirce took to be defining it as the science of making pure hypotheses, though Chrystal used the term *conception* rather than *hypothesis* (3.558). Chrystal, he

said, "puts emphasis upon the definiteness of mathematical hypotheses. . . . I incline to suspect that Prof. Chrystal has confounded *definiteness* with *iconicity,* or the capability of being represented in a diagram" (NE 2:595).

(10) In 1885 Peirce published the second of his two papers "On the Algebra of Logic," with the subtitle "A Contribution to the Philosophy of Notation" (3.359–403). It begins with a section on "Three Kinds of Signs"—icons, indices, and tokens—whose thesis is that "in a perfect system of logical notation signs of these several kinds must all be employed." He gives his student O. H. Mitchell credit for introducing indices, and thereby quantification, into the algebra of logic. He goes on to say that by means of tokens and indices alone "any proposition can be expressed; but it cannot be reasoned upon, for reasoning consists in the observation that where certain relations subsist certain others are found, and it accordingly requires the exhibition of the relations reasoned with in an icon." The theory of signs and the logic of relatives thus lead to the further conclusion that all deductive reasoning, including that of mathematics, involves experiment and observation (3.363). In the main body of the paper, Peirce presents in the form of twelve "icons" the algebraic foundations of a system of material implication, including truth-table analysis and quantification. One of these "icons," the fifth (3.384), has come to be called Peirce's Law.

Every one of the icons consists of symbols (here called tokens) and *is* a symbol. Some of the elementary symbols are indices. But what Peirce wants to emphasize is the iconicity of each formula as a whole. The logic of relatives has opened the way for him to extend the notion of iconicity from quasi-geometrical graphs, whose iconicity was already obvious, to algebraic formulations of the laws of logic, whose iconicity is rendered obvious by the logic of relatives.

It follows that, just as the world does not consist of two mutually exclusive kinds of things, signs and non-signs, so there are not three mutually exclusive kinds of signs: icons, indices, and symbols. These are rather elements or aspects of semeioses that vary greatly in relative prominence or importance from semeiosis to semeiosis. We may therefore call a sign, for short, by the name of that element or aspect which is most prominent in it, or to which we wish to direct attention, without thereby implying that it has no element or aspect of the other two kinds.

(11) In 1886 A. B. Kempe published in the *Philosophical Transac-*

tions "A Memoir on the Theory of Mathematical Form" and sent an inscribed copy to Peirce, who annotated and indexed it. Kempe made an extensive use of graphs, and it was in part by critical study of this memoir that Peirce later arrived at his own two systems of graphs. As late as 1905, he called Kempe's "great memoir" "the most solid piece of work upon any branch of the stecheology of relations that has ever been done" (5.505).

(12) In 1889 Peirce contributed to *The Century Dictionary* the first dictionary definition of the new term *graph*:

> A diagrammatic representation of a system of connections by means of a number of spots, which may be all distinguished from one another, some pairs of these spots being connected by lines all of which are of one kind. In this way any system of relationship may be represented. Graphs are commonly used in chemistry, and have been applied in algebra and in logic.

(13) In 1894–95 Peirce drafted two textbooks: *Elements of Mathematics* (NE 2:1–232) and *New Elements of Geometry Based on Benjamin Peirce's Work & Teachings* (NE 2:233–473). In the former he describes mathematics as "the exact study of ideal states of things" and says his father's definition "comes to much the same thing" (NE 2:10). "Two kinds of icons are chiefly used by mathematicians, namely, first, geometrical *figures*, drawn with lines, and, second, *arrays* of points or letters . . . . upon which experiments and observations can be made" (NE 2.24; cf. 2:12).

(14) In 1896, in a paper "On Quantity, with special reference to Collectional and Mathematical Infinity," Peirce finally concedes that his father's definition of mathematics is defective in that it omits the framing by the mathematician of the hypotheses from which he proceeds to draw necessary conclusions (NE 4:271); and he offers a definition of his own that makes good that defect (NE 3:40–41).

> Mathematics may be defined as the study of the substance of exact hypotheses. It comprehends 1st, the framing of hypotheses, and 2nd, the deduction of their consequences. . . . [T]he definition I here propose differs from that of my father only in making mathematics to comprehend the framing of the hypotheses as well as the deduction from them. [Ms 16 p.1; Ms 18 p.3; cf. NE 2:595][21]

(15) In *The Monist* for January 1897, with references to Clifford and Kempe by name (3.468, 479n1) and to Sylvester by implication

(3.470*), Peirce presented the system of what he later called *entitative graphs*. While reading the proofs, he conceived another system, which he called *existential graphs*. Partial expositions of this second and more iconic system reached print in 1903 (4.394–417) and 1906 (4.530–72).[22]

(16) In the *Educational Review* for 1898 Peirce published "The Logic of Mathematics in Relation to Education" (3.553–62).

> Thus, the mathematician does two very different things: namely, he first frames a pure hypothesis stripped of all features which do not concern the drawing of consequences from it, and this he does without inquiring or caring whether it agrees with the actual facts or not; and, secondly, he proceeds to draw necessary consequences from that hypothesis. [3.559]

Peirce describes the "stripping" as "skeletonization or diagrammatization"; that is, iconization.

(17) In 1901, in a draft of "On the Logic of drawing History from Ancient Documents, especially from Testimonies," Peirce divided deductions into two kinds, corollarial and theorematic, and gave a detailed example of each, both drawn from the doctrine of multitude (NE 4:1–12). He took this to be the most important division of deductions, and his own most important discovery in the logic of mathematics (NE 4:38, 56). He had already "opened up the subject of abstraction" (NE 4:1), distinguished its two kinds, prescission and subjectifaction, and called the latter "the very nerve of mathematical thinking" (2.428). He now proceeded to divide theorematic reasoning into abstractional and non-abstractional (NE 4:49). Here again the theory of signs came into play. "Every subject partakes of the nature of an index. . . . The expressed subject of an ordinary proposition approaches most nearly to the nature of an index when it is a proper name. . . . Among, or along with, proper names we may put abstractions. . . ." (2.357). But this is matter for a separate long article or short book.

(18) In 1902, in the chapter of his *Minute Logic* on "The Simplest Mathematics," Peirce briefly restates the distinction between corollarial and theorematic deduction; speaks of the latter as "mathematical reasoning proper"; describes it as "reasoning with specially constructed schemata"; and says it "invariably depends upon experimentation with individual schemata," that is, with icons, whereas corollarial reasoning is largely "reasoning with words," that is, with symbols (4.233). In the same chapter, in an eleven-page passage omitted by the editors of the

Collected Papers (at 4.261), he introduces two notations for the sixteen binary connectives of the two-valued propositional calculus. One of these may be called his box-X, the other his cursive notation. He says it was his Hopkins student Christine Ladd-Franklin "who first proposed to put the same character into four positions in order to represent the relationship between logical copulas, and . . . it was a part of her proposal that when the relation signified was symmetrical, the sign should have a right and left symmetry." Peirce's own notations simply carrry out that proposal in a particular way (NE 3:272–75n at 272).[23]

(19) In his article on Symbolic Logic in Baldwin's *Dictionary of Philosophy and Psychology* in 1902, Peirce said the symbols should include graphical as well as algebraic ones, and that a system of symbols devised for the investigation of logic, as opposed to one intended as a calculus, "should be as analytical as possible, breaking up inferences into the greatest possible number of steps, and exhibiting them under the most general categories possible." "There must be operations of transformation. . . . In order that these operations should be as analytically represented as possible, each elementary operation should be either an insertion or an omission" (4.372–74).[24]

(20) In 1903, in his *Syllabus of Certain Topics of Logic*, there appeared the first published account of Peirce's existential graphs (4.394–417), including rules of transformation and code of permissions, from which it appears that in this system each elementary operation is an insertion or an omission. This is preceded by a section called "The Ethics of Terminology"—an ethics that applies to notations and other symbols as well as terms (2.219–26). And that is preceded by "An Outline Classification of the Sciences" (1.180–202). Logic is now a normative science, depending on ethics, as that does on esthetics. Above the normative sciences are mathematics and phenomenology.

All thought being performed by means of signs, logic may be regarded as the science of the general laws of signs. It has three branches: 1, *Speculative Grammar*, or the general theory of the nature and meanings of signs, whether they be icons, indices, or symbols; 2, *Critic* . . . ; 3, *Methodeutic*. . . . Each division depends on that which precedes it. [1.191]

(21) About 1904, in his καινὰ στοιχεῖα ("New Elements"), Peirce presents the best restatement so far of his general theory of signs (NE 4:238–63). Symbols are now genuine signs; indices are signs degenerate

in the first degree; icons are signs degenerate in the second degree. A symbol sufficiently complete always involves an index; an index sufficiently complete always involves an icon (NE 4:256). But "the icon is very perfect in respect to signification, bringing its interpreter face to face with the very character signified. For this reason, it is the mathematical sign *par excellence*" (NE 4:242).

(22) About 1905 Peirce begins "The Rules of Existential Graphs" (Ms 1589) with a preface and an introductory section on "The Nomenclature," in which he confesses a violation of the ethics of terminology in his previous expositions. The preface reads:

> The system of existential graphs is intended to afford a method for the analysis of all necessary reasonings into their ultimate elements. No transformations are permitted except *insertions* and *omissions*, and the formal signs are the fewest with which it is possible to represent all the operations of necessary reasonings.

(23) In 1906, in his "Prolegomena to an Apology for Pragmaticism," Peirce presents the fullest and most mature accounts both of his semeiotic (4.530–51) and of his existential graphs (4.552–72) that he succeeded in publishing. A sample sentence:

> Now since a diagram, though it will ordinarily have Symbolide Features, as well as features approaching the nature of Indices, is nevertheless in the main an Icon of the forms of relations in the constitution of its Object, the appropriateness of it for the representation of necessary inference is easily seen. [4.531]

(24) Up to this point, Peirce has concerned himself primarily with the classification of arguments. From the beginning he recognizes three kinds, which he calls at first *deduction, induction,* and *hypothesis.* The last he later calls *abduction,* and finally *retroduction.* He has set the logic of mathematics (that is, of analytic, deductive, or necessary arguments) over against the logic of science (that is, of ampliative or probable arguments, either retroductive or inductive). In 1908, however, in "A Neglected Argument for the Reality of God," he presents retroduction, deduction, and induction as successive stages of inquiry (8.468–73). To that extent, he absorbs the logic of mathematics into that of science. Deduction, he says, has two parts.

> For its first step must be by logical analysis to Explicate the hypothesis, i.e. to render it as perfectly distinct as possible. . . . Explication is fol-

lowed by Demonstration. .... It invariably requires something of the nature of a diagram; that is, an "Icon," or Sign that represents its Object in resembling it. It usually, too, needs "Indices," or Signs that represent their Objects by being actually connected with them. But it is mainly composed of "Symbols," or Signs that represent their Objects essentially because they will be so interpreted. Demonstration should be *Corollarial* when it can. .... *Theorematic* Demonstration resorts to a more complicated process of thought.

(25) The nearest thing to a retrospective summing up is in a long letter to J. H. Kehler in 1911 (NE 3:159–210), from which I quote two short passages.

I invented several different systems of signs to deal with relations. One of them is called the general algebra of relations, and another the algebra of dyadic relations. *I was finally led to prefer what I call a diagrammatic syntax.* [162]

He gives an exposition of the syntax of his existential graphs, in the course of which he remarks that

this syntax is truly *diagrammatic,* that is to say that its parts are really related to one another in forms of relation analogous to those of the assertions they represent, and that consequently in studying this syntax we may be assured that we are studying the real relations of the parts of the assertions and reasonings; which is by no means the case with the syntax of speech. [164f.]

In concluding this section, I trust that its twenty-five selected steps in the working out of the explanation of mathematical reasoning have made it sufficiently evident that Peirce's lifelong study of the logic of mathematics was conducted throughout within the framework of the general theory of signs.

7. THE REBIRTH OF PRAGMATISM (1898–1911)—A THIRD FOUNDING?

In the United States, at least, it was in 1898 that the word *pragmatism* was first used in a public address and then in print as the name of a philosophic doctrine and method. The speaker was William James, addressing the Philosophical Union at the University of California at Berkeley on "Philosophical Conceptions and Practical Results." His address appeared as the leading article in the *University Chronicle* for

September. It was widely circulated, and pragmatism soon became a movement, the liveliest so far in American philosophy.[25]

Though James gave him full credit, Peirce soon felt the need of restating his own pragmatism, both to distinguish it from James's and Schiller's and to correct certain errors and omissions in his original statement of 1877–78; above all to make fully explicit the semeiotic framework within which it had been worked out. Peirce held that his own strictly limited form of pragmatism was provable, and it was only within the semeiotic framework that the proof could be made evident.[26] With this in view, he gave two series of lectures in 1903, one at Harvard University in the spring, the other at the Lowell Institute in the fall.

In 1905 he began a series of articles on pragmatism in *The Monist*. In the first, "What Pragmatism Is," his own form of it was renamed *pragmaticism* (5.411–37 at 414). In the second, "Issues of Pragmaticism," two doctrines that he had defended before he first formulated his pragmatism back in the 1870s—namely, critical common-sensism and scholastic realism—were now treated as consequences of it. The chief novelty in this article is the semeiotic of vagueness, one of the characters of critical common-sensism (5.438–63 at 446–50).

These two articles were meant only to prepare the way for the proof of pragmaticism in a third article. But after the second had appeared, Peirce decided that the best way to present the proof was by means of his existential graphs. So he devoted the third article to further "Prolegomena" to the proof. These, as we saw in step (23) of section 6, were a restatement of his general theory of signs—the last he succeeded in getting into print—and a much fuller exposition of his system of existential graphs.

But, alas! Though there are drafts of a fourth article and promises of a fifth and sixth, the third was the last to reach print. One of the unfinished tasks of Peirce scholarship is to construct the proof, largely from manuscripts not yet published, and to show how the graphs would have functioned in the exposition of it.

In sheer volume, his writings on the theory of signs in the nine years from 1903 through 1911—many of them still unpublished—exceed those of the preceding forty years. The most striking features of these later writings are the high frequency of focus on pragmaticism and the development of a semeiotic realism out of the type–token distinction.

In any case, the semeioticians who were soon to begin thinking of Peirce as founder of modern semeiotic had in mind chiefly his published writings of this last period, rather than those of what I have called the first and second foundings.

Meanwhile a relevant change had taken place in Peirce's view of the relation between logic and semeiotic. I report that change in the following section.

8. BACK TO LOCKE: FROM LOGIC-WITHIN-SEMEIOTIC TO LOGIC-AS SEMEIOTIC (1865–1911)

We have seen in section 2 that Peirce at first refused to follow Locke in identifying logic with semeiotic, and defined it rather as one of the three parts of a symbolistic which in turn was one of the three parts of semeiotic. By the mid-1880s, however, as we saw in step (10) of section 6, he had come to realize that logic requires indices and icons; that it cannot do business with symbols that are neither indexical nor iconic. About 1894, in the chapter on signs in his only finished treatise on logic (the so-called Grand Logic), he argued that in all reasoning we must use a "mixture" of icons, indices, and symbols. "We cannot dispense with any of them" (Ms 404 p.46). So the symbolistic trivium became the semeiotic trivium, with logic as its mid-science, and Peirce was halfway back to Locke.

But we have also seen in step (20) of section 6 that by 1903 he had gone the rest of the way. Logic was now semeiotic, as Locke held, and what Peirce had previously called *logic* he now called *Critic*. When and how did his conversion come about?

It was a gradual transition rather than a conversion. Even on the second half of the way back there was an intermediate stage, beginning about 1896, in which Peirce was saying such things as: "The term 'logic' is unscientifically by me employed in two different senses" (1.444). "The word logic is ambiguous. It is at once the name of a more general science and a specific branch of that science" (Ms 751 p.1). During this two-sense transitional stage, logic in its narrow sense was the mid-science of the semeiotic trivium; in its broad sense it was general semeiotic, embracing all three sub-sciences. But even the narrow sense was by no means as narrow as that which Peirce had given to logic in what I have called the first founding.

The journey back to Locke was completed when in 1902 he gave up the narrow sense altogether, identified logic unreservedly with semei-

otic, and adopted Locke's term *Critic* for what he had most recently
been calling "logic in the narrow sense" (NE 4.20f.). Since Critic in this
sense is the critic of arguments (4.9), and since this may need to be
distinguished from the critic of morals or of works of art or of craftsman-
ship, Peirce sometimes calls it *Critical Logic* (2.93); more often, *Logical
Critic* (6.475). To one occurrence of the latter phrase, however, he adds
"or let us say 'critic' simply, as long as we have to do with no other than
the logical kind" (Ms 852 p.2).

It is important to note, however, that though logic is now wholly
semeiotic, it is still not the whole of semeiotic. It is semeiotic variously
qualified as cenoscopic[27] (Ms 499 p.[15]), formal (NE 4:20f.), general
(1.444), normative (2.111), speculative (Ms 693 p.188). It is "General
Semeiotic, the *a priori* theory of signs" (Ms 634 p.14); "the quasi-necessary, or formal doctrine of signs" (2.227); "the pure theory of signs, in
general" (Ms L 107 p.24). In addition to cenoscopic semeiotic, there are,
or may be, idioscopic studies of signs as various as the idioscopic sciences themselves—physical, chemical, biological, geological, anthropological, psychological, medical, musical, economic, political, and so on.
None of these is any part of logic, though the reasonings they employ
may be made matter for logical study. Take psychology for example.

> Of course, psychologists ought to make, as in point of fact they are mak-
> ing, their own invaluable studies of the sign-making and sign-using func-
> tions,—invaluable, I call them, in spite of the fact that they cannot pos-
> sibly come to their final conclusions, until other more elementary studies
> have come to their first harvest. [Ms 675 pp.20f.]

Those, namely, of cenoscopic semeiotic.

The explanation Peirce most often gives of his move from logic-
within-semeiotic to logic-as-semeiotic is in terms of the classification of
the sciences.[28] This was always a concern with him, but increasingly so
after 1890, from dissatisfaction both with the definitions of science and
with the classification of the sciences that he had contributed to the
Century Dictionary. He came to think of science no longer as knowledge already possessed or acquired and systematized, but as ongoing
investigation, as what research scientists do; and therefore to identify
a given science not with a particular body of knowledge but with a
social group, a subcommunity of the larger community of investigators.
As he wrote Lady Welby in 1908, "the only natural lines of demarcation
between nearly related sciences are the divisions between the social
groups of devotees of those sciences" (8.342). But of course, in attempt-

ing to place a given science, the classifier would consider not only what the subcommunities are severally doing at present, but what changes are in progress, and how far they are likely to go in the near future.

"A great desideratum," he wrote in 1909, "is a general theory of all possible kinds of signs, their modes of signification, of denotation, and of information; and their whole behaviour and properties, so far as these are not accidental" (Ms 634 p.14). The task of supplying this need must be undertaken by *some* group of investigators. Nearly all that had hitherto been accomplished in that direction had been the work of logicians. No other group was so well prepared to take on the task, or could do so with less diversion from its previous concerns.

For examples, though "a piece of concerted music is a sign, and so is a word or signal of command," and "logic has no positive concern with either of these kinds of signs," it must nevertheless "concern itself with them negatively in defining the kind of signs it does deal with; and it is not likely that in our time there will be anybody to study the general physiology of the non-logical signs except the logician," who is in any case "obliged to do so, in some measure" (Ms 499 p.[15]).

So it came about that the last of Peirce's major unfinished works, which he hoped would in the twentieth century have some measure of the success that Mill's *System of Logic* had had in the nineteenth, was *A System of Logic, considered as Semeiotic* (Ms 640 p.10; NE 3:875); considered, that is, not as the whole of semeiotic, but as the whole of cenoscopic semeiotic.

9. THE LOGIC OF MATHEMATICS AGAIN (1903)

At this point we return briefly to section 6, step (14). How could Peirce defend his father's definition so long and then so abruptly change it? Because of the change in his conception of science that we have just been tracing. As he put it in 1903,

> if we conceive a science, not as a body of ascertained truth, but, as the living business which a group of investigators are engaged upon, which I think is the only sense which gives a natural classification of sciences, then we must include under mathematics everything that is an indispensable part of the mathematician's business; and therefore we must include the *formulation* of his hypotheses as well as the tracing out of their consequences. [NE 3:343]

10. VICTORIA LADY WELBY AND SIGNIFICS (1903–1911)

In May 1903 Victoria Lady Welby published *What is Meaning?*, had a copy sent to Peirce, and wrote him asking for criticism. He replied, and he reviewed the book in *The Nation* along with Russell's *Principles of Mathematics*. The correspondence thus begun lasted eight years, until her final illness.[29]

Along with the rebirth of pragmatism, his having at last a responsive correspondent was almost certainly a factor in Peirce's concentration on semeiotic in the last decade of his life, from his Harvard and Lowell lectures of 1903 onward. It may also have been a factor in the directions this concentration took, and in its characteristic emphases. Some of his best expositions are in letters to Lady Welby, and among his last creative efforts were drafts of a paper for a *Festschrift* in her honor.

After first trying *sensifics*, Lady Welby had adopted *significs* as the name for the field to which she was devoting the latter part of her life. She had contributed a brief article under that title to Baldwin's *Dictionary* in 1902. She later contributed a much longer one to the *Britannica*, in which she distinguished "three main levels or classes" of "expression-value"—"those of Sense, Meaning, and Significance." Peirce wrote her that these nearly coincided with his own division of interpretants (W111). And in a letter to James about the same time, he referred to her distinction in an illuminating passage on the sign-object and sign-interpretant relations, and on the relations between the two relations (NE 3:844).

Lady Welby wrote on December 4, 1908: "You have always been kindly interested in the work to which my life is devoted" (W65). Peirce replied on the 23rd:

> But I smiled at your speaking of my having been "*kindly* interested" in your work, as if it were a divergence—I should say a *deviation*, from my ordinary line of attention. Know that from the day when at the age of 12 or 13 I took up, in my elder brother's room a copy of Whately's "*Logic*," and asked him what Logic was, and getting some simple answer, flung myself on the floor and buried myself in it, it has never been in my power to study anything,—mathematics, ethics, metaphysics, gravitation, thermodynamics, optics, chemistry, comparative anatomy, astronomy, psychology, phonetics, economic, the history of science, whist, men and women, wine, metrology, except as a study of semeiotic. ... [W85–86]

Or, as he put it in a postscript not mailed, "when I have myself been entirely absorbed in the very same subject since 1863, without meeting, before I made your acquaintance, a single mind to whom it did not seem very like bosh" (8.376).

11. THE SOP TO CERBERUS (1908)

Responding to questions about his work in logic, Peirce wrote to Philip E. B. Jourdain on December 5, 1908:

> My idea of a sign has been so generalized that I have at length despaired of making anybody comprehend it, so that for the sake of being understood, I now limit it, so as to define a sign as anything which is on the one hand so determined (or specialized) by an object and on the other hand so determines the mind of an interpreter of it that the latter is thereby determined mediately, or indirectly, by that real object that determines the sign. Even this may well be thought an excessively generalized definition. The determination of the Interpreter's mind I term the Interpretant of the sign (NE 3:886).

Less than three weeks later, in his letter of December 23 to Lady Welby, Peirce wrote:

> I define a Sign as anything which is so determined by something else, called its Object, and so determines an effect upon a person, which effect I call its Interpretant, that the latter is thereby mediately determined by the former. My insertion of "upon a person" is a sop to Cerberus, because I despair of making my own broader conception understood. [W80–81]

What was that broader, that more generalized, conception? Negatively, it is apparent that it did not involve "the mind of an interpreter" or "an effect upon a person." Did it also not involve an utterer, a sign-giver? In the last account of his theory of signs which Peirce had published, as a framework within which to introduce his existential graphs, the place of the sign-utterer or sign-giver had been taken by the Graphist.

> Morever, signs require at least two *Quasi-minds*; a *Quasi-utterer* and a *Quasi-interpreter*; and although these two are at one (*i.e. are* one mind) in the sign itself, they must nevertheless be distinct. In the Sign they are, so to say, *welded*. Accordingly, it is not merely a fact of human Psychology, but a necessity of Logic, that every logical evolution of thought should be dialogic (4.551).

What, then, was the sop to Cerberus? If we recall that the original motive of subsuming logic under semeiotic in 1865 was to avoid basing it on psychology, we can give a tentative and at least partial answer. The sop to Cerberus was lapsing from sign-talk into psych-talk—from semeiotic into psychology. Since Peirce was himself an experimental psychologist, perhaps the first on the American continent, and once thought of giving up logic for psychology,[30] no disparagement of psychology is implied. Certainly it was no disparagement of psychology to place it lower than semeiotic in the classification of the sciences, just as it was no disparagement of semeiotic to place that below mathematics.

If we were attempting to give a more positive and complete answer, we might well begin with Peirce's 1902 application to the Carnegie Institution for a grant to enable him to write a series of thirty-six memoirs on logic; and more particularly with his brief descriptions of Memoirs No. 11, "On the Logical Conception of Mind," and No. 12, "On the Definition of Logic."

> If the logician is to talk of the operations of the mind at all . . . he must mean by "mind" something quite different from the object of study of the psychologist. . . . Logic will here be defined as *formal semiotic*. A definition of a sign will be given which no more refers to human thought than does the definition of a line as the place which a particle occupies, part by part, during a lapse of time (NE 4:20).

A few sentences from one of the drafts of the application offer further hints.

> We must begin by getting diagrammatic notions of signs from which we strip away, at first, all reference to the mind; and after we have made those ideas just as distinct as our notion of a prime number or of an oval line, we may then consider, if need be, what are the peculiar characteristics of a mental sign, and in fact may give a mathematical definition of a mind, in the same sense in which we can give a mathematical definition of a straight line. . . . But there is nothing to compel the object of such a formal definition to have the peculiar feeling of consciousness. That peculiar feeling has nothing to do with the logicality of reasoning, however; and it is far better to leave it out of account (NE 4:54).

If that does not answer our question, it sets us off on the right track. But we return from it to pursue the question how Peirce came to be recognized as a founder of semeiotic.

12. OGDEN AND RICHARDS: THE MEANING OF MEANING (1923)

Almost from the beginning of their correspondence in 1903, Lady Welby gave her visitors accounts of Peirce's letters, and frequently enclosed copies of extensive extracts from them in her letters to other correspondents. On May 2, 1911, she wrote Peirce that she thought she had found a disciple for him in C. K. Ogden, then still a student at Cambridge University (W138–39).

In Peirce's letters to Lady Welby, one of the most striking passages is that concerning his early reading of Whately's *Elements of Logic*. Ogden was so impressed by it that in *The Meaning of Meaning* in 1923 he and Richards made Whately and Peirce the culminating figures in the movement "Towards a Science of Symbolism"—the nominalistic movement from Ockham through Hobbes, Locke, Leibniz, Berkeley, Condillac, Horne Tooke, and Taine. (In order to pass directly from Whately to Peirce, they depart from chronology by taking up Taine before Whately.) They quote a passage from Whately's introduction in which he professes to know nothing of any universals but signs. Signs, he says, are the instrument of thought, not merely the vehicle of expression and communication. In any case, the only logic he understands "is entirely conversant about language" and other signs. It knows nothing of "abstract ideas" or of non-semeiotic mental processes. Ogden and Richards then say:

> It was doubtless this insistence on Signs, in which few subsequent logicians have followed him, that appealed to C. S. Peirce, the most notable of all the thinkers who have approached the question of Symbolism from the logical side.

After misquoting the Whately passage from Peirce's letter to Lady Welby, they continue:

> There cannot be thought without signs, he insists; and when William James drew attention to the work of Taine as the first writer to emphasize the importance of symbol-substitution in 'thought,' the objection was put forward that already in 1867 Peirce had treated "all logical thought as an operation upon symbols consisting in substitution."[31]

They do not call Peirce a nominalist, but they suggest that his "scholastic realism" and his exclusion of psychological considerations may account for a lack of clarity at certain points in a semeiotic that was otherwise the final upshot of the nominalistic tradition they have been sketching. In an appendix they offer a thirteen-page digest of his theory of signs in the form of extracts from his published papers (chiefly from the "Prolegomena" of 1906) and from three of his longer letters to Lady Welby, one of which contains the Whately and the "sop to Cerberus" passages.

The Meaning of Meaning was the first book in any language from which it was possible to get a grasp of Peirce's semeiotic at first hand, in his own terms. F. P. Ramsey, reviewing the book in *Mind*, rightly said that its "excellent appendix on C. S. Peirce deserves especial mention."[32] (Ludwig Wittgenstein may have known something of Peirce through Ramsey.)

The authors misquote three passages from Royce's *The World and the Individual*. Had they also looked into *The Problem of Christianity*, its chapters on interpretation would surely have led them to Peirce's cognition series of 1868–69, in which the doctrine that all thought is in signs was most fully argued and developed.[33] This is much more fundamental than anything they do quote. Had they known of it, they would surely have asked themselves where Peirce got that doctrine, and would have given what is almost certainly the right answer: He got it from Whately at the age of twelve. But at least they were on the right track in approaching Peirce from Whately and from Whately's nominalistic predecessors. It is unfortunate that no other writer on Peirce's theory of signs has taken the same approach.

13. CHARLES MORRIS: FOUNDATIONS OF THE THEORY OF SIGNS (1938)

The movement variously called logical positivism, logical empiricism, scientific empiricism, and the unity of science movement, began in German-speaking middle Europe in the 1920s, started a westward migration in the 1930s, and for a time found its main resting place, at least in English-speaking countries, at Chicago. Its chief single monument is the *International Encyclopedia of Unified Science*, edited by Otto Neurath, Rudolf Carnap, and Charles Morris, and published by the University of Chicago Press. After an introductory monograph called "Encyclopedia and Unified Science" (by six authors—Neurath,

Bohr, Dewey, Russell, Carnap, and Morris), its first systematic monograph was *Foundations of the Theory of Signs* by Morris in 1938.[34]

The position of Morris's monograph in the *Encyclopedia* was no accident. It was the outstanding feature of the very design of the *Encyclopedia*. The foundations of the theory of signs were the foundations for
the unification of the sciences.

Morris had studied under George Herbert Mead and had written his
dissertation on *Symbolism and Reality* in 1925. He had been "helped to
identify the contours of a general theory of signs by *The Meaning of
Meaning*."[35]

The first six volumes of Peirce's *Collected Papers*, edited by Charles
Hartshorne and Paul Weiss, had come out in the earlier 1930s; the first
in 1931, the sixth in 1935. (Hartshorne was a colleague of Morris's at
Chicago.) Morris acquired each of the six volumes as it appeared, and
annotated it extensively.[36] There were semeiotic materials in all six volumes, but especially in the second and fifth. By the time Morris wrote
the *Foundations*, therefore, he had examined a much more nearly adequate body of evidence for Peirce's theory of signs than had been ac-
cessible to Ogden and Richards. But the same evidence was now in the
hands of many other students, and interpretations or criticisms of
Peirce no longer passed unchallenged.

Morris had a student named Estelle Allen De Lacy, who wrote her
dissertation in 1935 on *Meaning and Methodology in Hellenistic Philosophy*, giving prominence to Philodemus. She assisted Morris for several
years in collecting materials for a history of semeiotic. This was never
written, but she and her husband, Phillip De Lacy, edited and translated Philodemus's *De signis*.[37]

Morris's later work, *Signs, Language and Behavior* (1946), has an
appendix with a section on Peirce, which begins: "Peirce was the heir
of the whole historical analysis of signs and has himself had a major influence upon contemporary discussion." In this book, as in the *Foundations*, Morris rightly took off from semeiosis, but about the same
time Dewey challenged his earlier account of "the pragmatic dimension" of semeiosis as "the relation of signs to interpreters." Morris replied to Dewey and other critics in 1948 in "Signs About Signs About
Signs," which brought Peirce to the center of semeiotic controversy,[38]
as Morris's two books had brought Peirce to the center of fresh construction.

Another student of Morris's, Thomas A. Sebeok, has become the most productive and influential semeiotician of the present day. A special field of his, which he will forgive me for spelling *zoösemeiotic*, is one that farmer Peirce entered now and then with his horses and dogs, but found no time to cultivate systematically.

14. THE GESTATION PERIOD
(1851–1865)

Whately's *Elements of Logic* was studied in the spring semester of the junior year in Harvard College. In September 1851, when about to enter upon his junior year, Peirce's older brother Jem (James Mills Peirce) bought his textbooks for the year, including Whately. Charles, who was turning twelve that month, came into Jem's room, glanced at the new textbooks, and asked what logic was. Jem's answer led Charles to stretch himself upon the carpet there in Jem's room, with Whately open before him. As Charles wrote F. A. Woods in 1913, in a few days he got all the good he could out of it, "so that 6 years later when I was, with the rest of my class, required to answer at recitations on the book, I needed no more than a slight rereading of the lessons" (Ms L 477).

There was no other episode of his boyhood that Peirce so often recounted. In other accounts he speaks of himself as having "in a few days mastered that illuminating work" (Ms 905, canceled p.5), as having been "intent" upon reading it "on several days" (Ms 842[s]), as having "buried" himself in it (W85), as having been "delighted" with it (Ms 1606 p.11), as "poring over" it (NE 4:vi); and in at least four other accounts as "devouring" it.[39]

The logicians of Peirce's youth, however critical they were of particular points in Whately, ascribed to him the revival of logic at Oxford and elsewhere after a century or more of stagnation. As early as 1833, Sir William Hamilton wrote that by the publication of Whately's *Elements* in 1826 "a new life was suddenly communicated to the expiring study," and that the decade in which it appeared had "done more in Oxford for the cause of this science than the whole hundred and thirty years preceding."[40] In 1854 George Boole, in the preface to his *Laws of Thought*, said that for "a knowledge of the most important terms of the science, as usually treated, and of its general object . . . . there is no better guide than Archbishop Whately's *Elements of Logic*," to which "the present revival of attention to this class of studies seems in a great measure due." Augustus De Morgan in his article on logic in the *English*

Cyclopaedia in 1860 wrote that Whately possessed "the talent of rendering a dry subject attractive in a sound form by style, illustration, and clearness combined. And to him is due the title of the restorer of logical study in England." Peirce's Harvard teacher, Francis Bowen, had written in the *North American Review* for October 1856:

> The revival was not confined to England, but extended to the colleges in this country. The study of Whately's *Elements* here almost immediately superseded that of Hedge's *Logic*, a little compend which did not profess to give more than a few definitions of the most frequently recurring technicalities of the science.[41]

Besides the passages in his introduction from which Ogden and Richards quoted, Whately had a chapter criticizing realism, and treating conceptualism as a variant of it.[42] He made the same distinction between fact and arrangement[43] to which Peirce appealed in two of the most nominalistic passages of his *Popular Science Monthly* series: the application of the pragmatic maxim to the conception "hard" and the comment on Gray's "Elegy" (5.403 and 409 at end; cf. 7.340). In later stages of his long progress from nominalism into realism, Peirce corrected or rejected these (5.453, 457, 545; 1.27n1, 615; 8.216).

To keep from sliding into realism unawares, Whately prescribed the prophylactic measure of using "description" when tempted to say "kind" or "nature."[44] Peirce never quite lost the habit so formed, in spite of having gradually become more and more of a realist (1.27n, 204, 549n; 5.127, 483, 486; 8.251).

When Peirce recited on Whately's *Logic* in the spring of 1858, it had been the Harvard logic text, and nominalism had been "the Cambridge Metaphysics,"[45] for a quarter of a century. But the *Logic* was not the only book of Whately's on which Peirce had to recite. In the first term of his freshman year, he recited twice a week on Whately's *Lessons on Morals and Christian Evidences*. In both terms of his junior year and perhaps also in his senior year he recited on Whately's *Elements of Rhetoric*, which had a passage advocating nominalism more vigorously even than the one that Ogden and Richards quoted from the *Logic*. Here is the latter half of it:

> The full importance, consequently, of Language, and of precise technical Language,—of having accurate and well-defined "names for one's tools,"—can never be duly appreciated by those who still cling to the theory of "Ideas"; those imaginary objects of thought in the mind, of

which "Common-terms" are merely the names, and by means of which we are supposed to be able to do what I am convinced is impossible; to carry on a train of Reasoning without the use of Language, or of any General-Signs whatever.

But each, in proportion as he the more fully embraces the doctrine of *Nominalism*, and consequently understands the real character of Language, will become the better qualified to estimate the importance of an accurate system of nomenclature.[46]

The rhetoric text in Peirce's sophomore year, George Campbell's *Philosophy of Rhetoric*, inculcated similar views.

While still in college, Peirce had in his private library at least two other books of Whately's. One was *A Selection of English Synonyms*, by Whately's daughter Elizabeth Jane Whately, revised throughout by Whately himself, who said in his preface that it was "very much the best" work that had appeared on the subject, but that

> the importance of that subject itself . . . and of all that relates to language, will be much less highly estimated by those who have adopted the metaphysical theory of *ideas*, and who consider the use of language to be merely the *conveying* our meaning to *others*, than by those who adhere to the opposite—the *nominalist*—view . . . and who accordingly regard words—or some kind of *signs* equivalent to words—as an indispensable instrument of thought, in all cases, where a process of *reasoning* takes place.[47]

It was doubtless this book that prompted Peirce in October 1857, early in his junior year, to begin writing "A Scientific Book of Synonyms in the English Language" (Mss 1140–42).

Also in Peirce's private library was Whately's *Historic Doubts Relative to Napoleon Buonaparte*, a parody of Hume's scepticism concerning miracles. This was almost certainly the germ from which Peirce's theory of historical method developed (2.625, 634, 642, 714; 5.589; 8.194f., 380, 382; Mss 1319–20).

Peirce also read the nominalists that Ogden and Richards later reviewed on their way to Whately and Peirce. Take Horne Tooke, for example. On January 1, 1861, Peirce's "Aunt Lizzie" (Charlotte Elizabeth Peirce) gave him a copy of the 1860 edition of *The Diversions of Purley*.[48] Though Horne Tooke was a follower of Locke, his thesis was that everything Locke had said in terms of ideas should rather have been said in terms of words. Though Peirce did not jettison the language of ideas, even in the article in which his pragmatism was first put forward

—"How To Make Our Ideas Clear" (1878)—he could write as late as 1896: "What do we mean by an idea being clear? It is not needful to inquire first what an idea is. We can dispense with the word idea, and can ask what we mean by attaching a clear signification to a word" (Ms 953 p.8).

Peirce frequently said in later years that it was the extreme nominalists such as Ockham, Hobbes, Leibniz, and Berkeley who had especially urged the doctrine that "every thought is a sign" (5.470), that "thoughts *are* signs" (4.582), that "Any concept is a sign" (8.332), but that there is nothing inherently or peculiarly nominalistic about the doctrine, and that "the realists are, for the most part, content to let the proposition stand unchallenged, even when they have not decidedly affirmed its truth" (4.582).

Of Peirce himself it may be concluded that he committed himself in youth to a theory of cognition which he knew to be *prima facie* nominalistic, and that he at first conceived himself to be a nominalist in so doing; but that, step by step over a period of forty years or more, beginning in 1868, he transformed that nominalistic doctrine into a more and more realistic one.

In any case, he remained a nominalist throughout what I have called the gestation period of his semeiotic.[49]

15. A FOURTH FOUNDING? (1976–)

Peirce's *Letters to Lady Welby* came out in 1953. Volumes 7–8 were added to the *Collected Papers* in 1958, both containing further materials on the general theory of signs, including a long draft of a letter not sent to Lady Welby and therefore not included in the 1953 edition (8.342–79). A microfilm edition of the Peirce manuscripts at Harvard University became available in 1964, and a *Catalogue* of them came out in 1967. The first of four volumes of his *Nation* reviews appeared in December 1975. Carolyn Eisele's *The New Elements of Mathematics by Charles S. Peirce* (1976) consists almost entirely of papers not previously published, and much more of this new material is relevant to semeiotic than would be guessed from the title, from the indexes, or from a casual glance through the four-volumes-in-five. A microfiche edition of the papers Peirce himself published appeared in 1977. An edition of the Peirce/Welby correspondence by Charles S. Hardwick, containing Lady Welby's letters to Peirce as well as his to her, appeared later in 1977. Several anthologies of Peirce's writings on semeiotic, both in English and in translation, are being prepared.

It remains the case, however, that Peirce's still unpublished writings on the theory of signs exceed in quantity those that have so far been published. A new and more comprehensive edition of his writings is now in preparation, to be arranged chronologically in fifteen or more volumes to appear over a period of ten or more years, plus a two-volume biography and a volume of bibliographies and indexes. The semeiotic materials appearing for the first time in this new edition will exceed in quantity those which first appeared in the eight volumes of *Collected Papers*.

There is already an extensive body of secondary literature, some of it purely expository, some of it critical; some of it continuing where Peirce left off; some of it inspired in part by Peirce but making no attempt to distinguish Peircean from non-Peircean elements in the new constructions in progress.

The continuing confusion of tongues in the semeiotic tower of Babel is such that, for some time to come, it will be worthwhile for semeioticians and Peirce scholars to study the new materials as they become available, and to attempt some of the unfinished tasks of Peircean semeiotic scholarship. Eight of these occur to me as worth mentioning here.

(1) Most needed, and perhaps even a prerequisite to the rest, is an annotated bibliography of Peirce's own relevant writings, published and unpublished, followed by a bibliography of the secondary literature and by a lexicon that quotes Peirce's best definitions or explanations of the terms he uses and that gives references to other relevant passages in his writings and in the secondary literature.

(2) The present paper has briefly shown how Peirce's lifelong study of the logic of mathematics was conducted throughout within the framework of semeiotic. This is worth showing in greater detail. But Peirce's work in the logic of mathematics was for the sake of his more extensive work in the logic of the positive sciences, and it remains to be shown how that also was conducted throughout within the same framework.

(3) Peirce said that the proof of pragmaticism on which he embarked in his *Monist* series of 1905 was "the one contribution of value" that he had still to make to philosophy, "For it would essentially involve the establishment of the truth of synechism" (5.415). What, in full, was the unfinished proof? How did the theory of signs and the system of

existential graphs function in it? And how would it establish the truth of synechism?[50]

(4) What, more exactly, was the "sop to Cerberus"? And what, more exactly, was that broader, that more generalized conception of sign that Peirce despaired of making understandable and understood?

(5) Suppose that Peirce had succeeded in writing *A System of Logic, considered as Semeiotic,* or rather suppose that he were writing it today, in full knowledge of developments in logic and in semeiotic since his time. What would be its distinguishing features? Imagine the *System* already published, and a competent critic writing a careful review article on it. How would the article go?

(6) As an approach to (5), consider that nearly everything that has so far been written about Peirce's general theory of signs belongs to the first of the three parts of the semeiotic trivium, leaving the second and third empty. But Peirce said his hardest and best work had been done on the third (NE 3:207).[51] Interpreters and critics of his pragmatism and of his theory of the economy of research, for examples, have either detached them from semeiotic altogether or have failed to assign them properly, as he did, to its third part, Methodeutic, as presupposing the second, Critic. To what extent has our understanding of them been thereby vitiated? What were his other contributions to Methodeutic? And how about Critic?

(7) What were the steps by which Peirce passed from a nominalistic to a more and more realistic general theory of signs? "Everybody ought to be a nominalist at first, and to continue in that opinion until he is driven out of it by the *force majeure* of irreconcilable facts" (4.1). What was the *force majeure* at each step of the way?[52]

(8) Among the recurring topics in Peirce's writings, early and late, are "first impressions of sense" and "immediate perception." It is perhaps obvious enough that the sign theory of cognition entails rejection of the former. It is less obvious that it entails acceptance of the latter. But as late as 1905 Peirce not only claimed to have adhered from the beginning to the doctrine of immediate perception, as held by Aristotle, by Reid and Hamilton, and by Kant in his refutation of Berkeley (8.261), but said that in his own case it was viewing logic as semeiotic that led "at once" to this doctrine.[53] These matters are worth arguing out in detail, and our understanding of Peirce will remain imperfect until that has been done.

If the new materials becoming available are as illuminating as the old, and if oncoming semeioticians and Peirce scholars carry out such tasks as these, and others not less fundamental, may we not look for a fourth founding before the end of the century?

It is my belief that such a fourth founding has already begun.

NOTES

1. Imagine a small boy for whom shaping his letters is still fun. One day he draws a big O that pleases him, and he proudly calls to his older sister, "See my O, sis!"

2. "See *my* O, see!"

3. The boy puts a pair of eyes in his big O and says, "See, my O sees!"

4. The boy draws another big O with a quivering or zigzag line and says, "See my O tick! Hear the clock tick, but see my O tick!" See further Thomas A. Sebeok, " 'Semiotics' and Its Congeners," in his *Contributions to the Doctrine of Signs* (Bloomington: Indiana University and Lisse: Peter de Ridder Press, 1976), pp.47–58; and Luigi Romeo, "The Derivation of 'Semiotics' through the History of the Discipline," *Semiosis* 6:37–50 (1977).

5. Peirce in a letter to his father without date but about April 15, 1877, in Ms L 333.

6. Letter to J. E. Hilgard, Secretary of the Academy, August 6, 1877, in the C. S. S. Peirce folder in the Archives of the National Academy of Sciences.

7. Max H. Fisch and Jackson I. Cope, "Peirce at The Johns Hopkins University," in *Studies in the Philosophy of Charles Sanders Peirce*, edited by Philip P. Wiener and Frederic H. Young (Cambridge: Harvard University Press, 1952), pp.277–311.

8. He uses the singular *representamen* once, in 1.557 (1867). The plurals *representamina* and *representamens* do not yet occur. He uses both later. By 1904 he has dropped this term, but he picks it up again at least once, in 1911 (Ms 675). He continues to use *represent* and *representation*, but seldom technically.

9. In 1.555 Peirce places these three categories between Being and Substance, making five in all; but he makes no *use* of the first and fifth *as categories*. By the time he wrote his 1870 paper on the logic of relatives, it was evident to him that, in any sense in which the central three are categories, the first and fifth are not; and they never reappear as such after 1867. They are hardly ever even mentioned in connection with the categories. In at least one account, however, Peirce explicitly says that "Being and Substance are of a different nature" (Ms L 75, Carnegie Application, "Statement," p.4 of longer draft with that heading). The best account of this matter is still that by Manley Thompson in *The Pragmatic Philosophy of C. S. Peirce* (Chicago: University of Chicago Press, 1953), pp.29–36. (Other questions concerning Peirce's theory of categories are dealt with in my essay "Hegel and Peirce," in *Hegel and the History of Philosophy*, edited by Joseph J. O'Malley, Keith W. Algozin,

and Frederick G. Weiss [The Hague: Martinus Nijhoff, 1974], pp.171–93, at 173–78.)

10. The last clause is here corrected from an errata list not found by the editors of the *Collected Papers*.

11. Josiah Royce, *The Problem of Christianity* (New York: The Macmillan Co., 1913), vol. 2, pp.107–325. See especially vol. 1, p.xi, and vol. 2, p.114. See also the last paragraph of section 12 below.

12. *Popular Science Monthly* 12:1–15 (November 1877), 286–302 (January 1878), 604–15 (March 1878), 705–18 (April 1878); 13:203–17 (June 1878), 470–82 (August 1878). *Collected Papers* (with later revisions and notes) 5.358–87, 388–410; 2.645–60, 669–93; 6.395–427; 2.619–44.

13. The first two papers appeared also in French in the *Revue philosophique* 6:553–69 (December 1878), 7:39–57 (January 1879), under the titles: *La Logique de la Science, Première partie: Comment se fixe la croyance; Deuxième partie: Comment rendre nos idées claires.*

14. To be sure, there *are* differences, but they might not strike a reader unacquainted with Bain's theory of belief. See Max H. Fisch, "Alexander Bain and the Genealogy of Pragmatism," *Journal of the History of Ideas* 15:413–44 (1954), at 438–40.

15. See Max H. Fisch, "Peirce's Arisbe: The Greek Influence in his Later Philosophy," *Transactions of the Charles S. Peirce Society* 7:187–210 (1971), at 190–91, 203.

16. Next in importance was Augustus De Morgan's fourth memoir on the syllogism, in 1860, which opened up the logic of relations (NE 4:125) and elaborated the syllogism of transposed quantity (4.103). A distant third was Sir William Hamilton's quantification of the predicate (1.29) and the controversy to which it gave rise (2.532–35).

17. "Substitution in Logic," *The Monist* 15:294–95 (1905), signed by Francis C. Russell but written by Peirce. See further steps (3), (19), (20), and (22) below. See also note 31 below.

18. *American Journal of Mathematics* 1:126n (1878).

19. Ibid., 4:97–229 (1881); for errata see p.iv.

20. *Johns Hopkins University Circulars* 1:178–80.

21. For an explanation of this step, see section 9 below.

22. See Don D. Roberts, *The Existential Graphs of Charles S. Peirce* (The Hague: Mouton, 1973).

23. Cf. Ms 530, "A Proposed Logical Notation." (An American psychologist and logician, Shea Zellweger, is about to publish a new notation for the same connectives, which he calls "the logic alphabet." He accepts four of Peirce's criteria for a good notation, and follows Peirce in calling two of them *iconicity* and *cursiveness*. The other two, in substance contained in Peirce's box-X, he calls *frame consistency* and *eusymmetry*. Although his logic alphabet differs from Peirce's notations, he conceives his own notation as directly continuing Peirce's work.)

24. See step (1) above and steps (20) and (22) below. Peirce submitted a long article on "Mathematical Logic" for the same *Dictionary*, but Baldwin

printed only the first five words of it and the appended bibliographical note. The article included a five-step analysis of the mathematician's procedure. The account of the peculiarities of mathematical reasoning ended: "Of still greater importance is the practice of making operations and relations of all kinds objects to be operated upon" (NE 3:742–50 at 749f.).

25. Max H. Fisch, "American Pragmatism Before and After 1898," in *American Philosophy from Edwards to Quine*, edited by Robert W. Shahan and Kenneth R. Merrill (Norman: University of Oklahoma Press, 1977), pp. 77–110.

26. Max H. Fisch, "The 'Proof' of Pragmatism," in *Pragmatism and Purpose: Essays Presented to Thomas A. Goudge*, edited by John G. Slater, Fred Wilson, and L. W. Sumner (Toronto: University of Toronto Press, forthcoming).

27. For Peirce's use of Bentham's cenoscopic-idioscopic distinction, see 1.241f., 8.199.

28. For Peirce's classification of the sciences as of 1902–1903, see 1.180–283. This is presented in tabular form between pages 48 and 49 of Thomas A. Goudge, *The Thought of C. S. Peirce* (Toronto: University of Toronto Press, 1950). See also the illuminating Ph.D. dissertation by Beverley E. Kent, *Logic in the Context of Peirce's Classification of the Sciences* (University of Waterloo, 1975); *Dissertation Abstracts* 36:2899-A, November 1975).

29. Charles S. Hardwick, ed., *Semiotic and Significs: The Correspondence between Charles S. Peirce and Victoria Lady Welby* (Bloomington: Indiana University Press, 1977).

30. Fisch and Cope (note 7 above), p.292.

31. C. K. Ogden and I. A. Richards, *The Meaning of Meaning* (London: Kegan Paul, Trench, Trubner & Co.; New York: Harcourt, Brace & Co., 1923), p.125, referring to the article cited in note 17 above.

32. *Mind* 33:109 (1924).

33. See sections 2 and 3 above.

34. Two hundred and sixty monographs were contemplated, to be collected in twenty-six volumes, but World War II and Neurath's death intervened. The ten monographs of Volume I were collected in 1955. When nine of the ten for Volume II were ready in 1969, it appeared along with a reprint of Volume I under the title *Foundations of the Unity of Science: Toward an International Encyclopedia of Unified Science*. The remainder of the project was indefinitely postponed. Meanwhile the monographs of both volumes had been appearing singly, as they became ready, beginning in 1938. Morris's monograph appeared in that year as Volume I, Number 2.

35. Charles Morris, *Writings on the General Theory of Signs* (The Hague: Mouton, 1971), p.7. (The *Foundations* and other writings mentioned below are reprinted in this volume.)

36. Morris has recently given a collection of his correspondence and other papers and a part of his library, including these volumes, to Indiana University–Purdue University at Indianapolis.

37. *Philodemus: On Methods of Inference; A Study in Ancient Empiricism*

(Philological Monographs published by the American Philological Association, Number X, 1941). Estelle Allen De Lacy, "Meaning and Methodology in Hellenistic Philosophy," *Philosophical Review* 47:390–409, 1938.

38. *Philosophy and Phenomenological Research* 9:115–33 (1948). On the controversy between Morris and Dewey about Peirce see Max H. Fisch, "Dewey's Critical and Historical Studies," in *Guide to the Works of John Dewey*, edited by Jo Ann Boydston (Carbondale: Southern Illinois University Press, 1970), pp. 306–33 at 330–32.

39. Mss 842 p.7, 848 p.9; W77; letter to Samuel Barnett, December 20, 1909, in Emory University Library.

40. Sir William Hamilton, *Discussions on Philosophy and Literature* (New York: Harper & Brothers, 1860), p.126.

41. In 1864 Bowen began the preface to his own *Treatise on Logic* (Boston: John Allyn): "The revival of the study of Logic, at least in England and America, as an important element of a University education, dates only from the publication of Dr. Whately's treatise on the subject, little over thirty years ago."

42. *Elements of Logic* (New York: Harper & Brothers, 1856), Book IV, ch. V, pp.294–303, at p.299*.

43. Ibid., pp. 296f.

44. Ibid., pp. 294*, 298, 302, 347.

45. Amos Bronson Alcott, writing to William Torrey Harris on April 2, 1868, and commenting on "Nominalism *versus* Realism" (*Journal of Speculative Philosophy* 2:57–61, 1868 [6.619–24]), says: "I take the author . . . to be the son of the Cambridge Mathematical Professor, and speaking the best he has for the Cambridge Metaphysics. . . ." (quoted from a typewritten transcript sent to me by Harris's daughter, Edith Davidson Harris, in 1949. She gave her Alcott–Harris collection to the Concord Free Public Library in 1952, but the entire collection, including this letter, has been missing since 1960.) In a draft of this letter among the Alcott Papers in the Houghton Library of Harvard University, Alcott puts it as follows: "I take Peirce to be the son of the Cambridge mathematics Professor, and perhaps defending as he best can the Professor's metaphysics, if not of the College." So Benjamin Peirce, too, was understood to be a nominalist.

46. *Elements of Rhetoric* (London: John W. Parker, 1846), pp.20f.

47. Editor's preface to Elizabeth Jane Whately, *A Selection of English Synonyms*, 4th ed., rev. (London: John W. Parker and Son, 1858). Peirce's own copies of four of the five Whately books are listed in Ms 1555. All are of editions published in Cambridge, or Boston and Cambridge; the *Napoleon* in 1832, the *Logic, Rhetoric*, and *Synonyms* in the 1850s.

48. The call number of this copy in the Harvard University Library is 9265.11.

49. Max H. Fisch, "Peirce's Progress from Nominalism toward Realism," *The Monist* 51:159–78 (1967), shows that he was espousing nominalism under that name in 1867, well into the period of what I have called the first founding. (Among the defects of this article are that it pays too little atten-

tion to the theory of signs, fails to mention Whately and Harvard nominalism, and ignores the gestation period altogether. Moreover, its title was misleading. It was short for "Peirce's progress toward that degree—or that extremity —of realism which he eventually reached." But it was also meant to leave room for a subsequent paper, not yet written, on "Peirce's Lifelong Nominalism.")

50. See section 7 above and note 25.

51. Lines 9–11 of p.207 should read: "The third branch of logic is *Methodeutic* which shows how to conduct an inquiry. This is what the greater part of my life has been devoted to, though I base it upon Critic." The preceding sentence was left unfinished. From another draft of the same letter (Ms 231): "In my own feeling, whatever I did in any other science than logic was only an exercize in methodeutic and as soon as I had the *method* of investigation thoroughly shown, my interest dropped off." From an earlier draft letter to William James (NE 3:874): "I have done a lot of work in Methodeutic that is valuable and very little of it is printed. This will be the most widely useful part of my Big Book."

52. See section 14 above and note 49.

53. Draft letters to James, July 22 and 26, 1905, in Ms L 224.

II.   Methodology

Semiotics: A Discipline or an Interdisciplinary Method?

Umberto Eco

In 1974 the editorial board of *VS* set out to compile a comprehensive bibliography of semiotic research and asked scholars from Israel to the USSR to Denmark to Australia to pull together their resources and prepare a critical list of works produced in their respective countries. Although the stylistic criteria were stipulated by *VS*, certain questions posed by the collaborators were left unanswered, such as: "Which books or papers are considered to be those dealing with semiotics—the ones which explicitly use the term *semiotics* within their title? Or those that we consider useful to our own semiotic perspective? For example, is Locke's *Essay Concerning Human Understanding* a book on semiotics, since its last chapter proposes that semiotics be one of the three main branches of science? Is Husserl's *Logische Untersuchungen* a semiotic work even though the term *semiotics* is never used, while another of this scholar's works, entitled *Semiotik*, has barely influenced semiotic thought? On the one hand, there seem to be books that are explicitly designated as pertaining to the 'semiotics of the visual arts' but that only reiterate the traditional clichés of academic art criticism, while, on the other hand, there are other books, such as Gombrich's *Art and Illusion* and Goodman's *Languages of Art*, that are masterpieces of visual semiotics but do not even mention the word *semiotics*. Please give us some guidelines." In response to this dilemma, we answered: "No, gentlemen, that's your business! Why do you think we are preparing this special issue if not to find out how semiotics is defined?"

Frequently, while traveling, I meet people who ask: "Semiotics? [Those in the U.S. sometimes say "symbiotics"; less frequently, on the Bloomington campus, they say "sebeotics."] What's that? A disease?" Although I suspect that my friend Tom Sebeok and I feel that semiotics is our Apollonian disease, this is not the point. Semiotics does not concern any irregularity in human functions. On the contrary, it deals with the most characteristic human function, that is, the sign-function, or, in more elementary terms, *signs*. According to C. S. Peirce, a sign is "something which stands to somebody for something in some respect or capacity." In other words, to have a process of communication between two human beings (or, perhaps, between two living beings in general) requires the material presence of a certain object, be it an artifact or a natural event, which refers back to something that is not itself. This process of referring back may change from phenomenon to phenomenon, and the type of rule (or convention or attitude) that allows one to correlate a given presence to a supposed object or concept may assume different forms. In any case, there is an object for semiotic curiosity every time there is, as Roman Jakobson has stated, a *"relation de renvoi"* or—in more classical terms—when *aliquid stat pro aliquo*.

This relationship of referring back must be taken into account by the linguist, who studies the connection between *signans* and *signatum*; by the meteorologist, who infers from certain clues forthcoming atmospheric conditions; by the medical doctor, who establishes the relation between a given spot on an X-ray and an anatomical peculiarity; by the political scientist, who is concerned with the links between a given public behavior and an ideological attitude; and so forth. Therefore, when speaking of the semiotic field today, one is compelled to list an impressive, wide-ranging array of approaches, all of which are concerned in some way with the process of signification (*aliquid stat pro aliquo*) at different levels of complexity and discernibility.

When we take a closer look, there seems to exist, from studies of the genetic code to those of information theory, an underlying foundation to the 'pseudo-communication' between an unintentional sender and an unintentional receiver. Zoosemiotics (as studied particularly by Sebeok), in its turn, analyzes all the processes involved in the exchange of information between nonhuman beings. On other fronts, research is being conducted on olfactory signs (Hall), tactile communication (Frank), gestural codes (Efron), and culinary conventions (Lévi-Strauss). Motor signs used by handicapped people have been found to be ruled by complex codes that are independent of linguistic ones (Stokoe, Bellugi). Paralinguistics has listed and systematically organized every kind of suprasegmental feature and toneme (Trager, La Barre, Fónagy); and medical semiotics, established since the time of Hippocrates, is now considered a highly developed branch of general semiotics. Following the linguistic reinterpretation of Freud that was undertaken by Lacan, psychoanalysis now claims to be a semiotics of the unconscious. Kinesics, from its first pioneers De Jorio, Kleinpaul, and Mallery through the work of Efron to the recent researches of Birdwhistell, Ekman, and others, has made it clear that to gesture is to speak according to certain precise codes. In addition, proxemics (Hall) has revealed that spatial distances (that can be qualified) acquire different significations within the framework of different cultural systems. There is even a growing school concerned with the semiotics of music (even though musicology has been, from the time of Pythagoras and Boethius, nothing more than a theory of musical codes), as well as of grammatology (from the work of Gelb to Derrida), which deals with the autonomous roles of those writing conventions that cannot be considered uniquely dependent on the verbal codes that they translate into another medium. The study of iconic signs is reaching more and more complicated levels of sophistication (cf. the work of Panofsky and the rediscovery of the iconological tradition as one of several possible approaches to the study of signification in painting; Gombrich, Goodman, Metz, Krampen, Eco, and others have dealt with the dialectics between motivation and convention in images). Further, those visual signs that are more clearly and simply coded, such as traffic signs, have been investigated extensively and reduced to strict logical rules (Prieto).

It therefore goes without saying that from formalized languages to natural ones, logic and linguistics are two basic aspects of the semiotic endeavor. I am not arguing here whether these disciplines are two branches of a general semiotics (as maintained by Saussure) or whether semiotics itself should be posited under their headings. It should be enough to realize that each throws light on the problems of the others. When linguistics does try to go beyond its boundaries and to elaborate either discourse analysis or text grammars, it is unable to resolve all the questions raised without comparing the verbal issues with the complex of semiotic circumstances that makes a text understandable (for

instance, think of the concept of *behavioreme* in Pike or of the recent
analyses of Petőfi). The comprehension of a text—which constitutes not
only a semantic problem but also a pragmatic one—is strictly dependent
upon a series of cultural codes that constitute a semiotic typology of
cultures (e.g., Lotman and the Tartu School). As far as social systems
are concerned, let us recall the semiotic approach used in cultural anthropology (Lévi-Strauss) and the semiotic notion of coding applied to
social interaction as presented by Bernstein.

In the last decade a semiotics of architecture and of various objects
has been elaborated (Eco, Prieto, Garroni, De Fusco); the various research projects on film are well known (Metz); and studies on verbal
texts as well as other visual phenomena converge toward a more articulated study of mass media in general. And, I hardly need to cite the
semiotic research done in literature (Jakobson, Barthes, Todorov,
Segre) and on the more general problems of esthetics and the philosophy of art, as well as rhetoric.

I have so far outlined a complex field of interrelated research that
advocates a semiotic perspective. Is it enough to state that therefore
a discipline (or a science) called semiotics exists, or are we simply
witnessing the passing of a rather snobbish fad? What are, in fact, the
criteria for a discipline? First, one needs to have a precise subject; and
second, a set of unified methodological tools. We could also list among
the requirements—since a discipline is a science—the capability of
producing hypotheses, the possibility of making predictions, and—as in
the hard sciences—the possibility of modifying the actual state of the
objective world. With regard to this latter set of requirements, let us
take it for granted that many semiotic inquiries have produced, along
with their hypotheses, the conditions for their falsification, as well as
for their successful prediction. What seems to be more urgent is the
need to establish whether there is a unique subject and a unique set of
categories, and I will conclude my essay by also asking whether semiotics is even able to permit the practical transformation of its own object, that is, whether semiotics is a form of social practice.

1. First of all, let us consider the unity of the object. If one looks at
the problems approached by the disciplines I have listed above, one
realizes that in every case the core of each problem revolves around the
process of referring back (*aliquid stat pro aliquo*). That is, that there is

a semiotic phenomenon every time something present can be used in order to lie—to refer one back to something that does not correspond to an actual situation. In other words, there is a semiotic phenomenon every time it is possible to speak of a *possible* world.

One could say that genetic processes cannot lie. That is true, and in fact I am not convinced that the genetic code should really be considered a code. The representation of the genetic process by geneticists, however, is a semiotic event. Chromosomes and DNA cannot lie; geneticists can. I am not sure that a machine can lie to another machine, but a man can lie to a computer (software being smarter than hardware); and perhaps the same applies to animals. The possibilities given above are not being excluded by any means, but the doubts raised also need to be examined. We are sure that one can lie using words, that it is possible to ring a bell in a church even though transubstantiation has not even taken place, to gesture like a Russian although one is a CIA agent, to dress like a bishop while being an atheist, to emit odors by chemical means, to mistake the social status of a person because of the megalomaniac size of his desk, to build a restaurant as though it were a pagoda (a very American performance indeed!), to show a photograph of John and say that it is a picture of Paul, to touch up a photograph of Paul, to edit a film by presenting the effects as the causes, and so forth. Let us look at another analogy: if two molecules of hydrogen combine with one molecule of oxygen, the result is water; there is no alternative because, in this case, nothing stands for something else: something stands *with* or *against* something. But the chemical formula of water stands *for* water, and there is the possibility of representing the same compound by another conventionalized formula. Making chemical reactions is not a matter for semiotics; the representations for these reactions are.

In this sense, many disciplines are concerned with semiotic phenomena even when no one realizes it. Let us now consider two fields that are usually examined from the viewpoint of material interaction rather than symbolic interaction: the production of material tools and the exchange of these tools as commodities.

When an Australopithecine used a stone to split the skull of a baboon, there was as yet no culture—even if the Australopithecine had in fact transformed an element of nature into a tool. We would say that culture is born when (i) a thinking being establishes the new function of the stone (irrespective of whether he works on it, transforming it into a flint stone); (ii) he calls it "a stone that serves for something" (irrespective of whether he calls it that to others or to himself); (iii) he recognizes it as "the stone that responds to the function F and that has the name Y" (regardless of whether he uses it as such a second time, it is sufficient that he recognizes it). These three conditions result in a semiotic process of the kind shown in Fig. 1.

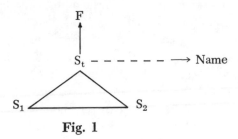

Fig. 1

S_1 represents the first stone used for the first time as a tool, and S_2 is a second stone, different in size, color, and weight from the first one. Now suppose that our Australopithecine, after having used the first stone by chance and having discovered its possible function, comes upon a second stone (S_2) some days later and recognizes it as a *token*, an individual occurrence of a more general model (S_t), which is the abstract *type* to which S_1 also refers. Encountering S_2 and being able to subsume it (along with S_1) under the type S_t, our Australopithecine regards it as the *sign vehicle* of a possible function F.

S_1 and S_2, as tokens of the type S_t, are significant forms *referring back to* and *standing for* F.

The possibility of giving a name to this type of stone (and to every other stone having the same properties) adds a new semiotic dimension to Fig. 1. A name denotes the stone-type as its content, but at the same time it connotes the function of which the object-stone (or stone-type) is the expression. In principle, this represents no more than a *system of signification* and does not imply an actual *process of communication* (except that it is not possible to conceive the reason for the institution of such signifying relationships if not for communicative purposes). These conditions, however, do not even imply that two human beings actually exist: it is equally possible for the same situation to occur in the case of a solitary, shipwrecked Robinson Crusoe. It is necessary, though, for whoever uses the stone first to consider the possibility of 'transmitting' to himself the information he has acquired; and in order to do so he would elaborate a mnemonic device that was able to establish a permanent relationship between a given *type* of object and a given *type* of function. A single use of the stone does not constitute culture. To establish how the stone can be used again and to transmit this information to himself again does imply culture. The solitary man then becomes both transmitter and receiver of a communication (which is based on a very elementary code).

The moment that communication occurs between two men, one might well imagine that what can be observed is the verbal or pictographical sign with which the sender communicates to the addressee, by means of a name, the object-stone and its possible function (for example: 'headsplitter' or 'weapon'). In fact, the sender could communicate the function of the object even without necessarily using its name, by merely showing it. Thus, when the possible use of the stone has been conceptualized, the stone itself becomes the concrete sign of its virtual use. That is, once society exists, every function is automatically transformed (as Barthes has said) into a *sign of that function*. This is possible once culture exists, but, at the same time, culture can exist only when such transformations are possible.

We shall now move on to other phenomena as economic exchange. Here we need to eliminate the ambiguity whereby every 'exchange' is a communication (just as some people think that every communication is a 'transfer'). It is true that every communication implies an exchange of signals (just as the exchange of signals implies the transfer of energy); but there are exchanges such as those of goods in which not only signals but also consumable entities are transferred. It is possible to consider the exchange of commodities as a semiotic phenomenon not because the exchange of goods itself implies a physical exchange, but because, in the transaction, the *use value* of the goods is transformed into their *exchange value*—and therefore a process of signification, or *symbolization*, takes place, this later being further refined by the appearance of money, which *stands for something else*.

The economic relationships ruling the exchange of commodities (as described in the first book of *Das Kapital* by Karl Marx) may be represented in the same way as was the sign-function performed by the tool-stone (Fig. 2).

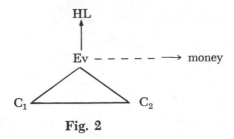

Fig. 2

C_1 and C_2 represent two commodities devoid of any use value. In *Das Kapital*, Marx not only shows how all commodities in a general exchange system can become signs standing for other commodities, but also suggests that this relation of mutual significance is made possible because the system of commodities is structured by means of *oppositions* (similar to those that linguistics has elaborated in order to describe, for example, the structure of phonological systems). Within this system, Commodity #1 becomes the commodity *through which* the exchange value of Commodity #2 is expressed (Commodity #2 being the item *of which* the exchange value is expressed by Commodity #1). This relationship is made possible by the existence, in culture, of an exchange parameter that we shall designate Ev (exchange value). If in a use value system all the items referred back to a function F (corresponding to the use value), in an exchange value system Ev refers back to the quantity of human labor necessary for the production of both C_1 and C_2 (this parameter being labelled HL). All these items can be correlated, in a more sophisticated cultural system, with a universal equivalent, i.e., money (which corresponds in some respects to the cultural name representing both commodities and their abstract and 'type' equivalents, HL and Ev). The only difference between a coin (as a sign-vehicle) and a word is that the word can be reproduced outside of an economic context while a coin is irreproducible (it therefore shares some of the properties of its commodity-object). This simply means that there are different kinds of signs that must be differentiated according to the economic value of their *expression-matter*. The Marxist analysis shows, in addition, that the semiotic diagram ruling a capitalistic economy distinguishes both HL and Ev (which are in fact mutually equivalent) from a third element, the *salary* received by the worker who performs HL. The gap between HL, Ev, and *Salary* constitutes the *plus value*. But this fact, although highly significant from the point of view of an economic inquiry, does not contradict our semiotic model; on the contrary, it shows how semiotics can clarify certain aspects of cultural life and how, from a certain point of view, a scientific approach to economics consists in discovering the one-sidedness of some obviously apparent semiotic codes—i.e., their *ideological* quality.

Therefore the relation of referring back may be the subject of a science called semiotics, even though, in any case, it is the object of other disciplines. Every discipline at a certain stage of its metatheoretical development should be concerned with semiotic phenomena, and if one does not want to consider semiotics as a discipline *per se*, one should at least consider it as a methodological approach serving many disciplines. But in order to do this, semiotics must have a unified set of methodological tools; this takes us back to our second criterion.

2. How does one go about establishing a unified set of categories for a 'pseudo' science that has grown incognito for 2,000 years under the headings of the other sciences? One could start by saying that there exist at least three *systematic* approaches to semiotics, each distinguished by a growing degree of abstraction—i.e., the ones propagated by Peirce, Morris, and Hjelmslev, respectively. Each approach takes into account, by a unified point of view and the use of a coherent ensemble of categories, *all* possible systems of signs. I can now see your disappointment and frustration: lured by the promise of the revelation whether semiotics is indeed a science or an interdisciplinary method, we find that it is in fact *three* sciences.

It may be more challenging, perhaps, to say that, given the present state of its growth, semiotics is moving toward a merger of all three perspectives in order to establish a more flexible set of tools. It is, moreover, undergoing a series of transplantations from various scientific domains, of which linguistics is only one. It should be mentioned here that the scholar who has recognized this merger to the greatest extent and who therefore has been the most influential in establishing a unified set of methodological tools is Roman Jakobson.

Let me list among the paraphernalia of this methodological *koiné* the following: the overwhelming use of the synonymous terms *signans/signatum, signifiant/signifié, expression/content, sign-vehicle/significatum*, and so forth, to describe the semiotic relationship in any sign system; the linguistic criterion of *pertinence* as applied to other code systems from gestural to folkloristic; the psychological notion of *frustrated expectation*, the mathematical one of *information*, and the poetic one of *deviation from the norm,* applied together to the analysis of messages; the list of the *functions of language* from Bühler to Jakobson as applied to any form of communication; the extension of the notion of *binarism* to certain syntactic systems and even to structural semantics; the concept of *distinctive feature* working outside the domain of phonology, from visual signals to genetic units; the opposition between *selection and combination* to explain phenomena of various languages, from movies to music; the unified use of the Peircean notion of *interpretant,* which, even in linguistics, does not work if not viewed as an intersemiotic substitution of a sign by another sign and so on; and, finally, the pair *code/message* originally derived from the mathematical theory of communication, borrowed by linguists, and subsequently used in other semiotic analyses. The list could go on and include other categories that come from other disciplines and are widely used today as 'pansemiotic' categories.

Many of the categories are very specific, but it is still possible to foresee a more wide-ranging and universal application of them. The notion of *presupposition* (linked with referential indices), for instance, has proved to be useful outside of its original domain, the logic of natural languages. It is impossible not to consider presuppositions when analyzing pictorial texts, for example. In the same way many researchers have borrowed from rhetoric the classical figures of speech and applied them to visual phenomena, such as are found in advertising. On the other hand, by analyzing visual communication, it was found that mathematical tools such as *transformation* (from geometry) and *isomorphism* between graphs (from topology) as well as the more elementary notions of *spatial* and *temporal directionality* or *vectoriality,* could be applied to explain the phenomenon of iconicity as well as certain verbal phenomena. One cannot, for instance, represent the relations of *command* and *embedding* in deep semantic structure of a phrase without referring to these notions.

At present, there are many semiotic methods, each of which is focussing on the same object and yet is organizing the same set of categories differently.

3. As for the third requirement, a science (be it a hard science or a soft one) should be able to change the state of things of which it speaks. Let me say that semiotics is not a science in the same sense as anatomy is. It seems to me a scientific carrefour more similar to medicine, which does not limit its task to a given state of affairs but attempts to improve

it—it is concerned with the way in which the human body functions and tries to influence that in a specific way.

Obviously I am not saying that semiotics is like a medicine of signs, or a therapy of the processes of communication. Such a utopia has already been advocated by general semantics, and I do not trust it. My metaphor (in which *aliquid* stood *pro aliquo*, as in every figure of speech) suggests that semiotics, more than a science, is an interdisciplinary approach—even though I could have also surreptitiously put forth the idea that it may be a sort of unified metatheoretical point of view governing a new encyclopedia of unified science. In any case, this interdisciplinary tendency (this is the second aspect of my metaphor) cannot avoid, at least at certain levels, an operational destiny.

The semiotician should thus always question both his subject and his categories in order to decide whether he is dealing with the abstract theory of pure competence of an ideal sign-producer (a competence that can be posited in an axiomatic and highly formalized way) or whether he is concerned with a social phenomenon that is subject to changes and restructuring, resembling a network of intertwined incomplete and transitory competencies rather than a crystal-like, unchanging model. The object of semiotics may somewhat resemble either (1) the surface of the sea, where independent of the continuous movement of water molecules and the interplay of the underlying currents, there is an all-encompassing form called the Sea, or (2) a carefully or dered landscape where human intervention continuously changes the form of settlements, dwellings, plantations, canals, etc. If one accepts the latter, one must also accept another condition of the semiotic approach, which is not like exploring the sea, where a ship's wake disappears as soon as it has passed, but is more like exploring a forest, where paths or footprints *do* modify the explored landscape, so that the description that the explorer gives must also take into account the ecological variations that *he* has produced.

The semiotic approach is ruled by a sort of indeterminacy principle: insofar as signifying and communicating are social functions that determine both social organization and social evolution, to 'speak' about 'speaking', to signify signification, or to communicate about communication cannot but influence the universe of speaking, signifying, and communicating.

The Contiguity Illusion

Décio Pignatari

> First comes the strength of *one* idea; then, if
> possible, its precision. And only after that, if
> you want, the precision of academic proce-
> dures.
>
> —AN OLD UNCLE

When I start with the warning, as so many semioticians now do, that
I am using language in its broadest sense, this seems to indicate that
verbal imperialism is starting to crumble, at last. . . .

It was David Hume who first distinguished the two basic forms of
association: association by contiguity and association by similarity or
resemblance. Charles Sanders Peirce defined them (7.391, 7.392) and
threw some darts at certain psychologists of his time who maintained
that the existence of two forms of association was contrary to science.
For them, association by resemblance was merely a subclass of the
only valid principle of association—association by contiguity.

Why is contiguity endowed with such a privilege? The reason lies
in a kind of logical illusion—the contiguity illusion—which we may
also observe in the works of many contemporary linguists and semiologists. This illusion, in all appearances, was born directly from Western
linguistic systems and has earned a *droit de cité* in the written notation
of these systems, that is, the alphabetic code (in this connection, the
fact that the unit *letter* was isolated many centuries before the unit
phoneme cannot be dismissed). These linguistic systems favor association by contiguity. What we formerly called classical logic—i.e., Aris-

totelian and linear—is the logic embodied in the Greek idiom: it is a contiguity logic. The alphabetic code—a most powerful logical machine —is a highly abstract discrete source of signs with digital and metonymic characteristics. Words are formed by combinatory permutations, that is, syntagmatically, and are linked together following the pattern of predication (especially when the verb *to be* is employed; "this is that"), the logical pattern *par excellence*. Predication units, in their turn, are articulated by linkage elements called *conjunctions*—first-class connections when hierarchy is implied (*hypotaxis*), and second-class connections when 'non-hierarchy' is implied (*parataxis*). From predication to sentences or propositions to concepts to Peircean arguments, we have the complete chain that has led ultimately to Western science and technology (at least if we believe in the verbalized histories of science and technology). *Ergo*, when we 'talk logic', or 'talk science', we mean that inferences have been drawn through contiguity. But is there no possibility of another kind of logic—that is, a logic by similarity?

The Western mind is contiguity-biased through language (the verbal code), which is itself based on contiguity. If we look at current European semiology, what we see is not so very different from the state of things as described by Peirce. What we see is 'semantics' nicknamed 'semiology', and Roland Barthes stating that semiology is a branch of linguistics rather than linguistics being a part of semiology. In fact, what we call *logocentrism* is another name for association by contiguity. When the word is taken as the central code, we are led to believe that all signs only acquire 'meaning' when translated into "Wordish," the verbal code. The rational mind, it follows, is the contiguity mind. When dealing with analogy, 'scientific' minds become very cautious: analogy is a dangerous path to follow—it is almost . . . non-scientific.

In Peirce's words:

> Uncontrolled inference from contiguity, or experiential connection, is the most rudimentary of all reasoning. The lower animals so reason. A dog, when he hears his master's voice, runs expecting to see him; and if he does not find him, will manifest surprise, or, at any rate, perplexity.

> Inference from resemblance perhaps implies a higher degree of self-consciousness than any of the brute possess. It involves somewhat steady attention to qualities, as such; and this must rest on a capacity, at least, for language, if not on language, itself. Primitive man is very industrious in this sort of reasoning. [7.445–46]

I doubt very much whether the Instinctive Mind could ever develop into a Rational Mind. I should expect the reverse process sooner. The Rational Mind is the Progressive Mind, and as such, by its very capacity for growth, seems more infantile than the Instinctive Mind. [7.380]

Firstness, secondness, thirdness. From sign to object to Interpretant; from icon to index to symbol. Firstness is form, the quality of a feeling (*feeling* = "the immediate element of experience generalized to its utmost" [Peirce, 7.364]). Similarity thus comes first:

> In this chaos of feelings, bits of similitude had appeared, being swallowed up again. Had reappeared by chance. A slight tendency to generalization had here and there lighted up and been quenched. Had reappeared, had strengthened itself. Like had begun to produce like. Then even pairs of unlike feelings had begun to have similars, and then these had begun to generalize. And thus relations by contiguity, that is, connections other than similarities, had sprung up. All this went on in ways I cannot now detail till the feelings were so bound together that a passable approximation to a real time was established. [Peirce, 8.318, "Letter to Christine Ladd-Franklin, On Cosmology"]

Associations by contiguity in the verbal code can therefore be summarized: to summarize a thesis is to retain its essence, to summarize a poem is to lose its essence (Valéry, 1954:1244). A summary cannot be made of a form. But what about a novel, or a short story? It is not by chance that in many Western idioms the term *argument* serves the reign of logic and the reign of fiction as well, to indicate the narrative line, the plot, the summary of a story. The work of Propp, for instance, has not been solely concerned with narrative functions, but also with the fact that narrative is built upon the predication pattern, upon associations by contiguity connected with cause/effect associations. Fairy tales and narratives in general present the same structure that can be found in predication, as well as in the sentence and the phrase (Propp, 1966: 121).

In 1968, I conducted a seminar at the Faculdade de Filosofia, Ciencias e Letras de Marília (São Paulo, Brazil) that was designed to analyze the phenomenon of *plot rarefaction* in modern fictional prose. Two major conclusions were reached:

1. The narrative depends on the number and the hierarchic structure of characters (*hypotactic structure*); and linear-discursive development is implied;

2. The reduction of the number of characters causes, at the same time, narrative 'impoverishment' (*plot rarefaction*) and simultaneity of actions (Joyce's *Ulysses*, the so-called French *nouveau roman*, and Alain Resnais' *L'année dernière à Marienbad*, serve as illustrations).

This is why French semiologists shun modern prose analysis and restrict their narrative analyses to plot analyses—the plot being understood as logical 'argument'. Once more, they fall victim to the contiguity illusion, which in the Western world is stretched to such a degree that contiguity is even smuggled into similarity. The most startling example is the so-called analogic dictionary, such as we have in Portugal and Brazil, in which terms and expressions are clustered around certain themes (i.e., ideas related by contiguity). It is interesting to observe that the organizing principle behind the making of these dictionaries is the same as that for the making of metaphors. Common dictionary entries and, even more so, those in a dictionary of rhymes, are truly analogic: they are organized following formal analogy, that is, following form similarity, in the same manner as ideogram organization. Their structure is *paramorphic*—the same structure that underlies poetic organization.

(*En passant*, it is worth noting, I think, that the written verbal code presents similarity patterns of its own, often quite independently of the sounds that they are supposed to represent [such as *bdpq* or *BDPR*]; we face here an almost autonomous language, with particular semiotic problems in modern poetry and communication [e.g., the iconization of the written verbal code]. In Mallarmé's *Un coup de dés*, all the *e*'s of a special typeface stand for spermatozoa; in Poe's *Berenice*, the thirty-two letters of the sentence *que toutes ses dents étaient des idées* stand for thirty-two teeth [Pignatari, 1974:95–96, 124]. A letter that is twenty feet high is no longer just a letter.)

Prose is contiguity's natural kingdom, as it were: fictional prose is a sort of non-antagonic contradiction, and poetry, an antagonic contradiction. When semiologists try to analyze what they formerly called the *narrative syntagm*, fundamental doubts arise in their minds—and in that of the poet—for a narrative syntagm seems not to be a common syntagm at all, but rather a paradigm, an icon—or, at least, a paradigmatic syntagm. Semioticians analyze a plot as if it were a concept—but we are dealing here with a model. A model is a nonverbal concept: that is, the equivalent of a concept based on contiguity is a model based on similarity. Fictional prose, or a biography, is a model, an icon. Of what?

Of life, the reader's life. One's life is seen and felt as an immediate icon, an immediate model (Peirce's *phaneron,* or "quality of feeling"). This is why a novel, not to speak of a play or a movie, may claim our attention even when there are no special stylistic features observed in it. To read a novel is to compare models, to exchange models—not to compare and exchange 'ideas' or concepts.

It was Paul Valéry, it seems, who first called attention to the necessity of an *Analogic*—not mere analogy. To him, da Vinci was a nonverbal philosopher:

> À peine notre pensée tend à s'approfondir, c'est à dire, à s'approcher de son objet, essayant d'opérer sur les choses mêmes (pour autant que son acte se fait choses), et non plus sur les signes *quelconques* qui excitent les idées superficielles des choses, à peine vivons-nous cette pensée, nous la sentons se séparer de tout langage conventionnel . . . *penser profondément . . . est penser le plus loin possible de l'automatisme verbal.* [1959:1263]

Philosophic systems are no more than written or scriptural systems, even when philosophy tries to assure itself against the "danger de paraître poursuivre un but purement verbal" (Valéry, 1959:1268). What Valéry says about the *graph* may be said of Peirce's *interpretant*—it is almost a definition:

> Le *graphique* est capable du continu dont la parole est incapable; il l'emporte sur elle en evidence et précision. C'est elle, sans doute, qui lui commande d'exister, qui lui donne un sens, qui l'interprète; mais ce n'est plus par elle que l'acte de possession mentale est consommé. [*Ad marginem,* he notes, "et de plus une *analogique*," and proceeds.] On voit se constituer peu à peu une sorte d'idéographie des relations figurées entre qualités et quantités, langage qui a pour grammaire un ensemble de conventions préliminaires (échelles, axes, réseaux, etc.); pour logique, la dépendence des figures ou des portions de figures, leurs propriétés de situation, etc. [Valéry, 1959:1266–67]

The paradox of Peirce's interpretant is that it is a meaning process, at the level of law and generalization and, at the same time, something like a moveable verbal and iconic supersign that is guiding the whole process, a dynamic model of signic relationships—an icon. As the meaning of a sign is another sign (cf. the dictionary), as one sign saturates into another of the same nature, so one code continually saturates into another, the verbal into the iconic and vice versa. Ultimately, thirdness saturates into firstness (cf. Valéry's graph). For Peirce, artists and scientists alike are creators of icons, and, in this light, we can understand Einstein's view:

> I seldom think in words at all . . . I work out the idea first . . . and then, much later, I try to explain it in words. [Metheny, 1968:15]

And this also helps to shake Benveniste's apparently matter-of-course idea that:

> Une chose au moins est sûre: aucune sémiologie du son, de la couleur, de l'image ne se formulera en sons, en couleurs, en images. Toute sémiologie d'un système non-linguistique doit emprunter le truchement de la langue, ne peut donc exister que par et dans la sémiologie de la langue. [1969:130]

From this we may deduce that metalanguage (the interpretant) is always and necessarily verbal in nature. This is not so. Any translation from code into code implies a metalingual operation (*metasignic* seems to be a more precise term). Any object—a work of art, for instance— will always resist (i.e., will always be different from) its description or analysis. The smile of Mona Lisa is metasignic in relation to critic and critics; semiotic is not "the study of relations between code and message," as Umberto Eco states (1968:94).

Semiotic is the study of the relations among sign systems; semiotic is always intersemiotic. Moreover, to what *langue* is Benveniste referring? The system of spoken utterances or that of written words? Or both? Here we have two different sign systems: a vocal, continuous, analogical, iconic sign is translated into a visual, discrete, digital, arbitrary sign. This is a semiotic fact, not a linguistic one. Phonological units may be translated as well—and even better—into iconic codes through phonogram plates or frequency apparatuses, such as a video-phonogram. Sign systems exist and are created for the sake of knowledge and information; each must have its own untranslatable 'bits' of information. Meaning results from the confrontation of sign systems—and difference is always implied in the process. Consequently, we are free to raise the following questions: Can a "sémiologie de la langue" exist without the written code? When we talk about 'red', are we not dealing first of all with the word *red* rather than with the visual phenomenon of color?

Is not Benveniste's statement a 'normal' sample of verbal automatism and contiguity illusion? Is it possible for human beings to build a house with words? Can a bird do this? Was da Vinci an iconic thinker?

The contiguity illusion reigns everywhere among the works of semiologists. Let us illustrate this once more with some statements of Eugen Bär, from his "The Language of the Unconscious According to Lacan." Bär begins by assuming a 'scientific' posture, as always seems to happen in those soft sciences called the 'human sciences':

> I shall make a distinction between what Lacan wants to convey and the way he says it. First, he purports to be scientific, but presents his theory in the form of a literary text, sacrificing clarity not for accuracy, but for aesthetic ambiguity. . . . For this reason, *Ecrits* should be read as a literary text and, for scientific purposes, be presented in a clearer form. Some such form is attempted in my article. [1971:243]

Here we see the traditional mistake—the dichotomy *form/content*, *signifier/signified* leading to the contiguity illusion that it is possible to translate form by translating 'content'. But the following lines suit our purposes better:

> Lacan refers the reader to the works of R. Jakobson, who (1956:58) distinguishes two fundamental operations of speech: (1) to select certain linguistic units and to substitute one for another; and (2) to combine the selected linguistic units into units of higher complexity. The operation in (1) is based on the principle of similarity. For instance, substitutive reactions to the stimulus "hut" in a psychological test were the following: the tautology "hut"; the synonyms "cabin" and "hovel"; the antonym "palace" and the metaphors "den" and "burrow." The operation in (2) is based on contiguity. For instance, to the stimulus "hut," the combining operations result in metonymic appositions such as "burnt out," "is a poor little house," "thatch," "litter," or "poverty" (1973:249–50). For Jakobson, and subsequently for Lacan, metaphor is an instance of the operation in (1); metonymy, an instance of the operation in (2).

First, we must ask:

$$\text{why } hut \; - - - - - \to \; \text{cabin, hovel, palace, etc.,}$$
$$\text{and not } hut \; - - - - - \to \; \text{hat, hit, hot?}$$

Secondly, Jakobson's discovery is based on the formal similarity of phonemes: would this not lead to *paronomasia* rather than to metaphor? Third, it is interesting to note that the same process seems to underlie operations of predication, synonym, and metaphor—from the Western point of view, of course. Chinese and Japanese ideograms have no synonyms and no predication, only *paronomastic metaphors,* or better, *paramorphic metaphors.* It is not my intention here to discuss the consequences of the contiguity illusion on the study of Lacan's ideas by Bär. If, however, we compare the different renderings of the Freudian formula, *Wo es war soll Ich werden,*

(a) *Where id was there ego shall be* [Freud, Standard Edition];
(b) *Là ou s'était, c'est mon devoir que je vienne à être* [Lacan];
(c) *There where IT WAS ITSELF, it is my duty that I come to be*
[Bär's rendering of Lacan's];

we can see that Lacan is not only saying, but *showing* what and where unconscious language is, with all its reverberations and varying hues of certainty: *Là où/ Là haut, c'était/ s'était, mon de/ voir.* Vienna (*vienne*) is hinted at as a compliment to the master—so does poetry. One must approach it with the instruments of Analogic, not simply with those of Logic (from *logos,* word, verb—that is, contiguity sign, or *symbol,* in Peircean terms). And when one says Analogic, icon is implied. (I agree, by the way, with Sebeok [1976:9–10] on the issue of the expression of nonverbal communication, in the sense that I see no use whatsoever in discussing it if it points to either body or gesture languages or to other iconic sign systems. I do not, however, quite agree with him when he talks about 'iconicity'; on the same ground, we would be entitled to talk about 'verbalicity'. For the sake of semiotic, the distinction 'verbal/ nonverbal' should be abolished once and for all; 'verbal/iconic', or 'symbolic/iconic' should replace this dichotomy—with the verbal and the iconic being the two central sign systems.

Unconscious language is basically paralanguage, pre-verbal, iconic, paratactic, and paronomastic—a quasi-sign if we are talking about poetry (Pignatari, 1974:56–59). Hence Freud's special affection for *parapraxes,* as Bär puts it (1971:265) and as Freud himself has put it in so many instances. What is common to the languages of the arts, of children and primitive peoples, of schizophrenics and of the Unconscious, is the paratactic, iconic organization of signs. Even Lacan is too 'word'-minded, but his poetic language is the only way to reach and try to apprehend the transverbal, or iconic. A psychoanalysis of Iconic Man (not only in works of art) should be possible. Perhaps it would also be a psychosynthesis of psychoanalysis.

Words, especially written words, are the most abstract instances of signs; poetry is the most concrete instance of words—and icons are the 'eastern' side of signs, as words are their 'western' counterpart. Recent discoveries in brain structure seem to point to the fact that this organ, too, is divided into a contiguity lobe (i.e., the left one) and a similarity lobe (the right one). It is high time that semiologists, critics, and pedagogues started making efforts to develop their right ones.

The contradiction of the 'scientific' attitude that is derived from the contiguity bias lies in the fact that its champions are inclined to consider puns, that is, paronomasia, almost as a nonscientific language. At the same time, they state that mathematics is the model for scientific thinking. Mathematical statements operate by actual similarity among signs: algebraic expressions are algebraic puns, iconic puns. Algebra is a science of the eye, Gauss used to say. And a mathematician who is not also a poet will never be a creative mathematician, Poincaré would have added. And then Peirce would have rejoined:

> a great distinguishing property of the icon is that by the direct observation of it other truths concerning its object can be discovered than those which suffice to determine its construction. Thus, by means of two photographs a map can be drawn etc. Given a conventional or other general sign of an object, to deduce any other truth than that which it explicitly signifies, it is necessary in all cases, to replace that sign by an icon. This capacity of revealing unexpected truth is precisely that wherein the utility of algebraical formulae consists, so that the iconic character is the prevailing one. [2.279]

> The reasonings of mathematicians will be found to turn chiefly upon the use of likenesses, which are the very hinges of the gates of their science. The utility of likenesses to mathematicians consists in their suggesting in a very precise way, new aspects of supposed states of things. ... [2.281]

For this reason, the icon is the sign of all possible lies as well as the sign of all discoveries—the heuristic sign, the *open sign* (4.531) *par excellence*:

> They [the icons], one and all, partake of the most overt character of all lies and deceptions—their Overtness. Yet they have more to do with the living character of truth than have either Symbols or Indices.

I am too much indebted to Roman Jakobson to dare disagree with him. Nevertheless, I must dare—and may my errors and eventual nonerrors alike be as so many more homages to him. Peirce suggests that metaphors are linked to predication (7.590). Furthermore, he makes a distinction between a pure icon ("a possibility alone is an Icon purely by virtue of its quality; and its object can only be a Firstness") and iconic signs, or *hypoicons*, which are divided into three types: *images*, *diagrams*, and *metaphors*. In this connection, metaphors are thirdnesses among firstnesses: they refer mainly to symbols (i.e., words). In semiotic terms, we could define metaphor as a hypoicon by contiguity, meaning a similitude or parallelism between certain supposedly observed features of the *referents* of the signs ('semantic' similarity or likeness of the signified), as when we say "John is an eagle." But the case would be different if we were to say "Neagle is an eagle." Here it is as if an external similarity were internally embodied in signs: sound and image tend to mimic certain features supposedly existent in the referents. Paronomasia establishes syntactic similarity or likeness between signifier and signified. What we see here is the process of iconization of the verbal. Even if we take formal similarity as metaphorical (ultimately, resemblances among sounds and letters have little to do with resemblances among features of objects which are compared), even then the phenomenon is entirely different in quality, because it represents the passage from contiguity to similarity association, from symbol to icon—*an icon of the process of similarity*. Metaphors point to; paronomasia attempts to portray. The "de-wording" of a word does not occur by common metaphor alone: paronomasia (paramorphism) must be introduced. Moreover, paramorphism alone may assume the complete role, discarding metaphors entirely (hence poetic "music"). It follows, or so it seems to me, that on the verbal level, paronomasia (paramorphism on all levels) and not metaphor characterizes the paradigmatic axis.

Paronomasia disrupts discourse (hypotaxis), spatializes it (parataxis), and creates a non-linear, analogical-topological syntax. In a poem, horizontal paronomasia (alliteration, colliteration) creates melody; vertical paronomasia, harmony. Rhyme is the most common vertical paronomasia. Mallarmé's *Un coup de dés* and the so-called concrete poems function on horizontal/vertical audio-visual paronomasias. Repetition of sounds is repetition of sounds in time, and this creates a spatial rhythmic grid—a diagram, a topological syntax. Rhythm is an icon. Sound-timing is rhythm, as is space-timing (e.g., in dance, cinema, or an assembly line) and space-spacing (in architecture or in a picture). Rhythm is thus a relational icon.

Summing up, sound similarity causes space similarity and correspondences—and here we have the basis for the iconic syntax that underlies poetry and such prose works as *Tristram Shandy, Ulysses,* and *Finnegans Wake.* Paronomasia is the bridge from the verbal to the iconic; for this same reason, it is said to be 'poetic', literary, and, chiefly, 'nonscientific'. Yes, most people believe that science is essentially verbal. They do not seem to realize that verbalized science is a translation of iconic science.

Thus, translating the famous Jakobsonian 'poetic function' from linguistics into semiotic, we have:

Verbal/properly—Peircely symbolic language acquires a so-called poetic function when an iconic system is infra-intra-superimposed on it.

Corollary: . . . when an analogical syntax is superimposed on a logical one.

NOTE: In certain iconic systems, like painting, phenomena seem to occur in reverse. For instance, 'metaphoric' surrealism is rather literary (by contiguity); 'metonymic' cubism is rather paronomastic (paramorphic).

SOME EXHIBITS/EVIDENCES/ HYPOTHESES

(a) Paratactic construction tends to destroy linearity:

John looks around, jumps, says good morning, cleans his collar, spins, stands still, starts running, waves at someone.

Here we see that verbs tend to "commonounize," framing interchangeable shots of equal value. The Brazilian linguist Myriam Lemle, in trying to establish a Basic Portuguese of some sort, has observed that parataxis prevails in the speech construction of the lower social classes.

(b) Sound organization creates space organization.

In Byron's "And *where* he gazed a gloom pervaded space," apparent linearity of sound turns into a nonlinear, spatial panorama—a space–sound landscape. Moreover, we cannot dismiss its calli-typographical dimension: here, we can 'hearsee' the eyes in *gloom*, as in Dante's

> Parean l'occhiaie anella senza gemme;
> chi nel viso delli uomini legge OMO
> ben avria quivi conosciuta l'emme.
>
> [*Purg.* XXIII, 31]

In Byron's verse, *gloom* stands also for "eye(s)," as commonly happens in poetry, where we find a kind of *ad hoc* meaning. Poetry creates a semiotic *ad hoc* dictionary, with semiotic *ad hoc* synonyms: words do not mean what they are expected to because they are no longer words. They acquire iconic features—and I insist on the idea that sound features are iconic features, as we can observe in music, singing, noise, *and* speech.

(c) Freud's parapraxes have the same iconic structure, as we can see, among so many instances, in the classic deciphering, by Aristandros, of Alexander of Macedon's dream: Satyr = *Sa Tyros* = thine is Tyros (Freud, 1950:11). Until recently, and despite Lacan's efforts, analysts, essayists, and semiologists have been speaking of the "association of ideas." Strictly speaking in semiotic terms, there is no such thing, but only *association of forms*: the meaning of a sign is another sign, and this meaning is exerted by the interpretant, which, in turn, is iconic in nature and is a super- or metasign that continually establishes diagrams of meaning, as I have stated above and elsewhere (1968:93; 1974:32–35; and with Lucrécia D'Alessio Ferrara, 1974:3/24). Summing up: you cannot have a thought (thirdness) without its form (firstness).

At this point, I believe it is useful to remember that it is utterly impossible to understand Peirce's semiotic without taking into serious account what he called his *ideoscopy*—his overall trichotomic system. Besides, like Marx, he came from Hegel (not without objections): "My philosophy resuscitates Hegel, though in a strange costume" (1.42). And I find also that it is not completely void of sense to say that Peirce did for language what Marx did for history. For this reason, it is difficult to accept Jakobson's suggestion that Peirce, ultimately, follows the old classic and Saussurean logic concerning the dichotomy *signifier/signified* (1975:8). As for secondness (reaction, real fact, antithesis, index, etc.), much work still needs to be done in the years ahead.

Form (another name for icon) is firstness, and its chief mode of organization is by co-ordination (parataxis). This does not mean that we do not have an iconic hierarchy; the difference is that the iconic hierarchy is established analogically, not logically. For instance, in architecture, hierarchy may be established, among other things, by likenesses and differences in size, volume, and quantity of elements; in photography, cinema, and television, by occupied space and by the whole range of distances and positions, from close-ups to panoramic shots. An analysis of a movie plot which does not take into consideration these iconic meanings is only an analysis of a verbalization. The same may be said of other sign systems, such as graphic and industrial design, music—or dreams:

> The ideas which transfer their intensities to one another are *very loosely connected*, and are joined together by such forms of association as are disdained by our serious thinking, and left to be exploited solely by wit. In particular, assonances and punning are treated as equal in value to any other associations. [Freud, 1950:448]

To be language-conscious is to be aware of iconic organization. To be truly language-conscious is to be free from the contiguity illusion.

In closing, I have roughly laid out the correspondence table represented in Fig. 1.

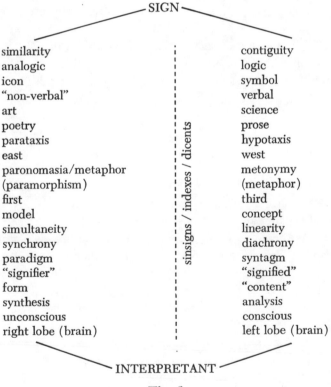

SIGN

	sinsigns / indexes / dicents	
similarity		contiguity
analogic		logic
icon		symbol
"non-verbal"		verbal
art		science
poetry		prose
parataxis		hypotaxis
east		west
paronomasia/metaphor		metonymy
(paramorphism)		(metaphor)
first		third
model		concept
simultaneity		linearity
synchrony		diachrony
paradigm		syntagm
"signifier"		"signified"
form		"content"
synthesis		analysis
unconscious		conscious
right lobe (brain)		left lobe (brain)

INTERPRETANT

Fig. 1

REFERENCES

Bär, E. 1971. "The Language of the Unconscious According to Lacan."
Semiotica 3(3).

Benveniste, E. 1969. "Sémiologie de la Langue." *Semiotica* 1(1).

Eco, U. 1968. *La Struttura assente*. Milan: Bompiani.

Ferrara, L. D., and Pignatari, D. 1974. "Études de Sémiotique au Brésil."
VS-Versus 8/9.

Freud, S. 1950. *The Interpretation of Dreams*, translated by A. A. Brill. New
York: Random House/Modern Library.

Jakobson, R. 1975. *Coup d'oeil sur le développement de la sémiotique* (=
Studies in Semiotics 2). Bloomington, Ind.: Research Center for Language
and Semiotic Studies.

Metheny, E. 1968. *Movement and Meaning*. New York: McGraw-Hill.

Peirce, C. S. 1931–58. *Collected Papers of C. S. Peirce*, 8 vols. Cambridge:
Harvard University Press.

Pignatari, D. 1968. *Informação Linguagem, Comunicação*. São Paulo: Perspectiva.

———. 1974. *Semiótica e Literatura*. São Paulo: Perspectiva.

Propp, V. 1966. *Morfologia della Fiaba*, translated by Gian Luigi Bravo.
Turin: Einaudi.

Sebeok, T. A. 1976. "The Semiotic Web: A Chronicle of Prejudices." *Bulletin
of Literary Semiotics* 2.

Valéry, P. 1959. "Léonard et les Philosophes." *Oeuvres* I. Paris: Gallimard.

Communication vs. Semiosis:
Two Conceptions of Semiotics

Alain Rey

SEMIOTICS AND LINGUISTICS

If one were to look at the recent history of the study of signs and sign systems one would see, under the headings of 'semiology' and 'semiotics', a range of scholarly activities. The two terms have in fact been used by various scholars interchangeably to mean the same thing or, sometimes, to mean different things (cf. Barthes's or Derrida's 'semiology', or Kristeva's 'semiotics'—the French *sémiologie* and *sémiotique*).

Beyond these terminological differences, which are meaningful only as indices of conceptual distinctions, there are other differences. How semiotics is placed among the sciences, for example, depends, in many ways, upon the definitions of 'science' itself. The Saussurean tradition uses the term *semiology* in accordance with the well-known passage from the *Cours de linguistique générale*, in which semiology is defined as a part of general psychology and includes the whole of linguistics. In the Peircean framework, semiotic is considered as a specific view of logic; Peirce, unfortunately, made no distinction between logic (as semiotics) and linguistics. If, however, we suppose that natural language is only a small, although important, part of the universe of signs, Peirce's semiotic would embrace many scientific fields, among which linguistics —even when defined in the broadest sense—would have a place.

Such a hierarchy may appear to be the only one possible. Nonetheless, an opposing view has been held by Roland Barthes and is explicated in his stimulating *Elements of Semiology*. Despite the wave of surprise that Barthes generated, his vantage point is far from isolated, although it had not been expressed before. An entire philosophical tradition has, in fact, come to us from the Greek concept of *logos*, that is, thought-language as reason, the feature that distinguishes man, the rational animal, from all other living beings (aside from the gods!). The Stoics and philosophers such as St. Augustine later established the principle underlying this tradition: that human language is the only relevant semiotic system insofar as the specificity of *anthropos* is concerned. Thus, depending upon one's view of the sign and of sign systems in general, and also upon one's view of knowledge as a relationship established by a subject (i.e., man) between himself and an object to be known, one of two hierarchies can be built: one in which language encompasses every other semiotic system (as the universal translator and mediator of knowledge) or one in which a multitude of semiotic systems exist, with language being only one of these systems.

Roman Jakobson, in his essay "Relations entre la science du langage et les autres sciences" chooses a position that is close to Saussure's, except that 'general psychology' is replaced by 'social anthropology' (Jakobson, 1973). Linguistics, then, defined as "the study of communication of verbal messages," is a part of semiotics—"the study of communication of any messages"—and is included in anthropology, the "study of communication," without any qualifications. Going a step further than Saussure, Jakobson joins anthropology to biology, linking the concept of (human) semiotics to zoosemiotics and ultimately to the study of the genetic code. Two problems seem to be raised by these definitions: (1) the central position of communication—rather than the sign—in such a conceptual framework; and (2) the status of social anthropology as the study of the communication of all things and beings (e.g., messages, women, goods . . .).

In any event, linguistics is indeed a part of semiotics, insofar as any verbal message is a subset of all messages. The relationship between semiotics and linguistics is therefore a function of *how* communication is defined.

ON DEFINING SEMIOTICS

How does Barthes's conception of semiotics differ from that of Saussure's, Jakobson's, and almost every other contemporary scholar's? First, what Barthes calls, in his *Elements of Semiology*, 'translinguistics'[1] is superordinate to semiology since any knowledge of the sign and its functions must be analyzed through the semiotic structures of natural language. Barthes includes under 'translinguistics'—which he does not actually distinguish from semiology—the study of "the great signifying unities of discourse" and "the objects of our culture inasmuch as they are spoken." (This is, in fact, an ambiguous way of defining two different levels in the domain of semiotics, that is, social processes as semiotic processes and their linguistic interpretants; the relationships between these two levels are themselves the objects of knowledge.) The implications stemming from Barthes's theory are numerous. Sebeok, for example, has noted, regretfully, the "absolute exclusion of sign processes among the speechless creatures from the semiotic universe." Barthes, it seems, based his analysis on signification, not on communication and coding systems, simply because restricting communication to the exchange of linguistic messages would have been too limiting (cf. the definitions of 'signification' and 'value' in the Saussurean [i.e., linguistic] sense).

Some scholars have tried to draw a line between two "groups of affinities" (e.g., Rulon Wells, 1971) or even between two fields for semiotics: communication, on the one hand; and signification, semiosis, or meaning, on the other. If we can rightly consider that an important difference exists between the two viewpoints and the theories that underlie them (for example, an extension of information theory vs. an extension of functional linguistics), it does not follow that there is any real opposition either in the terminological or in the methodological sense. It seems in fact impossible to accept a dichotomy in which "the science of communication" and the "science of signification"—whether called semiotics or something else—are two different intellectual activities, or even two separate methodological trends. If signification (or semiosis) has been the object of centuries of philosophical thought and discourse, communication as a delimited concept is a new epistemological problem. Of course, communication has been consistently defined in mathematical constructs, such as can be found in information theory, where the concepts of code, message, information, communication, etc., have been quantized. But once these same concepts are used in anthropology, biology, linguistics, and the other social sciences, their identity as single constructs is not so evident. Thus, a French sociologist once wrote: "the role of information theory being only the role of a segmental theory dealing with some necessary and instrumental conditions of communication, we must conclude that there is no such thing as a communication theory" (René Pagès, 1968). It therefore appears that, from the study of "some instrumental conditions of communication" to a general theory of communication, there is much work to be done, and semiotics is precisely the field where the groundwork could be laid. At present, there is nothing that forces us to contrast a semiotics of communication with a semiotics of signs and semiosis.

The idea of a semiotics of expression might prove more fruitful, since 'expression' as a pragmatic concept could divide the discipline with regard to the level of exchange (i.e., communication vs. expression). Even so, semiosis would still occur on another level. In any case, the word 'communication' has such a broad meaning that semiotics, if centered on this concept, would be identical to genetics (the exchange of information in genes), to social anthropology (the exchange of women), to economics (the exchange of goods), when, in reality, only a certain portion of such communication would be relevant. The works of Lévi-Strauss, Keynes, and others, for example, have many semiotic aspects, but they are not semiotic research. When the sign (or semiosis) becomes the underlying concept of semiotics, social anthropology, economics, medical semiology, etc., are semiotically relevant only if communication is described and analyzed according to precise (even if broad) definitions of the elements being communicated as signs. The definitions of the sign and of semiosis would thus replace the definition of communication in the delimitation of any semiotic discipline.

ON SOME CONCEPTIONS OF SEMIOTICS

The narrow conception of semiology in the Saussurean tradition—namely, that of Buyssens, Prieto, and other scholars (e.g., André Martinet), whose conception is akin to a "functional view of language"—is not a result of the fact that such a viewpoint considers communication as the starting point, but rather that the sign itself (and therefore communication) is narrowly defined. Buyssens (1970:12), for instance, states that "communication procedures" are "means used to influence somebody else and recognized as such by the person we want to influence. . . ." Accordingly, any process in which we act upon someone who is unwilling to recognize such an action has nothing to do with semiology. Signs are only signals; 'indices' are considered outside the field. On a much broader level, Charles Morris has divided communication into the following three concepts, each of which encompasses the one after it: (1) communication that covers "any instance of the establishment of a commonage, that is the making common of some property to a number of things"; (2) communication that is restricted to signs, defined as "the arousing of common significata by the production of signs"; (3) communication related to language, "when the signs produced are language signs" (Morris, 1971:195ff.). Morris's view of semiotics, even when restricted to his second concept of communication, embraces more than Buyssens's since it includes any process in which signs are used without regard to will, conscient knowledge (such a condition, by the way, would make zoosemiotics almost impossible). On the other hand, it should be noted that, since the use of signs gives way to communication (2) even when the commonage is not semantic (e.g., when signs of anger establish a commonage of feeling in another person—this is Morris's example), it seems that Morris does not consider the production of signification (i.e., of new signs) to be a relevant criterion for semiotics.

Morris's description of semiotics in *Foundations of the Theory of Signs* concerns, rather, a behavioral process in which "something takes account of something else mediately." The first 'something' is defined as the *interpretant*; the second 'something' as the *designatum*; and the mediator as the *sign vehicle* (see Peirce's 'interpretant', 'object', and 'sign' or 'representamen'). Morris's account of Peirce's theories of semiosis shows that the two scholars differ in their conceptions of semiotics, despite outward similarities. Morris's critical remarks about Peirce are centered on the latter's lack of precision in the following regard: (1) Peirce's definition of the sign as anything involved in the process of mediation includes, in the concept of sign, such phenomena as a conditioned stimulus; (2) the sign process, similarly, is defined by Peirce in such a way that it can be applied to nonbehavioral situations; and (3) the infinite number of triadic relations, implicit in the fact that one of the elements in such a relation is the starting point of another triadic relation, and so on, is unduly included by Peirce in his definition of the sign.

Let us look briefly at each of these points. Morris's first criticism was intended to restrict the concept of sign processes to a subclass of processes involving mediation, that is, of "restricting sign processes to those in which the factor of mediation is an interpretant" (Morris, 1971:338). His second point "illustrates the difficulties which appear when we leave the ground of behavior situations in attempting to define 'sign'." Morris's final criticism concerns the introduction into the definition of a sign of an "empirical question . . . as to whether signs always generate new signs" (1971:339). Even without examining Peirce's writings on these points, we must point out that all of Morris's remarks are grounded in a behavioral approach to science in which the philosophical concepts of Peirce's "phaneroscopy" cannot be accepted without important modifications. Let us consider, for example, the fact that a sign, according to Peirce, implies, in addition to an Object and a Ground, another sign (the Interpretant) that gives way to another sign process in such a way that: Sign 1 ⟶ Object 1 ⟶ Interpretant 1 ⟶ Sign 2 (⟶ Interpretant 1) ⟶ Object 1 ⟶ Interpretant 2 ⟶ Sign 3 . . . , *ad infinitum*. From Peirce's viewpoint, such a sequence of events is not at all an empirical fact, but is of a definitional character that has resulted from the infinite power, linked to Thirdness, and is entailed by a philosophy of thought whose foundations are metaphysical. The concepts of the sign and even of an object (as object-of-a-sign) are therefore defined by Infinity. Thus one must look at the problems raised by Peirce's broad definitions of the sign, semiosis, or the interpretant, within the context of the whole theory before these concepts can be used properly in other contexts (both philosophical and epistemological).

LOOKING FOR UNITY

Considering Saussure's 'semiology', Morris's, Jakobson's, Sebeok's, or Eco's 'semiotics', Tarski's or Carnap's 'semantics', Hjelmslev's 'glossematics', Barthes's project of 'translinguistics', or Thom's 'semantics' in topology, it is difficult to conceive of the unification of what would be the major organon to a unified science. This is especially true when methodologies vary, philosophical foundations oppose one another, and when even the focus of inquiry is not the same, ranging from signalling behavior to literature, from the logical structure of mental processes to the social history of ideas, from the genetic code to opera or film. At present, any definition of semiotics that is unable to take into account at least some of the various aspects of current semiotic research is too narrow; and any that is unable to work out a definition in which semiotics is distinct from the adjacent sciences (even if these sciences have distinctively semiotic parameters) is too broad. How narrowly or broadly semiotics is defined ultimately depends upon how the sign, the sign process, the sign system, and so forth, are defined—with communication by means of signs and sign systems being dependent on sign theories.

There is currently no other theory broad enough to cover the entire scope of empirical semiotics except Peirce's. His theory of signs, however, is not *the* solution to the problems of defining semiotics, but, instead, steers one toward the right questions and offers some powerful tools, such as the classification of signs and the concept of the interpretant. With semiotics defined as the science of the *semeion*, Peirce puts communication in his theory, inasmuch as the triadic processes imply the production and use of signs and are therefore implicitly included in the study of codes (even though the latter idea occurred sometime after Peirce) as sign structures. Considering semiosis in the Peircean fashion allows the epistemic "commonage" of science and philosophy in the universe of signs as well as an enlargement of semiotics without an epistemological break from language signs to anthropological signs, or from them to any sign in the living world. It allows, in addition, the inclusion of a diversity of viewpoints, such as Hjelmslev's conception of a hierarchy of semiotic systems.

In short, the disadvantages stemming from a broad definition of the sign—which are clearly evident when we try to look for a contrastive view of science—are compensated for by the power of a general, theoretically based framework. And, if such a frame of reference is paired with a comprehensive view of science—as is Peirce's—its power is difficult to match.

EPISTEMOLOGY FOR SEMIOTICS

What seems more important than asking if a certain theoretical view can supply a satisfactory (for whom?) definition of semiotics is to look at the types of knowledge required to study the different aspects of semiotics. This raises the well-known problem of the nature of knowledge in biology, pathology, psychology, sociology, and other disciplines. That is, how can these sciences be considered as epistemic unities, when their objects of knowledge, the observed data, and the observer (e.g., human vs. nonhominoid biology) may not be of the same nature? The problems raised by the fact that there is a continuum of matter from nonliving to living are of a different nature, since they would concern sciences in which nonhuman objects are always considered (see, for example, Pascual Jordan's *Die Physik und das Geheimnis des organischen Lebens* [1948][2]).

When a tentative definition of a unified semiotics is discussed, two classes of problems arise: first, how are certain trends in semiotics to be unified and what types of hypotheses, definitions, and rules are required of its domain? Second, if theoretical systems are able to produce consistent definitions that are broad enough, what are the empirical implications of the central hypotheses within each of these systems? The fact that Peirce's framework and philosophy are not only mentalistic (in Morris's terminology) but also idealistic—with the hypothesis of a Supreme Power—and metaphysical, is as important as the existential and "hermeneutic" character of Heidegger's philosophy when Peirce's theories of the sign as a tool, or instrument, are discussed. Yet the empirical nature of their respective definitions cannot be simply deduced from the theoretical structure of their work.

The power of a system is certainly distinct from its empirical and heuristic implications, which can be analyzed and criticized from other systematic viewpoints. What is more relevant here is not Peirce's metaphysical post-Kantian attitude or his 'pragmaticism', but the possible uses of his definition of the sign and of semiosis as the origin of any semiotic knowledge.

Whatever the system of reference may be, semiotic activities depend upon the epistemic relationship between the seeker of knowledge and his object of study. In a tentative and somewhat naive way, I would like to classify the basic types of relationships between the scientist, the scholar—man, in his own historical and cultural situation, with all of his psychological motives, including the unconscious ones—and the objects, considered here as signs, systems of signs, sign processes, sign behaviors, communication using signs, and so forth. The process of knowledge cannot itself be described without reference to the products of at least a few semiotic systems, either natural language—given that many types of 'discourse' are scientific, philosophical, mythical, political, pedagogical, etc.—and/or 'artificial' languages and formalized systems, with the addition of a few iconic ones. The fact that one of the main objects of semiotic inquiry (and the only one possible for Barthes) is natural language and its products, is relevant to the situation insofar as such a relation defines the only homogeneous epistemic relation: man, using the semiotic system of language, studies the products of his semiotic activities through the same type of semiotic system that he uses in the constitution of his knowledge. This last situation can be empirically observed in philology. *Literaturwissenschaft*, poetics, rhetoric, text-grammar and text linguistics, and, on a purely theoretical level, in "pure" linguistics.

Next to language, the semiotician may and does study the secondary codes and speech surrogates that can be easily translated into natural language. He can then deal with semiotic behaviors that are linked in an empirical manner to language behavior, with its conditions, its products, and its implications (on psychology, cultural structures, and so forth).

Human semiotic activity, including the use of any sign or sign system —be it symbolic, indexical, or iconic—is the broadest field in which the object of science is of the same nature as the scientist himself (this sameness is evident when he studies his own semiotic behavior, his own culture, his present time). Anthroposemiotics involves a detailed look at every human phenomenon, since man can be described as a logical, or semiotic, animal (if a broad definition of the sign, such as the one offered by Peirce, is accepted). (This does not imply, however, that other animals are not logical or that man is entirely logical.) We may then study zoosemiotics; here the object, a living organism, is in some respects identical to man, but in other respects different. The latter are of greater relevance where an epistemic relationship is concerned. We are certain of the specific character of *anthropos* when the semiotics of language is implicated and when historical data, considered as a major element in human social behavior, are involved; we can, in addition, accept or reject the fact that the human unconscious—if considered a major component of human psychology—is unique among bio-psychic structures.

When zoosemiotics is included in the scope of semiotics and not merely associated with it peripherally, all the problems of animal behavior (with respect to ethology, psychology, sociology) are introduced. If the knowledge of animal behavior and its underlying structure are to be considered as possible objects for scientific study, then sign processes —with an adequate definition of the sign—that are accounted for in observed animal behavior are indeed possible areas of inquiry for science. Any definition of semiotics, either including or excluding sign processes and systems outside the human world, is, of course, analytical since such a definition would depend upon what meanings are given to the sign and to semiosis. The attitude excluding nonhuman sign processes would require an anthropological definition of the sign, which is contrary to a great part of philosophical tradition and, of course, to Peirce's theories (it would be different with a Husserlian or Heideggerian starting point).

Zoosemiotics, with ethology, points to the continuity from animal to man, but as the relationship between knowledge changes from one object to the other, the methodology and issues raised must be different from those in human semiotics, where a linguistic interpretant can always be elicited even when the object is not language semiotics, or observed (e.g., in philology) when the data are available (which is an empirical, not theoretical, problem). With zoosemiotics, the central object of study is not and cannot be the sign and semiosis as such, but their effects in observable exchanges, in a behavioral approach, that is, in communication. The fact that other approaches, often criticized as mentalistic and introspective, which were rejected as far back as Auguste Comte's early works, are possible only in anthroposemiotics and are still the only possible ones in some respects (e.g., literary semiotics) clearly shows the existence of a gap. A behavioristic approach, with a communication-centered definition for semiotics, would be one answer to the problem. Unfortunately, behaviorism, in its extreme form, is unable to give answers to 'scientific' questions about man and his specific semiotic behavior, be it religious, mythical, poetic, psychotic, economic, political, or even scientific.

In 'external' knowledge patterns (that is to say, essentially not methodologically external), such as those found in the scientific study of animal life, the methods and approaches cannot be identical to those used in 'internal' knowledge patterns, such as in the study of human psychiatry. The hypothesis of a possible 'externalized' unified knowledge seems (at least in my own view of epistemology) (neo)positivist fiction.

Other fields are open to investigation where objects that may be considered signs—according to a specific definition—are at work. What Sebeok calls 'endosemiotics', in which the genetic code plays a central role, or a broad biosemiotical field where all living beings, including plants and protistae, could be studied as communication sources and receptors, give examples of objects quite different from man and his specific semiotic systems. In these fields, it is doubtful if, even with a broad definition of the sign and of semiosis, the underlying concepts of semiotics would still be the same. Thus, with the study of communication and communicative exchanges in non-living matter in the traditional domains of chemistry and physics, the assumed presence of the *semeion* would be a metaphor, even if an exchange of information could be considered.

The general patterns of mathematics or logic, on the other hand, belong to another type of epistemic relation in which the structures of the human brain are related to the structures of the world as object-to-human knowledge (which is the only possible meaning of 'world'). Here, semiotics, as in René Thom's stimulating work, appears at least in the abstract patterns through which phenomena are represented.

ON THREE EMPIRICAL
DEFINITIONS OF SEMIOTICS
AND SEMIOLOGY

The opposition between communication-centered and signification-centered semiotics or semiology is thus (a) irrelevant, since the central role of communication seems necessary when the knowledge relation is external and (b) unnecessary, if extremely relevant, when the object is man. The main object for semiotics, however, must be different from the object of the adjacent sciences, such as those concerned with information or communication theory: it must be specific, if semiotics is to be a science at all. The concepts of sign, signification, etc., can be discussed and criticized in their historical genesis, but they cannot be suppressed without suppressing the very idea of semiotics.

Among the various conceptions of semiotics currently in vogue, the following three seem to command the most importance:

(1) An overall study of "the exchange of any messages whatever and of the systems of signs which underlie them" . . . , "the key concept of semiotics remain[ing] always the sign" (Sebeok, 1974).

(2) A study of semiotic processes in culture, considered as an aspect of social anthropology and/or a critical analysis of human semiotic products especially in the sciences and in semiotics itself. Such a study puts stress on the sign and semiosis as human properties that are linked to history (in a post-Marxian sense) and to human psychology (viewed in a post-Freudian sense).

(3) 'Semiology' as the study of voluntary messages transmitted by means of certain signs that are defined in a restricted way as signals (as opposed to 'indices'); this may include nonhuman systems, but it excludes many situations in which symptoms, or indices, act, even in anthroposemiotics and in the semiotics of language.

The trend given in (1) corresponds to the Peircean and Morrisian traditions, which, although different in their philosophical foundations, are similar with regard to the scope of semiotics; included in this school of thought is the bulk of American semiotics, and, to a much lesser degree, European. Trend (2) is basically philosophically oriented and is well represented among the scholars in Western Europe, while (3) corresponds to a smaller school of Saussurean linguists, led by Buyssens and Prieto.

Each definition above is linked to a tradition: (1) is connected with structuralism in anthropology, the behavioral sciences, and structural linguistics (in a broad sense, including 'generative' linguistics); (2) comes from post-Husserlian philosophy, Marxist criticism of 'ideologies', and the Freudian analysis of human psychic nature; and (3) is derived from functional linguistics and a communicational approach of socialized codes. The influence of Peirce is stronger on (1), of Hjelmslev on (2).

Each of the three groups uses different definitions of the sign. (1) and (2) give greater importance to the sign process (semiosis); (2), in addition, considers semiosis from a genetic point of view (i.e., where does the sign, or significance, come from?) and emphasizes the systematic, theoretical aspects of sign studies. (3) focuses on the transactional aspects of sign studies in terms of functional descriptions. Each claims to be theoretical (or 'pure'); moreover, descriptive, 'applied' semiotics, according to the Morrisian view, is not sympathetic to the view espoused by (2).

With regard to the scope of semiotics, both (2) and (3) exclude nonhuman semiotics, even when animal sign behavior is closely linked to human sign behavior (e.g., facial expressions studied in the primates by Darwin). (2) shows a decided emphasis for natural language, while (3) is methodologically related to functional linguistics, a different view altogether.

Coming, finally, to the question of a unified semiotics, I would argue that Peirce's work, more than Morris's, Hjelmslev's, or Saussure's, gives some means for answering whether or not a definition for semiotics is possible, and with which key concept—semiosis or communication. In my opinion, semiosis, understood as a structural and genetic concept, is the only possible answer and implies communication when social factors are considered. Communication, in addition, is the only empirically centralized concept when methods for studying nonhuman semiosis are necessary. A narrow behaviorism and information theory technologism are proof, *a contrario*, of the gap between human and nonhuman semiotics; useful, perhaps even necessary in the latter, they are insufficient, if not irrelevant, in the former. The epistemic situation, then, is different when the semiotic object is natural language (and the social, historical phenomenon of 'discourse') and when another semiotic fact, human (such as iconic messages or music) and nonhuman, is considered.

NOTES

1. "Then (since the semiologist finds language in his way) semiology perhaps tends to be absorbed into translinguistics . . ." (Barthes, 1965:81).

2. It is interesting to note that Jordan tried elsewhere to apply to human psychology some key concepts of physics (*Verdrängung und Komplementarität*, 1947). His idealistic philosophy is not typical of unitarism in science; Engels's philosophy (with nineteenth-century concepts) shows a similar attitude.

REFERENCES

Barthes, R. 1965. "Eléments de sémiologie." In *Le Degré zéro de l'écriture*. Paris: Editions Gonthier, n.d. [1965], pp.77–176. First published in *Communications* (Paris: Editions du Seuil, 1964).

Buyssens, E. 1970. *La Communication et l'Articulation linguistique*. Brussels and Paris: Presses Universitaires.

Jakobson, R. 1973. *Essais de linguistique générale*, vol.2. Paris: Editions de Minuit, Part I, chap. 1, pp.9–76.

Jordan, P. 1948. *Die Physik und das Geheimnis des organischen Lebens*, 6th ed. Braunschweig: Friedrich Vieweg und Sohn.

Morris, C. 1971. *Writings on the General Theory of Signs*. The Hague: Mouton. On *Foundations of the Theory of Signs*, I and II, see pp.19–24. On communication, see pp.195–98; on *Signs, Language and Behavior*, IV and Glossary, pp.359–68. On Peirce, see "Charles Peirce on Signs," pp. 337–40.

Pagès, R. 1968. "Communication." In *Encyclopaedia Universalis*, vol.4, pp. 765–68.

Sebeok, T. A. 1974. "Semiotics: A Survey of the State of the Art." In *Current Trends in Linguistics*, vol.12. The Hague: Mouton, pp.211–64.

Wells, R. 1971. "Distinctively Human Semiotics." In *Essays in Semiotics— Essais de sémiotique*, J. Kristeva, J. Rey-Debove, and D. J. Umiker, eds. The Hague: Mouton.

III. Nonverbal Communication

Affective and Symbolic Meaning: Some Zoosemiotic Speculations

Peter Marler

Zoosemiotics potentially spans much of the subject matter of animal behavior (Sebeok, 1968, 1977). One topic, always present in the minds of those concerned with behavioral biology, is the role of external stimuli in the control of behavior. To focus on communicative events is to deal with a special case of the more general phenomenon of the stimulus control of behavior.

Two issues in particular recur frequently in zoosemiotic discussions of animal signaling. One concerns the relationship between external perceived situations and signaling about those situations. If one focuses particularly on the degree of exclusiveness of the relationship between signal production and denotations of that signal, the prevailing impression with animals is often of a lack of specificity. This may be linked in turn to the prominence of "affective" processes in animal signaling behavior, in contrast to symbolic processes more typical of our own species. I shall strive to show that these two issues are aspects of the same central problem.

In the discussion that follows I shall assume that there are two essential aspects to the semantic meaning that a word or statement has

The author is indebted for thoughtful discussion and criticism of this paper to Steven Green, Donald Griffin, William Mason, David Premack, and Thomas A. Sebeok. Research was supported by NSF grant number BNS75–19431.

for the one who utters it, as distinct from its "pragmatic" meaning to others (Cherry, 1966). We can distinguish them as *denotation* on the one hand and *connotation* on the other. Denotation is concerned with the object or event referred to, while connotation is concerned with the idea that is called to mind. The distinctions between "naming" and "meaning" (Quine, 1953), or "reference" and "sense" (Palmer, 1976) are equivalent to those between *denotation* and *connotation*.

BIRD ALARM CALLS

Some examples will serve as illustrations. Many small birds have two types of alarm call, one the "hawk-alarm call," the other a mobbing call; the former is often difficult to locate, the latter easy (Marler, 1955). The ventriloquial type is given especially on seeing a flying hawk. The locatable type is used with either a ground predator (such as a fox) or a stationary aerial predator (such as an owl perched in a tree). One might think of these two classes of calls as names for two classes of predators, but other factors complicate the issue. A male chaffinch, the species in which I first discovered this dichotomy between ventriloquial and locatable calls, will also give the "hawk-alarm call" in other situations. At the height of the breeding season, for example, he may give it if a person comes close to the nest containing his young.

At this point a sceptic, convinced of the inflexible automaticity of the animal as an unthinking machine, is likely to respond that this is hardly surprising if, as is surely appropriate, one views these alarm calls not as analogs for "symbolic" names but rather as "affective" signals, such as we generate in unconscious signs of emotion in voice, gesture, and expression. If there are two calls, so the thinking goes, they probably represent different levels of arousal. As I interpret this line of argument, two facts remove these calls from the naming process as manifest in our language. One is the lack of specificity in circumstances surrounding production of the "hawk-alarm call." The other is the apparent correlation with arousal levels, intense with the "hawk-alarm call," less so with the mobbing call.

The focus in this interpretation is on the denotative aspect of meaning. If we were to allow ourselves to entertain the notion that calls can have *connotational* meanings for animals (Griffin, 1976), then the lack of specificity could be viewed as in harmony with a more general meaning for the call than one particular class of predator. It might, for example, represent the abstract idea of a certain class of dangers, a class meriting a particular mode of response in those companions the signaler is presumably helping by its communications. The response of suddenly freezing in a crouched, cryptic position is as appropriate for nestling chaffinches threatened by a mammalian predator as it is for foraging adults threatened by a hunting hawk.

ALARM CALLS OF MONKEYS

Struhsaker (1967) discovered a remarkable array of alarm calls in the vervet monkey (Table 1). Inspection of the situations in which

Table 1. Alarm calls of the vervet monkey, stimuli evoking them, and responses of others. After Struhsaker (1967) and personal communication.

	UH!	NYOW!	CHUTTER	RRAUP	THREAT ALARM-BARK	CHIRP
ADULT ♂	yes	yes	yes (rare)	no	yes	no
ADULT ♀ AND YOUNG	yes	yes	yes	yes	no	yes
TYPICAL STIMULUS	Minor mammal predator near	Sudden movement of minor predator	Man or venomous snake –but the chutter is structurally different for man and snake	Initial sighting of eagle	Initially and after sighting major predator (leopard, lion, serval, eagle)	After initial sighting of major predator (leopard, eagle)
TYPICAL RESPONSE OF TROOP MEMBERS	Become alert, look to predator	Look to predator, sometimes flee	Approach snake and escort at safe distance	Flee from treetops and open areas into thickets	Attention and then flight to appropriate cover	Flee from thickets and open areas to branches and canopy

the four adult male alarm calls are uttered shows that they can be arranged in a series of increasing specificity. The first two, the "uh" and the "nyow," are evoked by rather generalized stimuli, and seem to function primarily to alert others. The third, the "chutter," is associated with either a man or a snake, especially the latter. The fourth, the "threat-alarm-bark," the only one that is the sole prerogative of the adult male, is given on sighting a major predator. It evokes not approach and mobbing, as is the case with a snake, but precipitant flight to cover. This series can also be interpreted in terms of an increasing level of arousal.

Such an interpretation is less straightforward with the alarm calls of the female vervet monkey, who uses all but one of the series. The "rraup" and the "chirp," for example, are given in rather specific circumstances, and evoke specific and contrasting responses—descent from the tree-tops in one case and ascent into the treetops in the other. It is not clear which is associated with a higher level of arousal. Perhaps here, more than anywhere else in vervet vocal behavior, one might begin to think of these two female alarm calls as serving as names for particular refer-ents. As with the chaffinch, however, each alarm call has more than one "denotational" referent.

In spite of this multiplicity of referents, may there not be "connota-tional" meanings to the vervets themselves with more unity than is immediately evident to us? One might think of alarm calls, not so much as having a large, ill-defined class of denotations, but rather as repre-senting the idea of a certain class of dangers favoring a particular escape strategy. In our own language, after all, the lack of one specific class of referents by no means disqualifies a signal from a naming function.

Even while entertaining this interpretation, there remains the corre-lation of different vervet alarm calls with independent signs of varying levels of arousal. Such correlations, regular and orderly, are well docu-mented in other kinds of primate signaling behavior (e.g., Green, 1975; Eisenberg, 1976). Still it is not clear to me whether the arousal asso-ciated with much animal signaling is best viewed as conflicting with a symbolic function or as supplementing it.

CALLS OF THE CHIMPANZEE AND THE GORILLA

Some primate vocalizations are notable for the relatively low arousal level with which they are associated. Chimpanzees have a vocalization I call "rough grunting," associated specifically with the discovery and eating of a highly preferred food such as a bunch of ripe palm nuts or, in an experimental situation, a bunch of bananas (Marler, 1976). Goril-las have a call with a similar acoustical morphology, labeled "belching" by Fossey (1972). While gorilla "belching" does occur during eating, it also occurs in a wide variety of other situations associated by Fossey with quiet relaxation, either while resting or while moving slowly through forage and feeding. The contagious chorusing of "belching," with no counterpart in the chimpanzee, apparently aids the gorilla group in maintaining contact. The referential designata for gorilla "belching" are more generalized than those for the "rough grunting" of the chimpanzee.

When we compare the social organization of these two species, a correlation with usage of the two calls emerges. The close-knit and coherent social unit of the gorilla is associated with the use of belching for maintaining contact while moving and resting in dense cover. The chimpanzee, with its much looser pattern of social organization, uses its version of the call in a more specific situation, thus assuming more of the function that we associate with a name. It is not hard to imagine the evolutionary transition from one condition to the other as social demands upon the vocalization vary with shifts in the pattern of social organization. Variations in referential specificity may thus be viewed as adaptive. This is true in our own languages, where a class of objects of indifferent detail for one culture, and a single name, may be subdivided into a multiplicity of separately named subclasses by a culture in which the added specificity assumes ecological importance.

AFFECTIVE STATES AND AROUSAL

It is not clear from the evidence on chimpanzee and gorilla behavior whether the two calls are associated with different levels of arousal. In both the levels seem to be low. But even if they were strikingly different, one can view such variations not as confounding the function of naming but rather as supplementing it. It potentially adds a valuable new communicative dimension. I can best illustrate what I have in mind with a quotation from Norbert Wiener (1948).

Suppose I find myself in the woods with an intelligent savage, who cannot speak my language, and whose language I cannot speak. Even without any code of sign language common to the two of us, I can learn a great deal from him. All I need to do is to be alert to those movements when he shows the signs of emotion or interest. I then cast my eyes around, perhaps paying special attention to the direction of his glance, and fix in my memory what I see or hear. It will not be long before I discover the things which seem important to him, not because he has communicated them to me by language, but because I myself have observed them.

With no other signaling elements than signs of arousal level and the deictic property of eyes and where they are looking, such behavior has rich communicative potential. The theme that we have underestimated the rich communicative potential of affective signaling is also discussed by Premack (1975). He opens a chapter on the origins of language as follows:

> Consider two main ways in which you could benefit from my knowledge of the conditions next door. I could return and tell you, "The apples next door are ripe." Alternatively, I could come back from next door, chipper and smiling. On still another occasion I could return and tell you, "A tiger is next door." Alternatively, I could return mute with fright, disclosing an ashen face and quaking limbs. The same dichotomy could be arranged on numerous occasions. I could say, "The peaches next door are ripe," or say nothing and manifest an intermediate amount of positive affect since I am only moderately fond of peaches. Likewise, I might report, "A snake is next door," or show an intermediate amount of negative affect since I am less shaken by snakes than by tigers.

He goes on to develop the difference between the two kinds of signaling, referential (= symbolic) and affective (= excited or aroused), suggesting that information of the first kind consists of explicit properties of the world next door; information of the second kind, of affective states, which he assumes to be positive or negative, and varying in degree. He goes on:

> Since changes in the affective states are caused by changes in the conditions next door, the two kinds of information are obviously related. In the simplest case, we could arrange that exactly the condition referred to in the symbolic communication be the cause of the affective state.

Premack makes the point that as long as there is some concordance between the preferences and aversions of communicants, a remarkable amount of information can be transmitted by an affective system. While he explicitly restricts his discussion to "what" rather than "where," one may note, harking back to the Wiener quotation, that incorporation of a deictic component in the signal—pointing or looking—not only indicates where, but also adds a highly specific connotation to the information—not just any apple tree, or all apple trees in the abstract, but this particular one.

FOUR DIMENSIONS OF "AROUSAL"

One drawback with arousal models of motivation is that although compelling in some respects (Mason, 1967, 1971) they leave unexplained a lot of *detail* of the natural behavior of animals. What are the simplest steps that could be taken to increase the efficiency of affective signaling, to specify its content more precisely? In Wiener's illustration there is one dimension. In Premack's there are already two. I tentatively suggest adding at least two more (Table 2).

Table 2. Four proposed dimensions of "affective" signaling

        (A)   Arousal/depression
        (B)   Locomotor approach/withdrawal
        (C)   Social engagement/disengagement
        (D)   Object acceptance/rejection

First, there is a level of arousal. Second, there is some indication of positive or negative sign, showing whether the signaler is inclined to approach the stimulus object or "referent" or to withdraw from it and opening up a similar set of alternatives for a responding companion. Beyond this point, already reached by Wiener and Premack, it would be advantageous if the signaler could give even a general indication of the class of referent being signaled about. Otherwise a hungry animal, for example, might approach a referent indicated by a companion as worthy of positive affect only to discover that it indicated not food but a social companion or a mate. Much time and effort would be saved if, at the very least, the signaler could give some indication as to whether the referent is environmental or social in nature. Environmental designata might include hazards such as predators or bad weather or resources such as food and drink or a safe resting place. Social referents, again with either positive or negative connotations, might include a mate or companion, an infant in need of care, all worthy of approach, or perhaps an enraged male of the species, who is to be avoided.

Intriguingly, some of the data on human emotional states and their classification are not incompatible with the four dimensions I have indicated. Fig. 1 is modified from Plutchik (1970), a psychiatrist interested in measuring the behavioral biases of different kinds of disturbed patients. His major emotional categories, which can be viewed in part as

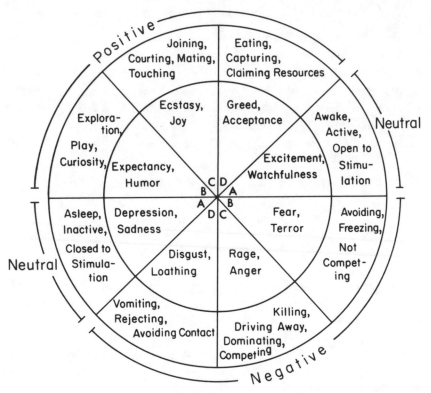

Fig. 1. Human emotional states (inner ring) with some equivalent ethological activities (outer ring) arranged according to whether their connotations are positive, negative, or neutral.

      A-A = a possible arousal/depression dimension
      B-B = a locomotor approach/withdrawal dimension
      C-C = a social engagement/disengagement dimension
      D-D = an object acceptance/rejection dimension.
      Modified after Plutchik (1970).

communicative devices, are shown, with minor changes, in the center of the diagram. In the outer ring I have added some equivalent ethological categories of ongoing behavior. Such a classification, crude though it is, encompasses most of the major sets of activities that constitute the ethogram of an animal. It is also compatible with the four affective dimensions of arousal/depression (A), approach/withdrawal (B), social engagement/disengagement (C), and object acceptance/rejection (D).

The details of these speculations are subordinate to the general point I am making—that, in some communicative circumstance there would be benefits to an increasing degree of specificity in the multiple relationships between production of a signal, its underlying physiological basis, and the kind of referential events contingent to its production.

"SPECIFICITY" IN SYMBOLIC AND AFFECTIVE SIGNALING

I believe that this theme of *specificity* is central in differentiating between what we are accustomed to think of as symbolic signaling on the one hand, and "affective" signaling on the other. As I have indicated in Table 3 there are at least four related aspects to this specificity.

Table 3. Features of "specificity" differentiating "symbolic" from "affective" signaling

1. Referential specificity (to the class of objects, events or properties represented)
2. Motor specificity (relation to other responses to the referent)
3. Physiological specificity (association with arousal and emotion)
4. Temporal specificity (coupling to immediate referential stimulation)

Symbols have a certain *referential specificity*. Thus to the extent that the vervet monkey chutter may be given to a man or a snake some no doubt feel that it fails to satisfy one of the conditions for a symbolic signal. However it may be a mistake to assume that vervet monkeys classify referential events or think about them, in our terms. Comparative studies of human cognition reveal many cultural disparities in the ways in which we view the world.

Another aspect of symbolic signaling is *motor specificity*. We generally require at least a potential ability to perform the motor act of signal production separately from the other behavioral responses that are associated with stimuli from the particular referent in question—an alarm call dissociated from acts of fleeing, a food call separate from eating. A third issue is *physiological specificity*, the potential dissociation from whatever degrees and qualities of arousal and emotion are associated with response to the referent. And these two relate in turn to what might be called *temporal specificity*, the fact that affective signaling, at least in animals, is usually closely bound in time to immediate or recent perception of the referent.

Signalers must themselves survive and reproduce, and a dissociation of signaling from other aspects of physiological and behavioral responding that contribute to individual fitness is likely to be dysgenic in most circumstances. Without temporal displacement of referential experience from signaling about that experience I find it hard to imagine the dissociation being other than disadvantageous.

There is one class of behavior in which such dissociation occurs regularly in animals, even constituting a useful identifying criterion. I am referring to play behavior, which often involves reorganization of the normal temporal relationships of signals, their usual referents, and the other behaviors typically accompanying them (Loizos, 1966). Thus such dissociation is not a physiological impossibility for animals. It may best be thought of as something that in most circumstances animals can well do without, other than in play, where youthful experimentation free of affective accompaniments may have beneficial ontogenetic consequences.

The point I am striving to establish is that symbolic and affective signaling should be thought of as differing in degree rather than kind. The particular constellation of relationships between referential, motor, and physiological specificity manifest in much animal signaling, often affective in nature, should not be thought of as something that animals do because they are physiologically incapable of going further in the direction of symbolic signaling. Rather it represents an adaptive compromise that, even in animals, can be seen to move to and fro along a continuum of specificity depending on which particular solution solves a given behavioral problem most efficiently. Furthermore, though animals are highly biased toward the "affective" extreme, they probably exhibit some simultaneous intermingling of "affective" and "symbolic" signal elements, much as intonation and gesture supplement the more symbolic components of our own communicative behavior.

REFERENCES

Cherry, C. 1966. *On Human Communication*. Cambridge: MIT Press.

Eisenberg, J. F. 1976. "Communication Mechanisms and Social Integration in the Black Spider Monkey *Ateles fusciceps robustus*, and Related Species." *Smithsonian Contributions to Zoology* 213:1–108.

Fossey, D. 1972. "Vocalizations of the Mountain Gorilla (*Gorilla gorilla beringei*)." *Anim. Behav.* 20:36–53.

Green, S. 1975. "Variation of Vocal Pattern with Social Situation in the Japanese Monkey (*Macaca fuscata*): A Field Study." In *Primate Behavior*, vol. 4, L. A. Rosenblum, ed. New York: Academic Press.

Griffin, D. R. 1976. *The Question of Animal Awareness*. New York: Rockefeller University Press.

Loizos, C. 1966. "Play in Mammals." Symp. Zool. Soc. London vol. 18. In *Play, Exploration and Territory in Mammals*, P. A. Jewell and C. Loizos, eds. New York: Academic Press.

Marler, P. 1955. "Characteristics of Some Animal Calls." *Nature* (London) 176:6–8.

————. 1976. "Social Organization, Communication and Graded Signals: Vocal Behavior of the Chimpanzee and the Gorilla." In *Growing Points in Ethology*, P. Bateson and R. A . Hinde, eds. London: Cambridge University Press.

Mason, W. A. 1967. "Motivational Aspects of Social Responsiveness in Young Chimpanzees." In *Early Behavior: Comparative and Developmental Approaches*, H. W. Stevenson, E. H. Hess, and H. L. Rheingold, eds. New York: John Wiley and Sons.

————. 1971. "Motivational Factors in Psychosocial Development." In *Nebraska Symposium on Motivation*, W. J. Arnold and M. M. Page, eds. Lincoln: University of Nebraska Press.

Palmer, F. R. 1976. *Semantics*. London: Cambridge University Press.

Plutchik, R. 1970. "Emotions, Evolution, and Adaptive Processes." In *Feelings and Emotions*, M. B. Arnold, ed. New York: Academic Press.

Premack, D. 1975. "On the Origins of Language." In *Handbook of Psychobiology*, M. S. Gazzaniga and C. B. Blakemore, eds. New York: Academic Press.

Quine, W. V. O. 1953. *From a Logical Point of View*. Cambridge: Harvard University Press.

Sebeok, T. A. 1968. *Animal Communication*. Bloomington: Indiana University Press.

————. 1977. *How Animals Communicate*. Bloomington: Indiana University Press.

Struhsaker, T. 1967. "Auditory Communication among Vervet Monkeys (*Cercopithecus aethiops*)." In *Social Communication among Primates*, S. A. Altmann, ed. Chicago: University of Chicago Press.

Wiener, N. 1948. *Cybernetics*. New York: John Wiley and Sons.

Facial Signs: Facts, Fantasies, and Possibilities

Paul Ekman

He looks like someone I can trust, and intelligent too. Must be about 50 years old, and I bet his family came from Norway. You can tell he's had a lot of laughs in his life, but right now he seems to be a little blue. He's a handsome fellow, and just look, he seems to be sexually interested in that woman.

Judgments like these are often made on the basis of facial appearance. Some of them may be accurate, correctly identifying something about the person. For example, gender is often accurately identified from facial appearance; accurate information may also be gleaned about a person's age, but there is more room for error. Some judgments may be based on stereotypes, with no grounding in fact. Some people may believe, for example, that a relatively large forehead indicates intelligence, or that crowsfeet wrinkles are evidence of a happy life. Some judgments may be quite idiosyncratic. There may be no shared beliefs, let alone accuracy. For example, the wrinkle that one person interprets as a sign of wisdom may be interpreted by another as a sign of dissolution.

Although some judgments have been subject to considerable study (e.g., judgments of emotion, personality, memory for faces), little is

The preparation of this paper was supported in part by a grant from NIMH, MH-11976. My research described in this paper was supported by that grant and by grants from ARPA, AF-AFOSR-1229, and a Career Development Award, MH 6092.

known about most judgments of the face. Which are accurate, which are stereotyped, and which are idiosyncratic? What facial clues does each type of judgment rely upon? Is it the wrinkles, the shape of the features, the skin texture, or the temporary movements of the skin that are the basis of judgments of age, mood, intelligence, etc.? Our research on the face[1] (Ekman and Friesen, 1969, 1971, 1975; Ekman, Sorenson, and Friesen, 1969; Ekman, 1972, 1973) has focused upon just one type of information available from the face—emotion—and just one source of that information—movements of the face (what are called the expressions). In this report I will consider many more types of information than emotion and many more sources than the facial expressions. Occasionally, research data will allow some precision in linking a type of information (e.g., emotion) to a particular facial source or sign vehicle (e.g., facial muscular contraction). Most often, only questions or hypotheses can be raised for consideration. In discussing each type of information an evaluation will be made as to whether judgments are likely to be accurate, stereotypical, or idiosyncratic. Usually these evaluations will be conjectural rather than based on data.

The sources of information, the facial sign vehicles, can be classified into four groups: static, slow, rapid, and artificial. The *static* signs listed in Table 1 are not completely immutable, but they change much less than the slow signs. There are changes in bony structure, features, and skin pigmentation with growth. And, these static signs can be modified by experience of one kind or another, but it is useful to separate them from the next two sets. The *slow* signs are the changes that occur with age, becoming pronounced in middle and old age. There is another group of slow changes, those that occur during infancy, childhood, and adolescence, which my lack of knowledge causes me to omit, although they belong in this scheme.

The third set of facial signs are the *rapid* changes, which can occur in a matter of seconds. Some of the rapid signs may be more visible than others. For example, some changes in muscle tonus may be quite subtle or not visible at all. Even if not visible, muscle tonus changes could provide information to another person through touch, or could provide information to the person himself through proprioceptive or cutaneous feedback. Temperature changes may be primarily a self-informative sign, although they are also available to others through touch.

The fourth set of facial signs are artificial in the sense that they interfere with the static and slow sign vehicles. Apart from optical glasses

Table 1.   Sources (sign vehicles) for facial information

STATIC SIGNS
Bony structure

Features: *Size, shape, and location of eyes, brows, nose, mouth.*

Skin pigmentation

SLOW SIGNS
Bags, sags, and pouches

Permanent creases

Blotches: *Color changes in specific areas.*

Texture: *Scaling, bumps, etc.*

Facial hair: *Changes in amount, distribution, and pigmentation.*

Scalp hair: *Changes in amount, distribution, and pigmentation.*

Fatty deposits

Teeth

Skin pigmentation

RAPID SIGNS
Movements: *Muscular contractions that move skin and change shape of features.*

Tone: *Level and pattern of electrical activity in non-mobile face.*

Coloration: *Blushing and blanching.*

Temperature

Sweat

Gaze direction

Pupil size

Head positioning

ARTIFICIAL SIGNS
Glasses

Facial hair: *Removal by permanent means or daily.*

Scalp hair: *Additions by hair-pieces or transplant or removal.*

Cosmetics: *To change skin coloration, cover wrinkles, redraw brow shape and location, etc.*

Face lifts: *To tighten skin, remove wrinkles, eliminate pouches and bags.*

used to improve vision, most of the artificial signs attempt to enhance beauty or combat signs of age, which, as we will discuss later, is often the same thing.

This listing of facial sign vehicles is not proposed as final or comprehensive, but it is useful for what we will discuss. If, for example, we were to discuss in any detail the facial signs of disease, the list of facial sign vehicles would have to be considerably elaborated.

The first four types of information that we will consider concern different aspects of a person's identity. The face identifies a particular person—"That is John walking down the street towards me." Even if we are not familiar with him, we may still judge that he looks so similar to someone we know that he might be a relative. Even if he did not look like a relative of someone we know, we may think we recognize something about his national origin—"He looks as though he comes from an

Italian background." The face also indexes race, at least in terms of such gross distinctions as Black, Caucasian, or Oriental. The unfamiliar face is informative also of whether the person is male or female. Age is another aspect of identity judged from the face, but we will consider it much later.

1. PERSONAL IDENTITY

We distinguish one person from another by their faces. It is probably the primary way we distinguish and remember each unique member of our species. This is not to suggest that there are not other signs of identity, e.g., fingerprints, or even identity signs requiring no special aids to perception, such as voice characteristics, posture, gait, etc. There is even research suggesting infants can identify particular persons from olfactory cues (Russell, 1976). I suggest that the face is the main, most commonly employed visual identity sign.[2]

People differ in their ability to remember faces and recall whether or not they have seen a particular face before. Memory for faces is the result of the interplay among the sex and race of the perceiver and the sex and race of the person perceived (cf. Cross, Cross, and Daly, 1971; Chance, Goldstein, and McBride, 1975; Malpass and Kravitz, 1969). A number of studies have examined the basis for the influence of race (in perceiver or perceived) in memory for faces. The amount of exposure to members of another race, one's social attitudes toward members of another race, and personality variables all seem to be relevant when the races of the perceiver and the perceived differ (cf. Galper, 1973; Lavrakas, Buri, and Mayzner, 1975; in addition to references cited above). Apart from race, faces rated as unique (Going and Read, 1974) or beautiful (Cross, Cross, and Daly, 1971) by one group of subjects tend to be better remembered by other comparable groups of subjects. Cognitive style, in particular measures of field independence–dependence, has been found to be related to memory for faces, but the results have not been consistent (Messick and Damarin, 1964; Lavrakas, Buri, and Mayzner, 1975). A more robust and consistent finding has been that people who are right-hemisphere dominant, or those having a left- rather than a right-hemispheric lesion, are better able to remember faces (see Levy, Trevarthen, and Sperry, 1972; Rizzolatti, Umilta, and Berlucchi, 1971; Yin, 1970). It is not certain, however, whether these findings are specific to memory of human faces or general to a type of information processing.

Children can discriminate their mothers' faces from the faces of strangers by the second month (Carpenter, 1973; Maurer, 1975), but little is known about the further development of facial recognition over the first few years of life. We do not know the limits of an adult's ability to discriminate and remember faces. Just how many different faces can we retrieve and identify as having been previously known?

Probably the chief source (sign vehicle) for distinguishing identity are the features (their shape, size, and relative location), and to a lesser extent the facial contours due to the underlying bony structure. Many other factors can aid identification, if salient, and yet many of the other facial signs also can erode the ability to identify.

Anything in Table 1 could aid or become the prime source for identifying a person, but it is unlikely that the rapid signs usually function in this fashion. They usually are not constant enough to be useful for distinguishing one person from another. It is more likely that rapid muscle contractions are a source of interference, sometimes so distorting the static facial signs as to render identification temporarily impossible. A manneristic rapid facial sign that characterizes a particular person or a tic could be an identity sign, but probably not an important one. The changes with age may also interfere with recognizing identity, but we will return to this later when we discuss the facial signs of age.

2. KINSHIP

Presumably, the very factors that permit identification of a person allow identification of his kin. The static facial sign vehicles are in part the product of heredity, and similarities in facial appearance among close relatives may be recognized. We do not know if this is possible throughout life. It is often said that infants show less individuality than do adults, suggesting the *possibility* that some facial identifiers may only emerge as the infant's face grows and differentiates. Are family resemblances evident at birth? Might these only become evident after certain growth? My hunch is that the answer depends on just how unusual the particular facial features are, but more of that line of speculation when we discuss facial age signs.

Not much is known about kin recognition from facial signs. There is no clear evidence that it is actually possible and not just a folk belief, but it seems obvious that at least some kinship recognition is possible from the face. How far does kinship recognition extend; to first cousins, second cousins, etc.? Popular belief is that not only can kin be recognized, but people who come from the same region (presumably because of inbreeding) have a particular facial appearance. To wit, the supposed difference in permanent facial signs for the southern European, the Nordic, etc.

If kinship recognition does occur with any degree of accuracy, inherited similarities in the static signs in the face are only one possible basis. It might be that people who live together develop the same facial habits. They may learn to show similar facial muscle actions or a similar pattern of muscle tone in the face at rest. (Birdwhistell [1970] has speculated along these lines; and Seaford [1975] has found similarity in the smiling faces in yearbook photographs among people from a particular geographical area.) Imitation of rapid signs not inheritance of static signs might be responsible for kinship recognition, if there is indeed kinship recognition. It would be interesting to determine whether the belief that husbands and wives have similar facial appearances is actually so. Can observers match spouses on the basis of their faces; is this possible early in their relationship, or only after they have lived together for some years?

3. RACE

Race is commonly recognized from the face, primarily by skin pigmentation, and probably to a much lesser extent by underlying bony structure and racial differences in the features. No one that I know of has followed Huber's (1931) suggestion of racial differences in the musculature, which, if true, could allow racial identification from either the rapid facial movements or differences in the appearance of the still face.

4. GENDER

Gender is also identified from the face, although obviously it can be identified from other sources. Facial hair is an obvious source for distinguishing the hairier, adult male from the female, although the extent of sex difference in facial hair varies among racial groups. It is curious that a dimorphic sign would be marked in only some racial groups and not be general to the species.

Various means can and often are used by males to eliminate facial hair and by females who have heavy or dark facial hair. Pelligrini (1973) found that young adult males were judged as more masculine, mature, dominant, courageous, liberal, nonconformist, industrious, and old when their faces were full-bearded than when their faces were clean-shaven. Pelligrini recognized the need to investigate the generality of his findings for older males and among various people who judge the faces. Some judgments (e.g., liberal) are likely to be quite specific to a particular point in time in the customs of a particular culture. The judgment of age on the other hand, is obviously biologically based. What about dominance—would any generality over time and across cultures be found in the attribution of dominance to bearded faces? It is interesting to note that female rulers in ancient Egypt attached goatees to their faces in ceremonial appearances to signify their power.

Scalp hair can also be used to distinguish gender. The length and styling of scalp hair for males and females has varied through history. Custom has usually prescribed a difference between what males and females wear. Recent styles, the so-called unisex, show this need not be so.

Males have proportionately bigger heads than females, but the overlap is considerable. The brow ridge is more prominent in males, but I do not know if there are other sex differences in bony structure that influence facial appearance. Are there sex differences in features, their size, shape, and relative placement? Liggett (1974) claims that the female nose is smaller than the male, and shaped differently than the male, more like the shape of the child's nose. He also claims that in females the mouth is smaller, the eyes larger, the features finer, and the skin more transparent. Unfortunately, Liggett neither cites the work of others nor provides any data of his own to support these assertions.

Cosmetics are employed by females to enhance or create marked sex identifiers in the face. It would be interesting to look at the use of cosmetics by males and females historically as well as cross-culturally. I know of only one such study, in regard to outlining the eye, which is not sex-specific (Coss, 1974).

Do the faces of males and females age differently? Can we tell gender from any of the slow signs listed in Table 1? Females have smoother skin than do males because of estrogen. What about the rapid signals—

e.g., do females characteristically blush more than do males? Freedman (1974) suggests that during infancy females smile more than do males, and he does not attribute this to different child-rearing. Korner (1969) reported that newborn females smiled almost three times as often as did males. If there are such sex differences in the rapid signal system, they probably are not the usual means by which people identify gender from the face.

It is not clear when gender facial signs become most pronounced. It is commonly believed that it is difficult to tell male from female infants from the face alone. In adolescence, when many other gender changes occur, it might be expected that the facial gender signs become most pronounced. It would be interesting to determine whether there is also a decline in the clarity of the facial gender signs later in life when sexual fertility declines.[3]

5. TEMPERAMENT, 6. PERSONALITY

There is much less argument about whether someone is male or female, Black or White, than about a person's temperament, personality, or moral character. Yet, through many periods of history people have believed that they could derive such information from the face, usually claiming that variations in the features show temperament or personality. In the eighteenth and nineteenth centuries physiognomy was scientifically respectable. While no longer credited by the scientific community, this idea has not died out: a number of recent books have told how to read moral character or personality from a mixture of static and slow facial signs (Jordan, 1969; Lefas, 1975; Mar, 1974).

It seems unlikely that static facial signs are actually related to temperament or personality. One would have to assume that temperament and personality are in some part inherited (more probable for the former than for the latter) and that there is some linkage between their inheritance and the inheritance of static facial signs. Such a linkage between temperament or personality and body type is maintained by some (Sheldon, 1954). A link between static facial signs and personality cannot be ruled out without better empirical study. No serious research has been done on this topic for forty years. Although the early studies obtained negative results, they suffered from serious flaws in sampling of faces or measurements of either the face or temperament and personality.

Quite apart from the question of whether the face provides accurate information about personality or temperament is the issue of whether people share beliefs that faces do so. Here, there has been considerable research, mostly by Secord and his associates in 1954 (see Secord [1958]). In their experiments they accumulated unquestionable evidence that people share a variety of beliefs about the personality characteristics associated with facial appearance. The amount of consensus amazed these investigators. Recently, Hochberg and Galper (1974) have found that people agree not just in trait judgments but also in attributing interpersonal intentions to particular faces. Shoemaker, South, and Lowe (1973) have found that people also share beliefs about the faces associated with different crimes, and about whether a person is innocent or guilty of a crime.

There has been much less progress in specifying the basis, the facial sign vehicles, for judgments of traits, intentions, crime, etc. Secord's work is all that is available, and while strong in questions asked, data analysis, and theoretical interpretation, it was remarkably weak in number of faces studied (only 24) and in the facial signs measured (ratings of just some aspects of facial appearance confounding in the same rating scale static with rapid signs). Secord's work was an important beginning in specifying facial signs relevant to the judgment of personality, although virtually no one has followed. To give a taste of his findings, consider the traits associated with young faces without forehead wrinkles (energetic, conscientious, warmhearted, friendly, intelligent, expressive, air of responsibility, easygoing) as compared to older faces with average forehead wrinkles (meek, studious, air of refinement). Now that new methods have been developed to measure static facial signs directly (for example, profilometrics described by Peck and Peck) and rapid facial signs (for example, The Facial Action Coding System developed by Ekman and Friesen), Secord's work should be redone with a much larger and more representative sample of faces.

Secord provided a very useful discussion of the possible bases for concensus about the facial appearance associated with different personality traits. One possible explanation, of course, is that these are accurate judgments not stereotypes, based on some biological link between facial appearance and personality. While Secord thought this unlikely he acknowledged the need for better study of this possibility. Pertinent here would be a determination of whether there are uniformities among different cultural groups in the way they associate appearance with personality. With the dispersion of mass media presentations of the visual appearance of different heroes and villains, such work had better be done quickly while uninfluenced groups still remain. Secord noted that media influence might explain his finding that dark complexioned, oily skinned faces were associated with negative traits (hostile, boorish, conceited, etc.), citing Berelson and Salter's (1946) finding that in fiction villains are dark and swarthy while heroes tend to be blond and fair.

Another explanation for consensus in judgment of personality from faces offered by Secord is what he termed temporal extension. If you see a smiling face you assume smiling might be an enduring or frequent occurrence and so judge the person to be friendly. A related idea is our hypothesis that permanent facial signs that resemble the rapid facial signs of emotion tend to give an impression related to that emotion. For example, a person with brows placed quite low, with inner corners close together and with lids covering the top part of the iris, may tend to appear stern, unfriendly, or even hostile. Such a stereotype might occur, because in anger the muscular contractions in that region of the face temporarily lower and draw the brows together.

While I doubt that anyone will uncover evidence that the static facial signs provide accurate information about temperament or personality, it is possible that personality or temperament may be revealed in one or another rapid facial sign. Let me give some examples, bearing in mind that each is speculative and without a shred of evidence.

One aspect of what is meant by temperament is some lifelong characteristic level of responsivity to stimulation, in particular, emotional responsivity. Some people may seem rather slow to respond while others seem to be rather quick to respond to emotional stimulation. The latency of facial muscular actions might be an index of such a temperamental difference in responsivity. Of course, we must first determine if there are stable individual differences in latency of facial movement.

Another possible sign of such temperamental differences in emotional responsivity or of personality might be the pattern or level of muscle tone in the face when it is not moving but is more or less at rest. Little is known about whether people characteristically maintain a particular pattern of facial muscle tonus in the resting face, and if so whether the pattern would indicate anything relevant to personality. In recent work Schwartz, et al. (1976a, 1976b) used electromyographic measures to study presumably nonvisible facial activity, which is relevant to what we have been describing as the muscle tone in the resting face. Schwartz found depressed patients differed from non-patients in electrical activity when instructed to think of different emotions. Work has still to be done to explore whether there is a facial set when the patient is not following an instruction to think about emotion.

Personality may be manifest also in what the face shows about the characteristic secondary emotion that closely follows the arousal of a particular emotion. Tomkins (1962) described affect about an affect, the feelings you have about a feeling. For example, when you feel angry, you may habitually feel disgusted at yourself for being angry, or afraid of your anger, or saddened that you are angry, or gleeful in your anger, etc. If these affects about affects are stable through periods of life (which Tomkins suggested), it seems reasonable to expect that they might be considered indexes of personality.

Personality *may* also be evident as a result of habits learned early in life to control rapid facial movements. We (Ekman and Friesen, 1975) have speculated that habits about managing facial movements can result in a number of chronic facial styles: people who typically inhibit the signs of certain emotional expressions or the signs of emotional expressions in general; people who typically substitute the signs of one emotional expression for another; people who almost manneristically, flash the signs of one emotion regardless of the input. If such styles do indeed exist (and as of now there is only sparse anecdotal evidence), it is likely that they would be considered signs of different personalities.

Psychopathology, in particular, severe depression or anxiety states, may be evident in another type of rapid facial sign. We have used the term *flooded-affect* to refer to a state in which the person shows the muscular actions of only one or two emotions with great frequency, often with little obvious external provocation, and seemingly in disregard of an environmental stimulus or in contradiction to the normative emotional reaction to such a stimulus. An affect is flooded if it is high in the person's response hierarchy, if it is difficult or not possible for the person to turn off or modulate once the expression has begun, and if it interferes with work, sleep, eating, etc. The evidence for flooded-affect as an index or symptom of psychopathology is clinical-anecdotal, but it seems promising to explore.

7. BEAUTY

The chief signs of beauty or ugliness in the face are probably the size, shape, and location of the facial features, and to a lesser extent surface manifestations of the underlying bony structure. There is much in the way of anecdote but little systematic study of changes in standards of beauty through history and across cultures. Just which features have been idealized as the beautiful? Is it shape, size, location, symmetry, or relationships among features that have always been considered the basis of beauty?

Many artists have described the characteristics of the beautiful face. Leonardo, Botticelli, and Dürer emphasized the relative proportion of the features, as well as particular shapes for particular features. Their ideas suggest that standards of beauty are quite variable. Presumably the advertising industry and the entertainment media today create beauty standards. We do not know how persuasive they are, or whether there are limits to what the media can inculcate about what constitutes a beautiful face. Could the media create a consensus that noses that have a large hump in the middle or very narrow lips are signs of beauty?

In our culture, facial hair, a male sign, detracts from beauty in females. Is that universal? Could the mass media create a new consensus that hairy female faces were beautiful? Should we expect that any other gender sign when manifest in the opposite sex is not beautiful? The phrase *pretty man* suggests that beauty standards can disregard sexual fit. Most of the slow signs listed in Table 1 are age symptoms and as such are the enemy of beauty, at least in Western cultures. Is that universal, or are there cultures that idealize the aged face as beautiful? Later we will briefly mention facial signs of disease. Are such signs always considered detractors from beauty? One instance where it is not was the value given to pallor in Victorian women.

I have found just a few empirical studies of facial beauty, and all of them focus on judgment of female faces. Iliffe (1960) had twelve photos of women published in British newspapers. More than 4,000 people mailed him beauty ratings. There was very high agreement about beauty regardless of the respondent's age, sex, occupation, or region of Britain. The same pictures were published in American newspapers, and Udry (1965) obtained comparable results with no difference from the British judgments. Obviously, such a study should sample more than a dozen faces. The faces should be a representative sample, or picked according to some explicit a priori set of descriptive or theoretical principles. While Landis and Phelps (1928) made this point forcefully, pointing to the possibility that investigators may unwittingly bias their results by their personal selection of a few faces, and it has been reiterated many times by others, it is usually ignored. If the Iliffe faces had been a representative sample, it would have been important to have them judged by people from a culture more removed from Britain than that of the U.S. If one were to seek a culture where there had been little influence by mass-media portrayals of the beautiful face, the investigator would have the problem of people of one skin color judging people of another skin color, and the potential influence of social attitudes on beauty (cf. Martin, 1963).

Recent work by orthodontists on facial beauty offers a solution to this problem and a promising method for study of many different aspects of the static facial signs. Not content with the consensus among orthodontists about what constitutes a pleasing face, Peck and Peck (1970) developed a method for measuring a number of aspects of facial appearance. Profilometrics, which can be done from a still photograph, yields quantitative scores on a host of static facial signs, e.g., facial proportions, relationships among the three curves in the facial profile, angle of nose to philtrum, etc. They found very little variability in the measurements of 52 people selected to represent the beautiful (beauty queens, models, actresses). Their methods could be used to study males considered beautiful, and most important, to measure a wide range of male and female faces. This larger sample of faces could be also judged on beauty, as well as personality, temperament, intelligence, etc.

8. SEXUAL ATTRACTIVENESS

By sexual attractiveness I refer to some consensus among a group of people that a particular face is sexually appealing. This is not the same as a flirtatious, coy, or coquettish facial action. We will discuss these later under facial symbolic actions, or what we term *emblems*. Presumably, it is possible to have a facial countenance regarded as sexy without engaging in a flirtatious action, and for a person with a face not generally considered sexually attractive, to emit a facial flirtation signal. Sexual interest might also be confused with sexual attractiveness. It is not clear whether there is a facial sign of sexual interest (in general,

in the sense of availability, or sexual interest in a particular person),
independent of facial signs of interest in almost anything, including
sexual activity. Another unknown is whether there are any facial signs
of sexual pleasure, independent of or different from facial signs of
pleasure from a non-erotic source. There is some data to suggest that the
face judged as sexually attractive is not identical with the face judged
as beautiful (see Dillon, 1974).

What makes for sexual allure in the face? Is it the static signs or can
it also involve muscle tone, or the lack of it, such as the droopy, bed-
room-eyed look? Secord reported that female faces with a lot of lipstick,
bowed lips, thick lips, or relaxed lips were rated as sexy. Are there
other signs than these? Are sexual attractiveness signs variable through
history and across cultures? Is there as much consensus about sexual
attractiveness signs for males as there is for females, at different points
in history and across cultures? Is there agreement between males and
females about sexual attractiveness signs for male and female faces?
If signs are uncovered that are in any way biologically related to gender,
would sexual attractiveness signs tend to be elaborations of them?
Should we expect to see the signs of sexual attractiveness in male and
female faces vary and exchange back and forth between male and
female over history and among cultures?

Goffman (1976) speaks of how the adult female is presented in the
advertising media as childlike in a variety of ways. This fits with the
observation that the cosmetic industry's presentation of the sexually
attractive female is one whose face is childlike, in terms of the relative
size of the eyes. I do not know whether this has been verified as truly
sexually attractive or arousing, or whether such an attractiveness sign
in females has been studied historically or across cultures.[4]

Hess (1975) has found that males prefer and judge most positively
a female face in which the eyes have been retouched to enlarge the
pupil. In discussing this finding, Hess noted that a large pupil characterizes the child's face. He also noted that pupil dilation is a sign of
interest in children or adults and appears to be so judged. We will return briefly to pupil dilation when discussing signs of emotion.

9. INTELLIGENCE

Intelligence, like personality and moral character, has long been
said to be manifest in the face. The eighteenth-century physiognomists
looked to the permanent facial signs, in particular the facial features,

for the smart versus dull countenance. I would be shocked if research ever found intelligence correlated with forehead expanse or nose length, or size of eyes, but no one has adequately checked. Pintner (1918) had physicians, teachers, psychologists, and laymen judge the intelligence of twelve children from photographs. He interpreted his results as negative, but the distribution of results he reported for the group of psychologists appears to me to show significant accuracy. Anderson (1921) reported that twelve college students' judgments of the intelligence of 69 faces were slightly better than chance—the correlation with I.Q. was .27. Gaskill, Fenton, and Porter (1927) reported that when 274 observers judged intelligence from facial photographs of twelve boys of the same age, the median correlation of judged intelligence with actual I.Q. was .42. Landis and Phelps (1928) correctly questioned these previous studies since the investigators may have unwittingly biased their results; instead of using random sampling they personally inspected the faces and then chose just a few. Landis and Phelps corrected this problem by selecting randomly eighty photographs from a college yearbook. Inexplicably, rather than study the ability to judge intelligence, they had their judges rate vocational success and type of vocation. Their judges failed on that task, but of course that does not tell us about intelligence. There is still no satisfactory test of the ability to judge intelligence accurately from a facial photograph.[5] When such work is done, some care should be taken to control for clothing clues, hair styling, and the absence or presence of any rapid facial signals.

Quite apart from the issue of accurate judgments of intelligence, there is little information about the basis for consensus about what constitutes an intelligent face. Again, Secord's studies are all that are available. They do demonstrate that people agree about what is an intelligent face, but provide relatively little information about the facial signs relevant to that judgment. While there is no obvious or apparent logical basis for the development of stereotypes about what the smart face should look like, stereotypes about the dumb face might be based on some version of the static facial configuration found with mental retardates suffering from Down's syndrome. Recently, Joseph and Dawbarn (1970) have systematically measured the unique static facial signs symptomatic of this disease.

Rapid facial signs might be related to intelligence. Haviland (1975) has suggested that many of the techniques used to measure intelligence in infants rely in some part upon rather unsystematic use of rapid facial signs of emotional expression. She suggests the importance of systematically measuring facial movement in infants and children in relation to intelligence, but she has not yet done so. In some of our recent studies in collaboration with pediatricians we have learned of their belief that mental retardation can be diagnosed not just from static facial signs, but from something about the rapid facial signs (Nyhan and Shear, pers. comm.). It would seem reasonable to explore whether the face of the mentally deficient or marginally intelligent person is characterized by: slower latency of muscular contractions for the emotion signs; less complex muscular contractions for the emotion signs; lower overall level of electrical activity in the face at rest (less muscle tone); different bony structure (which could in part, at least, result from retarded growth due to less muscular activity). If there are such indexes of low intelligence, it may be worth considering whether there are also signs of unusually high intelligence. We would suspect the rapid signals as the source.

10. DISEASE

Facial indexes of a variety of physical diseases are revealed through peculiarities in static, slow, or rapid facial signs (e.g., Goodman and Gorlin, 1970). It would take us too far afield to describe these here. It is worth noting, though, that the facial evidence of some diseases may not be an obscure signal system, interpretable only to the physician. For some diseases the facial sign that something is amiss may be evident to the person and others who view him.

11. EMOTION

Having spent all this time discussing matters which I have not studied, let me turn to something we have investigated, the facial signs of emotion. Temporary changes in feelings, emotions such as fear, surprise, anger, disgust, sadness, happiness can be signaled through the rapid contractions of the facial muscles, which move the skin about temporarily changing the shape and even the location of the features, causing wrinkles, pouches, bags and bulges to appear on the face. These facial expressions of emotions typically flash on and off the face in a matter of just a few seconds, often lasting less than one second. There is now considerable (I judge conclusive) evidence that these facial signs for emotion—the particular muscles likely to be recruited for each of a number of emotions—have evolved and are therefore universal.[6]

This is not to suggest that when an emotional event occurs you will see the same facial expression on everyone's face within a culture or in any two cultures. There are important differences within and between cultures in what is learned about the need to control facial expression in public places. Even when people feel the same way in the same situation, they may not all show the feeling on their faces. Some may mask it with another feeling, some may inhibit it totally, some may amplify it or deamplify it. Rules about controlling facial behavior are learned so well that usually we do not know of their operation except when someone fails to follow them. There are individual differences in the rules for controlling facial expression that probably reflect personality as well as social class. Clearly there are also differences between cultures in these rules about managing the appearance of the emotion signs. One of our main studies (Ekman, 1972, 1973: 214–18; Friesen, 1972) of facial expression examined the spontaneous facial behavior of Japanese students in Tokyo and American students in Berkeley, under conditions where they would and would not be likely to mask their facial behavior. The faces of students of both cultures were videotaped without their knowledge while they individually watched stress films. In one part of the experiment they thought they were alone, and in another part of the study a research assistant talked with them as they watched the film. When alone, rules for controlling facial behavior should be less operative, and we expected the universal form of the expressions would be shown. Indeed, we found a very high correlation between the specific facial movements emitted by Japanese and Americans when watching a stress film alone. When in the presence of another, in particular a representative of "science," we expected the Japanese more than the Americans to mask with smiles negative affect aroused by the film. Measurement of the spontaneous facial behavior confirmed this prediction. There were major differences in facial behavior between Japanese and Americans in the more public situation.

Another source of differences in facial expressions of emotion within cultures and between cultures has to do with the learned triggers of emotion. While there may be some universal or nearly universal emotion triggers (e.g., death of a child), even within a culture we are not all made angry, disgusted, sad, etc., by the same events.[7] Often we do not see the same facial sign of emotion in different people in the same situation, or when members of different cultures are in the same situation, because the situation calls forth a different emotion.

A third way in which cultures may differ is in the extent to which facial expressions of emotion are named. Rosch and Heider in their study of the Dani in New Guinea found evidence for the universality of facial expressions, but no names in the language for some of the emotions.[8]

My discussion of emotion has argued that the linkage between facial movement (sign) and emotion (significant) is natural,[9] with an evolutionary basis, rather than a conventional or arbitrary association. Much of the misunderstanding of this view of facial expression has been based on the assumption that if facial expressions are evolved behavior (as we claim), and if the relationship between sign and significant is natural (as we maintain), then we must also believe that facial expressions are impervious to the influence of culture. But, we have never said that facial expressions are *always* automatic or unwitting. Facial expressions of emotion are not fixed-action patterns or instincts of some kind, impervious to culture. They can be automatic, but not always or even usually.[10]

The facial nerve is connected to the very old and to the newer parts of the brain. Facial expressions of emotion are at times an involuntary automatic response, and at other times, a voluntary, well-managed response system. Facial expressions of emotion can be reflexlike in their speed. They also resemble reflexes because of the natural linkage between sign and significant. Facial expressions are language-like in that they often are voluntary, and the involuntary facial expressions are vulnerable to interference or modification by custom, habit, or choice of the moment. People can and often do put on false expressions to play with or seriously mislead another. Much of our current theorizing (Ekman and Friesen, 1975: chap. 11) has described the difference between simulated and felt facial expressions, and where to look for traces (what we have called leakage) of felt facial expressions that a person is attempting to conceal. While we have support for some of our ideas (Ekman and Friesen, 1974a), much of this theory is only now being subjected to empirical test.

The evidence on the universality of facial signs of emotion is limited to just the six emotions of happiness, fear, surprise, sadness, anger, and disgust. Interest is another emotion for which there may be a universal facial sign, but there are no conclusive data. We doubt that there are many more emotions that are universal in appearance, where sign and significant are naturally linked. Cultures may well differ in the extent to which they name other emotional states and by convention assign facial configurations to them.

Much of our work of the last few years has explored and described these rapid facial movements, which are signs of emotion. Our research and that of others suggest that people differ in their ability to interpret these emotional signs.[11] We have developed materials (Ekman and Friesen, 1975) to instruct people how better to recognize emotion signals. Such recognition is easy when the emotion is shown across the entire face, if the movement is held for a few seconds, without competition from words, body movements, voice tone, etc. Those conditions rarely happen. Difficulty in recognizing facial expressions of emotion occurs because the expression is usually brief and competes with other signals for attention, and because the expression is limited to one facial area, blended, or masked.

Facial expressions of emotion often are shown in just one area of the face, rather than across the entire face. This can happen early in the arousal of an emotion, or when the arousal of an emotion is slight, or when the person is attempting to control facial appearance. Emotions often occur in blends, and the face can show such blends of emotion. Sometimes each of the blended emotions registers within one facial area, such as a mouth movement that looks both fearful and surprised. Sometimes each of the blended emotions controls the muscles affecting a different facial area, so that, for example, the brows could register fear and the mouth surprise, or vice versa. The smile is shown not only when someone feels happy or wants to signal compliance or agreement, but often when a person uses it to mask the expression of a negative emotion. Determining whether these are blends or instances where the smile is a mask requires more information. It is necessary to evaluate the social context in which the expression occurs, other behavior coincident with the expression, the sequence of facial movements in the expression, etc.

We have recently developed a comprehensive system for describing and measuring the facial movements, and not just those that may be relevant to emotion (Ekman and Friesen, 1976, 1977). Much of the research on the face has been stymied by the lack of a tool for measuring facial movements. Previous attempts have catalogued a limited number of facial movements.[12] Usually there was little information given about how the author chose the type and size of his units of measurement, or why he chose to include or exclude one or another facial behavior. The Facial Action Coding System we have devised is based on how each muscle acts to change facial appearance temporarily. The units of measurement are based on visibly distinguishable changes produced by movements of the facial muscles. The measurement procedure tells us about the variety of rapid facial muscular movements that the human can make. The Facial Action Coding System distinguishes more than 10,000 different facial actions.

I have been discussing how the rapid facial muscular movements provide information of emotion. Let me mention five other rapid facial signs of emotion. Tomkins (1962) wrote about vascular changes in the face associated with emotion. We are all familiar with blushing, blanching, and hot and cold feelings in our face. Yet to my knowledge there has been little, if any, systematic study of thermal and coloration changes. Facial sweating, either hot or cold, could also be a sign for one or another emotion, but it too has not been studied. The muscular tone of the face when it is not moving, the particular pattern and/or level of electrical activity, might also be related to specific emotions. Schwartz's work (referred to earlier) suggests that this may be a promising line of study. Hess's (1975) work on pupil dilation, discussed earlier, shows that the pupil enlarges with emotional arousal. Increased pupil dilation is a sign of interest, but it is not clear whether it is a sign of only a positive interest or if it could also be a sign of negative interest. For example, if a person is afraid, but rather than fleeing he vitally engages in coping with the source of the fear, would there be pupil dilation just as there is when the person is interested in a pleasing stimulus?

While coloration changes and sweating are visible signals, the muscle tone changes and those thermal changes that do not produce visible changes in coloration may provide a sign only to the maker not to the viewer. Pupil dilation provides information to the viewer only in blue-eyed people, and recent work discussed by Hess found that pupil dilation variations were greater among blue-eyed than brown-eyed persons.

All five of these emotion signs—changes in temperature, coloration, muscle tonus, sweating, pupil dilation—are similar to facial expressions of emotion in that the link between sign and significant is natural not conventional. Unlike facial expressions, these five signs are very difficult to control or inhibit.

12. MOOD

Mood is a close relative of emotion but refers to a more enduring state than emotion. You feel sad for a few minutes, but you are blue for half a day. You feel angry for a moment or a few minutes, but you are irritable all day. Moods may be distinguished in terms of whether the specific emotion or blend of emotions is felt continuously or intermittently. In a mood in which there is an intermittent emotion, that emotion is not always apparent but is ready to become apparent, is easy to provoke, and is high in the person's response hierarchy. While not fuming continuously in an intermittent angry mood, the person is highly ready to become angry. Little provocation (sometimes any stimulation or environmental change) calls forth his anger. The intermittent mood should be signaled by the high frequency with which a particular emotion or emotion blend is shown in rapid facial movements within a given time interval.

A continuous mood may also show a high frequency of rapid facial movements, but we expect that those muscle actions will not be maintained continuously in a high state of contraction. The person who is continuously angry for two hours may frequently show *corrugator*, *procerus*, and *depresser supercilli* muscle contractions (which lower and draw the eyebrows together), but we would not expect that he could hold those muscles in a high state of contraction continuously. Fatigue would occur. Instead, there might be a slight increase in muscle tonus in those particular muscles maintained during his angry mood. Such a slight increase in muscle tonus might or might not be visible. If it were visible, it would be very subtle.

Note that this discussion of the facial signs of mood is conjectural, since this is largely an uncharted area.

13. EMBLEMS, 14. ADAPTORS

Let us consider some other types of information that are provided by the rapid facial muscular movements. There are a limited number of symbolic gestures, or what have been termed *emblems*,[13] shown in the face, although most such emblems involve the hands. The wink is a good example of a facial emblem. Emblems can signify anything, but the process of signification is such that the viewer believes that the maker did the movement to send him a message. You hold a person accountable for his wink, much as you would for his word. You believe he did it to tell you something. In this way emblems are the opposite of facial *adaptors*, movements in which the person engages in a non-instrumental, self-manipulative action. Lip sucking, lip biting, pushing the tongue around the cheeks and lips, using the tongue to wipe the lips, and a variety of lip movements can be considered what we have termed adaptors.[14] These are restless, nervous movements. They occur seemingly with little awareness. Individuals vary markedly in their typical rate of adaptors, but when a person becomes uncomfortable his rate of adaptors often increases above his own baseline.[15] These facial adaptors may provide information to the viewer. You may infer the person is ill at ease, but the knowledge is stolen, in the sense that the viewer does not believe the maker performed the movement to tell the viewer something.

15. ILLUSTRATORS

The face is used also to illustrate spoken conversation, much as the hands do. We distinguish among the following different types of hand illustrators:

batons, emphasis movements that accent a word
underliners, movements that emphasize a phrase or a clause
ideographs, movements that sketch the path or flow of thought
deictics, movements that point to an object, place, or event
spatials, depictions of a spatial relationship
rhythmics, depictions of the rhythm of an event
kinetographs, movements that represent a type or sequence of actions
pictographs, movements that draw a picture in the air to show the
  shape of the referent. (Cf. Ekman and Friesen [1972] for a
  detailed description of these illustrator sub-types.)

There is probably less variety in facial illustrators than in hand illustrators. It is possible, for example, to use your lips in a pictographic illustrator to show the size of an opening. But consider the impossibility of using a facial movement to draw a sphere or an hourglass figure, which are easy to depict by hand pictographic illustrators. There are probably just a few kinetic illustrators in which the face performs an action talked about in the conversation. For example, you can say that you spit the food out, and make a spitting movement with the lips. Obviously, the hands can perform many more different kinetic illustrators than can the face.

The commonest types of facial illustrators are probably the baton and the underliner, facial emphasis marks that italicize a word or a phrase, repeating in the face what is shown in the voice in loudness. The eyebrows are the most commonly used baton and underliner illustrators, most often either a raised or a lowered drawn-together brow action. Sometimes the upper eyelid is raised or the lower lid is tightened as a baton or underliner illustrator. Lip protrusions also are used seemingly as baton illustrators. Conceivably any other facial muscular action could be used as a baton or underliner illustrator, although we have not observed others.

16. REGULATORS

The face plays a role in regulating the flow of conversation. Facial signals convey whether the person is listening, understanding, or allowing the speaker to continue, or wishes to gain the floor. Dittman (1972) has studied such listener responses as specific muscular contractions (smiles), gaze direction, and head nodding. Duncan (1973) and Kendon (1973) have also detailed how these facial acts function in turn taking during conversation.

We believe that a number of facial emblems function as regulators provided by the listener to the speaker during conversation. These include, in addition to the agreement signs studied by Dittman and others, the facial emblems for exclamation, for questioning, and for incredulous disbelief. We have observed these in conversation, but we have not systematically studied their use or looked carefully for other such facial regulators.

The face may also provide syntax signs, although this has been studied only in conversation among deaf individuals using American Sign Language. Liddell (1975), working in Bellugi's laboratory, has found a particular facial movement that marks a relative clause. This facial action appears while the relative clause material is signed with the hands and disappears when the relative clause is over. There might be such facial syntax signs among hearing people as well. My experience when consulting with Bellugi's group on how to measure facial syntax signs suggests it will be very complex, requiring detailed and precise measurement to disentangle the various facial rapid movements that occur during conversation with deaf or hearing persons. During speech (or during ASL signing) some facial movements are emotional expressions, some are illustrators, some are regulators, some are emblems, and some may be syntax signs.

17. AGE

The face changes with age. The most rapid changes occur in the first few years of life, but changes occur throughout life. In Table 1 I have listed only those slow signs that index the changes in middle and older age. Individuals differ in the onset of these indexes of increasing age and in the particular pattern of signs that become permanently part of their face. We do not all develop the same set of permanent creases in the face or the same bags or sags. I do not know whether there are sex or racial differences in the amount or type of slow signs of old age. Anecdotally, it appears to Westerners that the Japanese do not show these age clues. It is difficult for Westerners to read age from a Japanese face; is it difficult for fellow Japanese?

What is responsible for the differences between people within the same culture in the slow facial signs of old age? I suspect that hereditary factors play the largest role. Some of the slow facial signs of age may result from the type of bony structure and the location and shape of the facial muscles. Skin elasticity, or the loss of it, may play an important role as well, and this may be influenced in part by heredity. Heredity also determines the pattern of fibers in the skin that may cause it to be more elastic when pulled in one direction than when pulled in another direction. Dermatologists and plastic surgeons say that exposure to the sun and wind decreases overall skin elasticity and facilitates permanent creases and bags. Nutritional factors are probably also relevant to skin elasticity, the shrinkage of the facial muscles, and the occurrence of blotching or textural changes in the skin. Usage of the muscles is another variable, but I will discuss it below, in relation to the notion that the face may show the emotional history of the person.

We believe that we can recognize the person across age changes, but can we? To what extent do the slow signs of age degrade the identity signal? If we divide life into the epochs of infancy, childhood, adolescence, young adult, mid-life, and old age, it is sensible to expect that identity can be recognized between adjacent epochs. To my knowledge no one has studied just how far identity signs can skip across developmental epochs.[16] I suspect that the answer will vary in part with how unusual a particular feature is and the likelihood that it will survive the appearance changes due to the ravages of time.

Quite separate from the matter of recognizing the same person over his life-span, is the issue of estimating a person's actual age from his face. Pittenger and Shaw (1975) found age estimates can be made with some accuracy when the ages of the persons whose faces are being judged ranged from 12 to 19. Age estimates were easiest around the years when physical changes are most rapid due to puberty. They were not able to determine the relative contribution of rapid, slow, and static[17] signs to the judgment of age, although their data suggested that all three types of facial signs may be relevant to age judgments.

In discussing beauty earlier, age signs were said to be the enemy of beauty in Western society. The goal of plastic surgery, cosmetics, and even exercise programs is to eliminate the appearance of the slow facial signs that inform about true age, in an attempt to appear younger. In the 1950s, adolescents and young adults in the United States would attempt to look older. Of course their purpose was not to appear middle aged. I have the impression that currently it is not as popular among adolescents to use cosmetics to try to look older, but this too has not been studied.

18. PREVIOUS EMOTIONAL LIFE

The notion of holding a man responsible for the appearance of his face after the age of thirty is attributed to Lincoln. The face is considered a tabula rasa on which is etched a person's emotional history, which is evident in the slow signs of middle age. Young women are sometimes cautioned not to frown or to smile too much, in order to avoid certain permanent facial creases.

I know of no research that has attempted to verify whether usage of the muscles affects in any substantial way the extent or type of facial signs of middle or old age. Certainly, the muscular contractions of the face occur not just for emotion. People move their facial muscles for a wide variety of reasons having nothing to do with emotion. Thus, it is unlikely that emotional life *per se* would determine the age signs, although usage might. Facial muscles, like other muscles, atrophy from disuse. It is possible that some of the sagging that does occur results from lack of muscle usage. It is also possible that non-isometric usage of particular muscles may increase the likelihood that certain permanent creases will develop. If someone has a particular facial style, a habitual set to the muscle tone maintained in his face in repose, or a particular facial movement that he habitually flashes in a manneristic fashion, then it is possible that the particular usage of his facial muscles might lead to some particular pattern in his face in old age. Yet, I suspect that heredity, climatic, and nutritional factors together play a larger role than usage in what happens to the face with age.

CONCLUSION

I have discussed eighteen types of information shown in the face. This is not a final list, nor is it the only list. There would be other ways to combine some of the categories I listed, or to subdivide them. No doubt the reader has already thought of a nineteenth or twentieth type of information revealed by the face.

My purpose has been to show how complex the face is as a vehicle for so many different types of information. Table 2 is a matrix indicating the relationships between facial sources and types of information. The pluses indicate knowledge, the minuses indicate that either evidence or logic suggests no relationship, the question marks show where possibilities seem worthy of study, and the blanks mean that I do not know what to think.

The matrix is my message. Consider how many blanks and question marks we have about our own faces.

NOTES

1. Friesen and I have collaborated for eleven years in our joint studies of facial expression and body movement.
2. I realize there is ambiguity in what is meant by "main" identity sign. Some of what I mean could be answered by research that determined whether people in general do better, are more accurate, at greater distance from the face than from other identity signs; or whether people tend to select the face as the source for identification when in a situation where there is free but limited choice.
3. Since writing this report, I have learned of research by Haviland and Lewis (in press) that has found that females have higher brows than do males,

Table 2

	Identity	Kin	Race	Gender	Temperament	Personality	Beauty	Sexual attractiveness	Intelligence	Disease	Emotion	Mood	Emblems	Adaptors	Illustrators	Regulators	Age	Previous emotional life
STATIC																		
Bony structure	?	?	?	?	−	−	?	?	?	+	−	−	−	−	−	−	−	
Features	?	?	+	?	−	−	+	?	−	+	−	−	−	−	−	−	−	
Skin pigmentation		?	+	−	−	−	+	?	−	+	−	−	−	−	−	−	−	
SLOW																		
Bags, sags, and pouches					−	−	?	?	−		−	−	−	−	−	−	?	
Creases					−	−	?	?	−		−	−	−	−	−	−	?	
Blotches					−	−	?		−	+	−	−	−	−	−	−	?	
Texture				+	−	−	?	?	−	+	−	−	−	−	−	−	?	
Facial hair	?	?	+	+	−	−	?	?	−	+	−	−	−	−	−	−	?	
Scalp hair	?	?	+	+	−	−	?	?	−	+	−	−	−	−	−	−	?	
Fatty deposits	?	?	?		−	−	?	?	−	+	−	−	−	−	−	−	?	
Teeth					−	−	?	?	−	+	−	−	−	−	−	−	?	
Skin pigmentation					−	−	?	?	−	+	−	−	−	−	−	−	?	
RAPID																		
Movements	−	?		?	?	?		?	?	+	+	?	+	+	+	+	?	
Tone	−	?	−	?	?	?	?	?	?	+	+	?	−	−	−	−	?	
Coloration	−	−	+	?	?	?				?	?	?	−	−	−	−		
Temperature	−	−	−	−	?	?				+	?	?	−	−	−	−		
Sweat	−	−	−	−	?					+	?	?	−	−	−	−		
Gaze direction	−	−	−	+	?	?		?	?		+	?	+	−	+	+		
Pupil size	−	−	−	−		?		?	?	+	+	?	−	−	−	−	−	
Head position	−	−	−	−		?		?			+	?	+		+	+		

and that their eyes are set wider apart than are males', and that these differences increase from infancy to adulthood. O'Sullivan (1976), in a study generated by this report, has found that untrained observers can accurately (83% correct) identify gender when judging photographs of college-age students in which facial hair has been eliminated. Guthrie (1976) has recently written many interesting and some far-fetched phylogenetic interpretations of facial static and slow signals, with particular reference to gender, beauty, sexual attractiveness, and age.

4. See Guthrie (1976) for another discussion of the childlike basis of beautiful facial appearance in women, although he also describes more "masculine" beautiful female faces.

5. A student of Dane Archer's, Michael Beller, recently found that observers could accurately judge I.Q. scores from photographs of the faces of children. This finding has not been replicated, was limited to ten children and there was no determination of whether the cues for intelligence were rapid, slow, or static signs.

6. The evidence regarding the universality of the morphology of facial expressions of emotion and their evolutionary basis comes from many sources. These include studies by psychologists, ethologists, and anthropologists of infants, children, people in different cultures, blind children, and nonhuman primates. Much of this work is reviewed in different chapters of Ekman (1973); also see Eibl-Eibesfeldt (1970) and Izard (1971).

7. In this way I disagree with Eibl-Eibesfeldt (1970), who believes that there are many stimuli that universally trigger specific facial expressions of emotion. Boucher (1975) has been studying cultural differences in what people say about the elicitors of emotion, and has found to his surprise more evidence of similarity than of difference if elicitors are classified in abstract terms rather than with regard to their specifics. Our current view (Ekman, 1977) emphasizes both the variability in specifics and commonality in the general characteristics of the emotion elicitors. For example, what is a disgusting taste, smell, or social act depends upon experience, but more generally disgust elicitors share the characteristics of being repulsive or distasteful rather than provocative or harmful.

8. Rosch and Heider's study has not been published, but is reported in Ekman (1972).

9. I use the term *natural* as it has been discussed and defined by Sebeok (1975). It is important not to misread my use of the terminology of semiotics as an implication that the facial signs are a linguistic system.

10. An expanded discussion of these theoretical issues can be found in "Biological and Cultural Contributions to Body and Facial Movement" (Ekman, 1977). Our formulation has been greatly influenced by Tomkins (1962).

11. Some of those studying differences in the ability to interpret facial expressions are Buck, Miller, and Caul (1974), Ekman and Friesen (1974b), Lanzetta and Kleck (1970), Shannon (1970), Zuckerman et al. (1975).

12. Many people have now proposed catalogues that list in words differ-

ent facial features, but most are based on the earlier ones presented by Bird-whistell (1970), Blurton Jones (1971), Brannigan and Humphries (1972), Grant (1969), or McGrew (1972). Some of these approaches were reviewed in comparison with other measurement techniques in Ekman, Friesen, and Ellsworth (1972:chap. 7) and are compared point by point in Ekman and Friesen (forthcoming).

13. Efron in 1942 (1972) first proposed the use of the term emblem to deal with a specific class of body movements. We have elaborated upon his distinction and conducted studies of emblems in a number of cultures (see Ekman, 1976; Ekman and Friesen, 1972; Johnson, Ekman and Friesen, 1976).

14. The distinction between emblems, adaptors, and illustrators was proposed on the basis of their origins, usage, and coding, although the hands, not the face, were considered (Ekman and Friesen, 1969, 1972).

15. Almost all the research on adaptors or emblems has studied the hands. The interpretations given here about facial adaptors is extrapolated from the evidence on hand adaptors (for evidence on hand adaptors see Ekman and Friesen, 1974).

16. O'Sullivan (1976) is currently analyzing data from a study that began to explore this question. If you know a person as an adult, you can accurately identify his baby pictures, but that is not so if you are just exposed to a photograph of a person as an adult and asked to identify his baby pictures.

17. It may seem peculiar that a static sign could be an age clue, yet recall that we included such very slow changing characteristics as facial shape and contours due to the bony structure as a static sign. As explained earlier, while such signs are not truly static since there are changes with growth, they are much slower than what we labeled as the slow signs.

REFERENCES

Anderson, L. D. 1921. "Estimating Intelligence by Means of Printed Photographs." *Journal of Applied Psychology* 5:152–55.

Birdwhistell, R. L. 1970. *Kinesics and Context*. Philadelphia: University of Pennsylvania Press.

Blurton Jones, N. G. 1971. "Criteria for Use in Describing Facial Expressions in Children." *Human Biology* 41:365–413.

Boucher, J. 1975. Personal communication.

Brannigan, C. R., and Humphries, D. A. 1972. "Human Non-verbal Behaviour, a Means of Communication." In *Ethological Studies of Child Behavior*, N. Blurton-Jones, ed. London: Cambridge University Press.

Buck, R.; Miller, R. E.; and Caul, W. F. 1974. "Sex, Personality and Physiological Variables in the Communication of Affect via Facial Expression." *Journal of Personality and Social Psychology* 30:587–96.

Carpenter, G. C. 1973. "Mother–Stranger Discrimination in the Early Weeks of Life." Paper presented at the Biennial Meeting of the Society for Research in Child Development, Philadelphia.

Chance, J.; Goldstein, A. G.; and McBride, L. 1975. "Differential Experience and Recognition Memory for Faces." *The Journal of Social Psychology* 97:243–53.

Coss, R. 1974. "Reflections on the Evil Eye." *Human Behavior* 3(10):16–22.

Cross, J. F.; Cross, J.; and Daly, J. 1971. "Sex, Race, Age and Beauty as Factors in Recognition of Faces." *Perception and Psychophysics* 10(6): 393–96.

Dillon, S. 1974. "Nonverbal Cues and Sex Role Stereotypes: Differential Perceptions of Masculinity, Femininity, Attractiveness, and Intelligence." Paper delivered at the meeting of the California State Psychological Association, Fresno.

Dittman, A. T. 1972. "Developmental Factors in Conversational Behavior." *Journal of Communication* 22(4):404–23.

Duncan, S. 1973. "Toward a Grammar for Dyadic Conversation." *Semiotica* 9(1):29–46.

Efron, D. 1942. *Gesture and Environment.* New York: King's Crown. Rev. ed., *Gesture, Race and Culture* (The Hague: Mouton, 1972).

Eibl-Eibesfeldt, I. 1970. *Ethology, the Biology of Behavior.* New York: Holt, Rinehart and Winston.

Ekman, P. 1972. "Universals and Cultural Differences in Facial Expressions of Emotion." In *Nebraska Symposium on Motivation, 1971,* J. Cole, ed. Lincoln: University of Nebraska Press.

———. 1973. "Cross Cultural Studies of Facial Expression." In *Darwin and Facial Expression: A Century of Research in Review,* P. Ekman, ed. New York: Academic Press.

———. 1976. "Movements with Precise Meaning." *Journal of Communication* 26(3):14–26.

———. 1977. "Biological and Cultural Contributions of Body and Facial Movement." In *Anthropology of the Body,* J. Blacking, ed. New York: Academic Press.

Ekman, P., and Friesen, W. V. 1969. "The Repertoire of Nonverbal Behavior: Categories, Origins, Usage, and Coding." *Semiotica* 1(1):49–98.

———. 1971. "Constants across Cultures in the Face and Emotion." *Journal of Personality and Social Psychology* 17:124–29.

———. 1972. "Hand Movements." *Journal of Communication* 22(4):353–74.

———. 1974a. "Detecting Deception from the Body or Face." *Journal of Personality and Social Psychology* 29(3):288–98.

———. 1974b. "Nonverbal Behavior and Psychopathology." In *The Psychology of Depression: Contemporary Theory and Research,* R. J. Friedman and M. M. Katz, eds. Washington, D.C.: Winston & Sons.

———. 1975. *Unmasking the Face.* Englewood Cliffs, N.J.: Prentice-Hall.

———. 1976. "Measuring Facial Movement." *Environmental Psychology and Nonverbal Behavior* 1(1):56–75.

———. 1977. *The Facial Action Coding System: A Manual for the Measurement of Facial Movement.* Palo Alto, Ca.: Consulting Psychologists' Press.

———. Forthcoming. *Analyzing Facial Action.*

Ekman, P.; Friesen, W. V.; and Ellsworth, P. 1972. *Emotion in the Human Face*. Elmsford, N.Y.: Pergamon Publishing Co.

Ekman, P.; Sorenson, E. R.; and Friesen, W. V. 1969. "Pan-cultural Elements in Facial Displays of Emotions." *Science* 164(3875):86–88.

Freedman, D. G. 1974. *Human Infancy: An Evolutionary Perspective*. Hillsdale, N.J.: Lawrence Erlbaum Assoc.

Friesen, W. V. 1972. "Cultural Differences in Facial Expressions in a Social Situation: An Experimental Test of the Concept of Display Rules." Unpublished doctoral dissertation, University of California, San Francisco.

Galper, R. E. 1973. "'Functional Race Membership' and Recognition of Faces." *Perceptual and Motor Skills* 37:455–62.

Gaskill, P. C., Fenton, N., and Porter, J. P. 1927. "Judging the Intelligence of Boys from their Photographs." *Journal of Applied Psychology* 11:394–404.

Goffman, E. 1976. "Gender Display." *Visual Anthropology*, in press.

Going, M., and Read, J. D. 1974. "Effects of Uniqueness, Sex of Subject and Sex of Photograph on Facial Recognition." *Perceptual and Motor Skills* 39:109–10.

Goodman, R. M., and Gorlin, R. J. 1970. *The Face in Genetic Disorders*. St. Louis: C. V. Mosby.

Grant, N. G. 1969. "Human Facial Expression." *Man* 4:525–36.

Guthrie, R. D. 1976. *Body Hot Spots*. New York: Van Nostrand Reinhold.

Haviland, J. 1975. "Looking Smart: The Relationship between Affect and Intelligence in Infancy." In *Origins of Infant Intelligence*, M. Lewis, ed. New York: Plenum.

Haviland, J. M., and Lewis, M. In preparation. "Sex Differences in Presentation of the Face."

Hess, E. H. 1975. "The Role of Pupil Size in Communication." *Scientific American* Nov.: 110–19.

Hochberg, J., and Galper, R. E. 1974. "Attribution of Intention as a Function of Physiognomy." *Memory and Cognition* 2(1A):39–42.

Huber, E. 1931. *Evolution of Facial Musculature and Facial Expression*. Baltimore: Johns Hopkins University Press.

Iliffe, A. H. 1960. "A Study of Preferences in Feminine Beauty." *British Journal of Psychology* 51:267–73.

Izard, C. 1971. *The Face of Emotion*. New York: Appleton-Century-Crofts.

Johnson, H. G.; Ekman, P.; and Friesen, W. V. 1976. "Communicative Body Movements: American Emblems." *Semiotica* 15(4):335–53.

Jordan, R. U. 1969. *Faces*. Emporia, Kansas: R. U. Jordan, Box 136.

Joseph, M., and Dawbarn, C. 1970. *Measurement of the Faces*. Spastics International Medical Publications Research Monograph, 3. Surrey: Wm. Heinemann Medical Books.

Kendon, A. 1973. "The Role of Visible Behavior in the Organization of Social Interaction." In *Social Communication and Movement*, M. Cranach and I. Vine, eds. New York: Academic Press.

Korner, A. F. 1969. "Neonatal Startles, Smiles, Erections, and Reflex Sucks as Related to State, Sex, and Individuality." *Child Development* 40:1039–53.

Landis, C., and Phelps, L. W. 1928. "The Prediction from Photographs of Success and Vocational Aptitude." *Journal of Experimental Psychology* 11:313–24.

Lanzetta, J. T., and Kleck, R. E. 1970. "Encoding and Decoding of Nonverbal Affects in Humans." *Journal of Personality and Social Psychology* 16:12–19.

Lavrakas, P. J.; Buri, J. R.; and Mayzner, M. 1975. "The Effects of Training and Individual Differences on the Recognition of Other-Race Faces." Paper presented at the Convention of the American Psychological Association.

Lefas, J. 1975. *Physiognomy: The Art of Reading Faces.* Barcelona: Ariane.

Levy, J.; Trevarthen, C.; and Sperry, R. W. 1972. "Perception of Bilateral Chimeric Figures Following Hemispheric Deconnexion." *Brain* 95:61–78.

Liddell, S. K. 1975. "Restrictive Relative Clauses in American Sign Language." Unpublished mimeo., Salk Institute.

Liggett, J. 1974. *The Human Face.* New York: Stein & Day.

McGrew, W. C. 1972. *An Ethological Study of Children's Behavior.* New York: Academic Press.

Malpass, R. S., and Kravitz, J. 1969. "Recognition of Faces of Own and Other Race." *Journal of Personality and Social Psychology* 13:330–34.

Mar, T. T. 1974. *Face Reading: The Chinese Art of Physiognomy.* New York: Dodd, Mead & Co.

Martin, J. G. 1963. "Racial Ethnocentrism and Judgment of Beauty." *Journal of Social Psychology* 63(59).

Maurer, D. 1975. "Developmental Changes in the Scanning of Faces by Infants." Paper presented at the Biennial Meeting of the Society for Research in Child Development, Denver.

Messick, S., and Damarin, F. 1964. "Cognitive Styles and Memory for Faces." *Journal of Abnormal and Social Psychology* 69(3):313–18.

Nyhan, W., and Shear, C. 1975. Personal communication.

O'Sullivan, M. 1976. Personal communication.

Peck, H., and Peck, S. 1970. "A Concept of Facial Aesthetics." *Angle Orthodontist* 40:284–317.

Pelligrini, R. J. 1973. "Impressions of the Male Personality as a Function of Beardedness." *Psychology* 10:29–33.

Pintner, R. 1918. "Intelligence as Estimated from Photographs." *Psychological Review* 25:286–98.

Pittenger, J. B., and Shaw, R. E. 1975. "Perception of Relative and Absolute Age in Facial Photographs." *Perception and Psychophysics* 18(2):137–43.

Rizzolatti, G.; Umilta, C.; and Berlucchi, C. 1971. "Opposite Superiorities of the Right and Left Cerebral Hemispheres in Discriminative Reaction Time to Physiognomical and Alphabetical Material." *Brain* 94:431–42.

Russell, M. 1976. "Human Olfactory Communication." *Nature* 260(5551):520–22.

Schwartz, G. E.; Fair, P. L.; Salt, P.; Mandel, M. R.; and Klerman, G. I. 1976a. "Facial Muscle Patterning to Affective Imagery in Depressed and Non-depressed Subjects." *Signs* 192:489–91.

————. 1976b. "Facial Expression and Imagery in Depression: An Electromyographic Study." *Psychosomatic Medicine*, in press.

Seaford, H. W., Jr. 1975. "Facial Expression Dialect: An Example." In *Organization of Behavior in Face-to-face Interaction*, A. Kendon, R. M. Harris, and M. Ritchie Key, eds. Mouton: The Hague.

Sebeok, T. A. 1975. "Six Species of Signs: Some Propositions and Strictures." *Semiotica* 13(3):233–60.

Secord, P. F. 1958. "Facial Features and Inference Processes in Interpersonal Perception." In *Person Perception and Interpersonal Behavior*, R. Taguiri and L. Petrullo, eds. Stanford: Stanford University Press.

Secord, P. F.; Dukes, W. F.; and Bevan, W. 1954. "Personalities in Faces: An Experiment in Social Perceiving." *Genetic Psychology Monograph* 49: 231–79.

Shannon, A. M. 1970. "Differences between Depressive and Schizophrenics in the Recognition of Facial Expression of Emotion." Unpublished doctoral dissertation, University of California, San Francisco.

Sheldon, W. H. 1954. *Atlas of Man: A Guide for Somatyping the Adult Male at All Ages*. New York: Harper & Row.

Shoemaker, D. J.; South, D. R.; and Lowe, J. 1973. "Facial Stereotypes of Deviants and Judgments of Guilt or Innocence." *Social Forces*, 51:427–33.

Tomkins, S. S. 1962. *Affect, Imagery, Consciousness*, vol. 1. New York: Springer Publishing Co.

Udry, J. R. 1965. "Structural Correlates of Feminine Beauty Preferences in Britain and the United States: A Comparison." *Sociological and Social Research* 49:330.

Yin, R. K. 1970. "Face Recognition by Brain Injured Patients: A Dissociable Ability?" *Neuropsychologia* 8:395–402.

Zuckerman, M.; Lipets, M. S.; Koivumaki, J. H.; and Rosenthal, R. 1975. "Encoding and Decoding Nonverbal Cues of Emotion." *Journal of Personality and Social Psychology* 32:1068–76.

Sign Languages and the Verbal/Nonverbal Distinction

William C. Stokoe

Sign languages have always held a fascination for the curious. As coded substitutes for elements of speech, they can easily be put to secret uses, and thereby take on the glamour of hidden intelligence. Making possible what seems impossible without speech, sign languages reveal at the same time to all who see them in use a mode of expression shared by primates, related to mammalian behavior, and ultimately tied to most visual communication of the animal kingdom. If only this were not true, if there were no relation between human gestural systems and animal behavior, then the whole matter could be dealt with and dismissed as Bloomfield thought he could do: Sign languages would simply be derivatives of spoken languages, with or without writing systems as intermediate stages. But the problem is more complex than that, and although a Bloomfieldian notion of sign languages is not now in favor, it is not completely mistaken—in many uses, sign languages are exactly and by intention coded substitutes for otherwise unexpressed language utterances. Books, pamphlets, and series have recently been published for those engaged in teaching deaf children; and in all of these gestural signs (gSigns) are presented as code substitutes, not just for individual words of English but also for inflectional suffixes like *-ing*, *-s*, and *-ed*

Much of the research herein reported has had the support of NSF Grant SOC 74 147 24.

and for derivational affixes like *-ity, -ment,* and *un-.* The authors of these codebooks are all proceeding from a tacit or open assumption that a sign language can be made into a complete, adequate, explicit, and simple code for representing English. Fortunately, or unfortunately, depending on one's point of view, they have not discovered that complete, adequate, explicit, and simple descriptions, codes, or grammars for any natural language are ideals not realized in practice. Also a code, but far older than these lexical coding efforts, is a system that makes use of the already existent alphabetical writing of spoken symbols. Employing gSigns made with one hand or both to represent the graphic symbols conventionally used, with or without additional instrumentality, is an ancient practice indeed and may be as old as graphic representation itself (Stokoe, 1975a:345–60).

If it were not for troublesome facts, all this could be put together and called *verbal*: Lexical gSign codes, manual alphabet codes, and graphic codes all represent *words*. In that case, the radically different use of the human body in face-to-face or group interaction would as obviously be nonverbal. But such a simplistic categorization is what this paper is intended to challenge. By directing attention to a number of studies of sign language, I hope to show that *verbal* and *nonverbal* are misused terms and that what they refer to are not categorical opposites but related matters. Just as we now know that space and time, like matter and energy, relate in ways that can be quantified, to realize that verbal and nonverbal behavior, so called, are related and not opposed may open the way to more rewarding research strategies.

Four uses rather than two are open to human gSigns: (1) They can substitute for some element or other of a spoken or written utterance. (2) They can denote emotions or certain general ideas directly. (3) They can do both of these at once. (4) They can also do something else not yet specified but to be discussed here. In the usual terminology of our day, the first of these four uses would be called verbal and the second nonverbal. There is little evidence that the third use has been carefully considered. But the fourth use is usually completely unsuspected, although it exists and has for a long time. This fourth use makes the simple bipolar nomenclature *verbal/nonverbal* inadequate, even with the admission of the third, mixed use of gSigns.

Examples of the first two uses beyond what has just been said are easy to find and have been written about increasingly of late by linguists and psycholinguists. The mixed use of gesture may take place when what is called a "natural" gesture enters into the performance of a code substitute; e.g., a "natural" gesticulation of a speaker talking about getting something is a grasping motion toward the body. In one or more Manual English lexical codes this motion is utilized with the addition of some manual alphabet configuration before the hand grasps—e.g., *g* for 'get', *o* for 'obtain', or *r* for 'receive', etc. The alphabetic may not blend perfectly with the emblematic use, but an observer unfamiliar with the alphabetic code may still interpret the action correctly—at least he is unlikely to mistake the gesticulation as an attempt to symbolize 'throw away'.

The fourth use of gSigns is distinct from all the foregoing. In it the individual sign does not denote or substitute for any element of a spoken or written utterance or structure, nor does it express an emotion or any such general idea, as emblems usually do. Instead the gSign in this fourth use directly and originally expresses an element of sign language itself, whether the element be lexical or grammatical.

One characteristic of language that distinguishes it from some other semiotic systems is its multiplicity of levels of organization, or strata, as they have been called. In this respect gSigns as linguistic manifestations are typical. If we take for the next portion of the discussion the hypothetical position of a native user of American Sign Language (ASL), we will find that the hand held with the thumb and first two fingers extended and spread apart is not a gSign at all but part of many such signs. If the hand is held palm out with the fingers pointing up, it becomes a *numerical*, not a *verbal*, sign and denotes 'three'. It need not mean 'three' to users of other sign languages or to nonsigners: Deaf signers in the Midi denote '3' by holding this hand in a horizontal position and moving it downward (Sallagoïty, 1975); hearing nonsigners are likely to denote '3' by holding the thumb over the pinky, leaving the three middle fingers upright.

The semantic element or unit (Chafe, 1970) '3' remains in the ASL sign for 'sergeant' when this hand is drawn across the opposite arm, suggesting the triple chevron. But 'three-ness' has nothing to do with other signs that also utilize this hand; e.g., NO, AWKWARD, LOUSY, BUG, ROOSTER, DEVIL, DENMARK, SAIL, PARKED-CAR, etc. (The use of capitals represents both signs of ASL and their conventional English gloss.) Most of these examples are taken from *A Dictionary of ASL* (Stokoe, Casterline, Croneberg, 1965, 2e 1976), but recent research by Battison, Markowicz, and Woodward (1974) has found out something even more characteristically linguistic about the "3-hand." It is not a simple symbol at all; it is more akin to a phonemic than to a phonetic symbol: Unlike the Morse code symbol for '3', which is always "di-di-di-dah-dah," but instead like English initial /θ/, which may occur as [θ] or as [f] in the childish pronunciation "free" for *three*, this hand is what appears when a portion but not all of ASL signers perform certain of the signs that other signers use the V-hand for. That is, in uttering SMOKE, READ, and other signs, many signers of ASL extend and spread apart only the index and second finger, keeping the thumb in. Other signers extend the thumb in these signs. This difference is analogous to such variations in English as *thing/ting* and *going/goin*, both in phonological and in sociological dimensions.

An even more striking identification of sign language phonology with universal phonology (see Battison, 1976) appears when another sign language community is considered. So far we have seen that two different hand configurations, the "3-hand" and the "V-hand," are used by ASL to keep meanings apart, e.g., TWO/THREE. But we have also seen that in specifiable circumstances the 3-hand can be substituted in the same sign for the V-hand by persons or groups also specifiable. As native users of the language we would know all this, out of awareness, and so be able to distinguish when the thumb extension was distinctive and when it was not distinctive.

With the same limited set of features (thumb, index finger, middle finger, extension/non-extension, spreading/non-spreading), ASL has also another set of signs and distinctions in which they are differentiated. The hand that has the extended index and middle fingers side by side and in contact (non-spread) composes out of these features another sub-morphemic element, the H-hand (so called in 1960 and 1965 descriptions, because when the context is alphabet coding it denotes *h* in horizontal presentation but *u* when upright and *n* when pointed downward). But this ASL H-hand as a phoneme has both thumb-extended and thumb-not-extended realizations.

The situation in American Sign Language may be summed up thusly: When the features are (1) closed fist, (2) extension or not of thumb, (3) of index finger, (4) of middle finger, and (5) spreading or not of fingers adjacent; then (a) ± *thumb extension* is sometimes phonemic and sometimes not, and (b) ± *thumb extension* in the context of − *spreading* is non-phonemic but can be accounted for by various sociolinguistic techniques.

If we now look at Danish Sign Language (DSL), we find that the feature ± *thumb extension* has phonemic force regularly, but the feature ± *spreading* seldom or never does. Thus in DSL, what we have called the V-hand and the H-hand are both used to realize one DSL phoneme, but what we have called the 3-hand has an unspread realization as well. This kind of relationship and organization of detail on feature, phonemic, and lexic levels is neither verbal, in the sense of relating to the word forms or word strings of another language, nor nonverbal, in the sense of unrelated to language.

Another reason that the terms *verbal* and *nonverbal* are misleading in the present context is that information that may be left implicit and matter that must be expressed in any utterance are differently distributed when the utterer moves from spoken to gestural expression. It is natural, note, for us who hear to consider moving from speech to signing—we outnumber the deaf by one thousand to one or two (Schein and Delk, 1974). But for the deaf, it is just as natural to start with signing and to consider speech and language from a signer's viewpoint (i.e., as alien and strange). Moreover, the large questions of both language origin and language evolution would be begged if sign language activity were to be called verbal and signs were to be accounted words. Sign languages contain material and relationships of kinds designated both verbal and nonverbal in unexceptionable usage of the terms. But it is time to deal in another way with these terms.

Semiotics as a discipline has been supportive of sign language studies, and Sebeok individually has been instrumental in furthering scientific investigation into ways that gSigns are used (see especially *Approaches to Semiotics* 14 and 21 and *Sign Language Studies*). Regarding *nonverbal* Sebeok has written:

> This deceptively simple phrase, widely bandied about and incorporated in a large miscellany of book titles . . . is well nigh devoid of meaning or, at best, susceptible to so many interpretations as to be nearly useless. [1975:9]

Logically the term *nonverbal* might become more satisfactory as its co-term *verbal* became more precisely defined. However, just as Sebeok finds *nonverbal* given unclear and conflicting interpretations, the term *verbal* is used as badly or worse. Worse, I think, if human consequences can be considered in judging a case of terminology. In the jargon of educators and counselors and interpreters who work with the deaf, *verbal* represents one end of a bipolar opposition, and their term *low-verbal deaf* both mislabels and condemns. Behind the term there may be a trace of sociolinguistic relevance: A deaf person's competence in English is likely to be much less than his competence in a sign language. But no person's competence should be judged solely on performance in a second language to which he can have little or no direct exposure, and the competence in sign language is completely ignored or is unsuspected by those who apply, and by many who hear or read, the label *low-verbal deaf* and who go on to infer deficits in language competence, cognitive skills, and intellect.

Rather than catalog the misuse of the term *verbal* and its compounds I would like to consider whether the term may have any legitimate application. Perhaps Sebeok is correct and we might better abandon the term *nonverbal* and so *verbal* too. Still it may be useful to look at what this distinction may have meant had there not been this confusion of tongues. The study of sign language has accomplished, I believe, what scientific investigation often does: It has found apparent opposites to be otherwise related.

In a large accomplishment, two such different creatures as dogs and dolphins were found alike in structure. In a small way, those who examine sign languages have found that verbal and nonverbal are not the opposites of Boolean algebra: It is not true that $U = v + \tilde{v}$ ('the universe of discourse consists entirely of verbal and nonverbal'). Behavior labeled with these terms may be related in more interesting ways than by simple negation.

One definition of *verbal* stems from classical studies, where one is, theoretically at least, bilingual in Latin and English and *verbal* is but the adjective form of the noun *word*. A word, then, is an idea that may be expressed internally in ways not yet well understood, or externally so as to be perceptible to others sharing the same convention of expression. In the preceding sentence, all that follows *idea* is restrictive; a word is not an idea only but an idea symbolized somehow, and so a sign in the full semiotic sense.

An idea may be expressed either in a vocal structure or in a gSign structure—we see in this the major contribution of sign language study. If *word* (of a language) and *gSign* (of a sign language) are equivalently expressions of, or signs for, ideas, the term *verbal* in its fullest sense should denote almost as much as does the term *language*. The abstraction language is larger, then, because the kinds of ideas we are discussing are related to each other in several kinds of ways. Some are nominal ideas, others verb-like (*verbal* in another sense of the word). Within this major classification are subclasses: Noun ideas contain, but do not consist entirely of, such features as potent, human, inanimate, uncountable; verb-ideas denote states of things, processes things undergo, or actions (Chafe, 1970). But besides the relation of idea to idea, words relate to words grammatically: State verbs appear in English sentences as adjectives placed after the pseudo-verb *be*; process verb ideas appear in English with a *patient* noun as subject; but verbs combining both process and action features require us to put the patient in English as object and the agent as subject. Thus it is indeterminate whether the term *verbal* should refer to semantic relations (between ideas) or to syntactic relations, both deep and superficial (between words).

When a word, however, is given vocal expression—not with one vocal sign for one denotatum of course but with the involvement of all kinds of submorphemic, doubly articulated structure—then it is simply a spoken word, and is called *verbal* in the sparse taxonomy of the legal profession. Semioticians may prefer to see *verbal* used as adjective standing for anything pertaining to words, but the legal term *verbal* does preserve the distinction of 'vocally expressed' as opposed to 'written' or otherwise documented. Curiously, in Italian common law, a gSign, viz., the index finger held up to the temple by a conspirator in a kidnap attempt, and used as surrogate for the phrase 'kill him', has been treated as "verbal" evidence (Leonard Siger, pers. comm.).

The source of much difficulty in terminology and in thinking about these matters is this polysemanticity of *verbal*. A word is both idea and the idea's expression. In triadic Peircean semiotics, a word is at once a sign interpreter, a significant, and a vehicle; i.e., Peirce includes our terms *idea* and *word* but also the possessor of the idea and the utterer or perceiver of the word. What is most disturbing about those who bandy about the term *verbal* is not so much their ignorance of Peirce's semiotic as the vicious assumptions their usage conceals. By the use of the terms *verbal, low-verbal,* and *nonverbal* they reveal perhaps their unconscious fear of the primitive animal side of human nature (Mindel and Vernon, 1971:83). But it is just from this part of human inheritance that gSign and vocal activity arises. Those who use these terms thus make speech (and hearing) instead of intellect and language the measure of man and the use of gSigns for language in their eyes is a badge of inadequacy.

To go back to a more satisfactory application, *verbal* pertains to words expressed either vocally or by gSigns. The essence of verbality is semiotic: The sign is denotatum, the sign is vehicle, the sign is interpreter—all in a special relationship normally called linguistic, though it is broader than normal linguistics concedes.

The term *nonverbal* then ought to describe whatever has nothing to do with ideas linked by grammar to spoken or to signed words. But the miscellaneous usage that Sebeok reviews in *The Semiotic Web* (1975) has no such logical consistency. Instead, for the most part, the best of current research into gestural, facial, bodily, and spatial behavior—though called nonverbal—is semiotic; i.e., it deals with ideas and their interrelation in nonvocal expression. Some of this research even deals directly with vocal expression—what the voice does as long as it is not the production of vowels and consonants, i.e., the segments of speech, now as closely guarded by syntacticists as they once were by phonemicists from identification with the phonology of sign languages.

To demonstrate that there are in sign languages of the deaf: (1) phonology as regular submorphemic structure, (2) grammar as the rules and transformations of syntactical patterns, and (3) semantics as a precise referential relation of the world of thought to the world of sound and sight—to demonstrate all this would take us in many directions.

One of these directions may even be backward. For some years the burden of proof was on students of sign language, and skeptics demanded "But is it really language?" Abbott (1975) puts the question less aggressively: "How highly encoded is a sign language? and In what parts of the system is there more abstract encoding, in what parts less?" The answers confirm the position taken here that words and gSigns of a deaf sign language are the same kind of signs. Abbott finds that sign language verbs are highly encoded; i.e., they contain several kinds of grammatical and semantic information in addition to their root meanings encoded in parallel, abstract, and economical ways. Questions like his about coding are more easily verified than bald inchoate questions about the nature of language.

In another part of sign language grammar a different degree of encoding is found, but even though person reference is less encoded than verb system, this part of a visually received language is interesting. Deaf signers designate self, person signed to, and others and do so singly, dually, trially, or plurally in the same basic way our whole species does, by looking, attending, pointing with hand or face or more saliently with finger pointing or eye gaze. Henderson (MS.) has identified nine semantic types and mapped the pronoun words, tokens, of a great many languages into the nine. Except for three-pronoun systems, he finds any number from two to nine linguistic tokens for the nine types. The usual case is for one of the tokens to represent two or more types; e.g., contemporary English *you* refers both to one addressee and to several or many. Users of American Sign Language express all nine types of person designation with distinct sign tokens (see also Friedman, 1975).

This matter, deixis, brings us back to another kind of distinction, sometimes referred to by the terms *verbal* and *nonverbal*, but for which the terms *language* and *non-language* (as Burling [1970] uses them) would be more exact. Human beings use language and are often the topics of language utterances, but they are not language. Even when a dyad or any larger group interacts, the roles of sender-of-signals, addressee-of-signals, and denoted-by-signals are non-language; but the terms being used by the sender-of-signals are language whether vocal signs or gSigns express them, if the sender is operating within the rules of a spoken or signed language. The same behavior, however (looking at addressee, gesturing self, or another), when used by a speaker who knows none of the forms and rules of a formal sign language, cannot be termed linguistic in the narrow sense of the term.

Another kind of encoding, commonly considered uniquely linguistic, is that expressed in dependent relative clauses further marked as restrictive. For a non-grammarian all this might be described as economy of effort or as packing information compactly. It differs in subtle ways from simple conjoining. Thus in the sequence of signs, EARLIER DOG CHASE CAT COME HOME, there are two propositions or sentences. Liddell (MS.) has found that if the head, face, and gaze of the signer are unmarked by difference from "normal" throughout the sequence's performance, the ASL sequence is equivalent to: 'The dog chased the cat and came home a while ago'. But if the signer tilts the head back a little, raises the eyebrows, and produces pronounced naso-labial folds by facial contraction while making the first four signs of the sequence, then returns all systems to "normal" for the last two signs, the equivalent in English is: 'The dog that chased the cat earlier came home'.

This discovery by Liddell will startle those who doubt that a language not symbolized vocally can have such structure. It also marks an important advance in sign language studies. I. M. Schlesinger (1970) concluded that Israeli deaf singers could understand correctly from drawings the kind of relation expressed in sentences containing subject, verb, direct object, and indirect object, but he found no evidence of any system for signaling these relationships in their signing. It is clear that he was looking for some equivalent in manual behavior of the same kind of units expressed in speech. Students of sign languages who know that manual sign vehicles are only part of the whole gSign linguistic system did not find Liddell's breakthrough surprising. Baker and Padden (MS.) have found that utterances in spontaneous ASL communication may show identical manual features but contrast in meaning and structure according to facial behavior and gaze. The same kind of head and face activity Liddell describes is to be seen in a videotape made in the Linguistics Research Laboratory at Gallaudet College in 1972. In the four-year-old transcription it reads: ME REFUSE GO UNLESS HE GO. The transcription suggests that UNLESS is a sign, but the tape shows no manual activity at this point; instead there is a backward head movement. In the light of Liddell's discovery it seems much more probable that the head tilt after the first GO puts the whole clause meaning 'unless he goes too' into a restrictive dependent relation to the refusal. Recent inspection of the tape also shows that the head indeed is held back-tilted to the end of the sequence and that with or a little after the energy peak of the GO sign at the end the head makes a forward sharp nod ('affirmative'?).

Gestural activity of the kind here described is neither nonverbal in one common usage of the term nor verbal in the sense of a directly coded substitution of visible action for normal English elements and structures. Restrictive relative clauses, or a contrast between relative dependency and coordinate conjunction (i.e., between embedding and conjoining), might with much more justice be termed *nonverbal*, because this contrast is a matter of logical relationship and so more abstract than any linguistic expression of it.

Another way in which nonvocal activity shows all the properties of language systems has been surveyed by Battison (MS.). He has found a class of words in ASL, i.e., signs, that have entered the language as loan words from English. Loan words generally make excellent indicators both of linguistic change and of cultural contact. Thus when a list of color terms in Kikuyu includes *buru*, the observer rightly guesses that before European contact there was no term for *blue* in the language. Also correct is the conclusion that *buru* is English *blue* passed through the Kikuyuans' phonological filtering system. But to take a word from a spoken language and make it a word of a sign language involves more change than that of replacing an *l* with an *r*. One channel for such lexical intercultural traffic is finger spelling. ASL signers use fully finger-spelled words to a greater or lesser extent in normal interaction. Abbreviated finger-spelled words came into ASL (and French SL before it) as borrowed signs simply by letting the hand in the configuration for the initial letter make some slight action; e.g., days of the week (except Sunday), color terms (except for black, white, and red: Stokoe, MS.), names of major cities.

But the several dozen loan signs Battison has found and described form a special class of ASL signs in formation, meaning, and functional distribution. Unlike finger spelling, which is used more in deaf-with-hearing interchanges, these loan signs are almost exclusively used in deaf-with-deaf interchanges. They are short words in English (usually needing only two, three, or four handshapes for complete finger spelling). They are signs of ASL belonging to a subclass formationally by virtue of using change of the active (*dez*: Stokoe, 1960) hand during performance. And some of them are highly polysemantic; in this the direct opposites of proper names, which are often reduced to initial-dez signs (Stokoe, Casterline, and Croneberg, 1976:291–93 [1965]; Meadow, 1975).

Three examples will be examined briefly here to show how meaning and form, or sign vehicle and sign denotatum, are related in this portion of a nonvocal but fully verbal system. The original words are *do, all,* and *what.* Battison finds that these have become naturalized in ASL as several signs, clearly related in formation but with distinctly different uses. Thus DO_1 means 'what shall I do?' DO_2 means 'what are you going to do (about it)?' DO_3 signifies 'things to do', 'chores', and DO_4 commands 'do something—anything!' *All* likewise becomes signs inflected to fit different structures of ideas and signs. AL_1 applies to the parts of a conceptual whole taken at once; AL_2 stands for all the items in a list or series; AL_3 designates all the people in a group facing the signer; and AL$_4$ means 'always' in the restricted sense of 'all the time from a past reference point'.

Battison reports (pers. comm.) that many of this class of loan signs in ASL are displacing signs long attested as being a part of the lexicon. One of the explanations he suggests is that the loan word AL is easier and less awkward in the making than ALL made with the two flat hands and a circle-touch action. Or it may be that because the older ALL is uninflectible it is being displaced by the one-handed AL, which can be varied in position, direction, and action to fit the idea of totality to different kinds of concepts—another example of parallel processing of information, i.e., encoding becoming highly abstract.

Another loan sign in the Battison study is WT 'what?' (In it a trace of the manual alphabet 'w' handshape appears as the open hand is closed to a 't' during horizontal movement.) The older sign WHAT (Stokoe, Casterline, and Croneberg 1976:235 [1965]) uses two hands but may always have had an equivocal status between true ASL and English manually encoded. I can remember being puzzled in the past when signers instead of using the WHAT sign I expected used a sign usually glossed 'name' but having a range of meanings and uses quite unlike that of English *name*.

The work of sign language researchers, only skimmed over here, makes it clear that applying the term *nonverbal* to sign languages is not only pointless but counterproductive. Members of a culture whose language has five or six inflected forms that translate English *all* and as many for *do* and several formationally different terms for *what* in all its uses cannot any longer be said to lack the ability to think abstractly, to operate on a "high-verbal" level, or to be skillful readers of "nonverbal" cues but without "verbal" skill.

If a clearer terminology should result from the study of sign languages, then semiotics will be repaid for its fostering of the at times scarcely tolerated study. And if a more humane, less egocentric and ethnocentric view of a special minority, the deaf, can displace prejudice, then studying sign language can be justified. But there is another implication in this semiotic strand that most engages me and others. Untangled it may lead toward better understanding of the origins and evolution of language and human behavior.

In the Fall 1975 number of *Sign Language Studies*, Goldin-Meadow and Feldman (see also Goldin-Meadow, MS.) report on a discovery that young deaf children, without access to any sign language and unable to hear, lip-read, or make any speech audibly, nevertheless use gestures. At first these gestures have only general referential relation to whole situations. Later they are specialized so that some express nominal ideas, others verbal ideas. Next, gestures of these two kinds are joined in two-sign structures. Still later, more complicated structures are made from a growing lexicon of gSigns. This behavior was not learned by the children from the mothers in the study; only some of the mothers ever did use two gestures syntactically, but those who did so combined gestures several six-week intervals after these structures appeared in the children's behavior.

This finding by Goldin-Meadow and Feldman should be considered along with two others: (1) Normally hearing children begin to put words together in two-word syntactic structures at the end of their second year of life; and (2) deaf children in homes where deaf parents sign without restraint begin to put their ideas into two-sign syntactic structures at the end of their first year of life.

In the Winter 1975 issue of *Sign Language Studies*, Adam Kendon describes another surprising discovery—not about deaf sign language but about another kind of gSign activity. That speakers gesticulate when speaking is common knowledge, but Kendon's analysis of both vocal and gSign activity on motion picture recordings shows that language utterances normally have two outputs: speech and gesticulation. He finds as well, that at those moments in a discourse when the vocal output is interrupted or suspended, the idea structure continues to be expressed in gSigns. Gesticulation, then, is not mere embellishment of spoken discourse with illustrative gestures but is the coeval or elder partner of speech in the work of expression.

Kendon reports this research in support of the gestural theory of language origins most fully articulated in the work of Hewes (1973, 1974). What Kendon has found perfectly matches the observations of deaf infants' language development in speaking and in signing households. To state the point simply: Communication in the human individual begins with gSigns, or gSigns in a behavioral matrix, not yet differentiated from touch. As well equipped as all human individuals are with a genetic propensity for language—even perhaps with an inborn ability to distinguish language sounds (Eimas, 1975)—they begin communicating in a less specialized way than that of adult language, using gSigns at first. Only later do (hearing) infants master the long-to-learn art of phonology and still later the whole grammar of the language adults around them use. But it is not through the study of development in the usual and the special individual only that we can see something like the phylogenetic development of gSign into speech-sign recapitulated. The gSign capabilities of chimpanzees and gorillas will tell us something more about languages and sign languages and about what is verbal and what nonverbal.

Prophets may be able to see ahead better than most because they are quicker to see what is presently around us all. Hewes suggested the use of sign language in raising a chimpanzee at the time when the Hayes experiment with Vicki was concentrating on teaching speech signs. The foresight of the organizer of this semiotic program is well known, but I would like to suggest that Sebeok's prophetic powers served semiotics well when he encouraged long ago the research of West (at Indiana University) in Plains Indians' sign language and of Stokoe in deaf sign language.

REFERENCES

Abbott, Clifford. 1975. "Encodedness and Sign Language." *Sign Language Studies* 7:109–20.

Baker, Charlotte. 1975. "Regulators and Turn-Taking in American Sign Language Discourse." MS. Working paper, Department of Linguistics, University of California, Berkeley.

Baker, Charlotte, and Padden, Carol. 1976. "Facial Features in ASL Conversation." MS. Working paper, Linguistics Research Laboratory, Gallaudet College.

Battison, Robbin. 1974. "Phonological Deletion in American Sign Language." *Sign Language Studies* 5:1–19.

———. MS. Ph.D. dissertation, University of California, San Diego.

Battison, Robbin, and Jordan, I. King. 1976. "Cross-Cultural Communication with Foreign Signers: Fact and Fancy." *Sign Language Studies* 10:53–68.

Battison, Robbin; Markowicz, Harry; and Woodward, James. 1975. "A Good Rule of Thumb: Variable Phonology in ASL." In *Analyzing Variation in Language*, R. Fasold and R. Shuy, eds. Washington, D.C.: Georgetown University Press, pp.291–302.

Burling, Robbins. 1970. *Man's Many Voices*. New York: Holt, Rinehart & Winston.

Chafe, Wallace L. 1970. *Meaning and the Structure of Language*. Chicago: University of Chicago Press.

Charrow, Veda. 1975. "A Psycholinguistic Analysis of 'Deaf English'." *Sign Language Studies* 7:35–46.

Eimas, Peter D. 1975. "Speech Perception in Early Infancy." In *Infant Perception*, L. B. Cohen and P. Salapatek, eds. New York: Academic Press.

Friedman, Lynn A. 1975. "Space, Time, and Person Reference in American Sign Language." *Language* 51:940–61.

Frishberg, Nancy. 1975. "Arbitrariness and Iconicity: Historical Change in American Sign Language." *Language* 51:696–719.

Goldin-Meadow, Susan. MS. "The Representation of Semantic Relations to a Manual Language Created by Deaf Children of Hearing Parents." Ph.D. dissertation, University of Pennsylvania.

Goldin-Meadow, Susan, and Feldman, Heidi. 1975. "The Creation of a Communication System: A Study of Deaf Children of Hearing Parents." *Sign Language Studies* 8:225–34.

Greenlee, Douglas. 1973. *Peirce's Concept of Sign. Approaches to Semiotics*, T. A. Sebeok, ed., paperback series 5. The Hague: Mouton.

Henderson, T. S. T. MS. "Pronoun Structure. Logical Terms and Language Types." Working paper, Department of Linguistics, Ottawa University.

Hewes, Gordon W. 1973. "Primate Communication and the Gestural Origin of Language." *Current Anthropology* 14:5–24.

———. 1974. "Language in Early Hominids." In *Language Origins*, R. Wescott, G. W. Hewes, and W. C. Stokoe, eds. Silver Spring, Md.: Linstok Press.

Kendon, Adam. 1975. "Gesticulation, Speech, and the Gesture Theory of Language Origins." *Sign Language Studies* 9:349–73.

Liddell, Scott. MS. "Dependent Clauses in ASL." Working paper, Salk Institute, California.

Meadow, Kathryn B. MS. "Name Signs as Identity Symbols in the Deaf Community." Paper presented at the "Culture and Language in the Deaf Community" symposium, Amercian Anthropological Association, Mexico City, 1974.

Mindel, Eugene, and Vernon, McCay. 1971. *They Grow in Silence*. Silver Spring, Md.: National Association of the Deaf.

Sallagoïty, Pierre. 1975. "The Sign Language of Southern France." *Sign Language Studies* 7:181–202.

Schein, Jerome D., and Delk, Marcus. 1974. *The Deaf Population of the United States*. Silver Spring, Md.: National Association of the Deaf.

Schlesinger, I. M. 1970. "The Grammar of Sign Language and the Problems of Language Universals." In *Biological and Social Factors in Psycholinguistics*, J. Morton, ed. Urbana: University of Illinois Press.

Sebeok, Thomas A. 1975. "The Semiotic Web: A Chronicle of Prejudices." *Bulletin of Literary Semiotics* 2:1–63.

Stokoe, William C. 1960. "Sign Language Structure." *Studies in Linguistics:* 8[o.p.]. Silver Spring, Md.: Linstok Press.

———. 1972. *Semiotics and Human Sign Languages. Approaches to Semiotics*, vol. 21, T. A. Sebeok, ed. The Hague: Mouton.

———. 1975a. "Classification and Description of Sign Languages." In *Current Trends in Linguistics*, vol. 12, T. A. Sebeok, ed. The Hague: Mouton, pp.345–71.

————. 1975b. "The Shape of Soundless Language." In *The Role of Speech in Language*, James F. Kavanagh and James E. Cutting, eds. Cambridge: MIT Press.

————. MS.   "Color Terms in American Sign Language."

Stokoe, William C.; Casterline, D.; and Croneberg, C. 1976[1965]. *A Dictionary of American Sign Language on Linguistic Principles*, 2d ed. Silver Spring, Md.: Linstok Press.

Woodward, James C., Jr. 1974. "Implicational Variation in American Sign Language: Negative Incorporation." *Sign Language Studies* 5:20–30.

IV.   Applications

Verbal Patterns and Medical Disease: Prophylactic Implications of Learning

Harley C. Shands

Physiological explanation has long been unsatisfactory in relation to two well-known groups of disorders: (1) the *disability* without demonstrable organic involvement that sometimes complicates the problem of compensation for industrial accidents, and (2) the so-called psychosomatic diseases (the group includes rheumatoid arthritis, hypertension, asthma, and ulcerative colitis most prominently). Both groups are often assigned to or claimed by psychiatrists, but in most instances those suffering from these disorders disclaim any neurotic symptoms.

For many years we (Shands and Meltzer, 1973) have been primarily interested in the applications of semiotic understanding to psychiatric and psychological problems. It has gradually become possible to find correlations in these two groups of suffering persons between the disease state and easily demonstrable deficiencies in higher semiotic functions. In the term used by Pavlov, these disorders are at the level of the "second signal system" instead of at that of the primary signal system of the reflex arc and physiological communication. The demonstrations presented below and elsewhere point up the close interrelation—for personal–social integration—of the two signal systems.

Since semiotic and cognitive functions in man are only developed slowly over many years in the process of intensive schooling, the inference from the hypothesis developed below is that education in a complex society has the implication not only of self-improvement but also of prophylaxis in relation to diseases that seriously impair and disable large groups of human beings.

An initial problem of interest is that of "emotion," since psychiatric "diseases" are alternatively classified as "emotional disorders." As Skinner (1963) has emphasized, the principal question in the scientific investigation of "emotion" is that of accessibility, in other words, how are emotions known? Ordinarily there are three routes: First, we infer emotional states from the facial expressions and postures of others; we say, "Does your scowl mean that you are angry?" or "You look depressed today." Second, there has developed, following the work of Cannon, a research tradition in which correlations between experimental states assumed to be "rage" or "fear" ("fight" or "flight") and instrumental readings (e.g., amount of adrenalin, level of blood pressure, gastric secretion, and the like) can be demonstrated "objectively."

Third, however, and somehow unexpectedly, many—but by no means all—human beings have access to their own inner states of emotion through the verbal description of inner physiological experience. To such self-observers the process seems "natural." In the obviously "neurotic," phobic patients are characterized by an exquisite sensitivity to their own inner states. Such a person may say, "My heart was pounding, my knees got all rubbery, my vision blurred, and my mouth was very dry," in describing an anxiety attack. This ability, in our experience, is remarkably different in different persons, and in the disabled and the psychosomatic it is characteristically absent. In the reports quoted below, it is apparent that when asked, "What does that expression on your face mean? Are you angry?" the psychosomatic patient may not know what the questioner is referring to. The inability to describe feeling has been given a Greek name by Sifneos (1967), *alexithymia*, from "no" "word" (for) "feeling."

This incapacity for self-description is specifically related to a lack of education, in two different degrees. In the disabled workman, we have routinely found not only the inability to describe feelings but also a severe cognitive lack. In Piaget's (1950) terminology, such a person when tested shows himself to be functioning at the preoperational level of cognitive sophistication, corresponding to the 7-year-old level in the normal, well-schooled child. Specifically, the disabled person characteristically cannot find simple similarities (apple and banana, dog and lion) and often cannot do simple serial subtraction: he is thus impaired in the logic of both classes and series (Shands and Meltzer, 1977).

The psychosomatic patient, on the other hand, may be highly intelligent and cognitively well trained, but show a major defect in affective function. He seems literally to know nothing about his own feelings and so little "consciously" about his relations to even his closest relatives. In Shands (1954) I suggested that losses of close relatives were often significant in the precipitation of psychosomatic disorders; now it is possible to add the suggestion that these losses are important because their affective implications cannot be taken into account. Patients of this sort are "unconscious" of their emotional situation, even when it is possible to infer a feeling state by examining their expressions. The situation has some resemblance to the neurological state of *anosognosia*, in which the patient does not know that he does not know. An internist specializing in the treatment of rheumatoid arthritis expressed this observation in saying that such patients were uniformly "inarticulate," even when they were highly sophisticated in the social sense.

What seems to emerge as the most interesting hypothetical explanation is that we see here a general lack of education in the disabled, so that while the person is obviously of good "native" intelligence, he is still totally unequipped to deal with complex changes in his own condition and social context. In the psychosomatic patient, there seems to be a marked deficiency in education to intimacy and to the description to others of his or her own feelings, positive or negative. Some patients, especially Case 4, below, clearly show an awareness of their own inability. But this man says specifically in relation to an overt hostile act, "I must have been angry" and "I don't think there was anything 'physical' about it."

The heuristic suggestion emerges that in a complex civilization there is an actual prophylactic effect of education to knowing one's own feelings and their implications of relatedness to others. These two groups of persons seem specifically handicapped; the problem can be described as another kind of "retardation." A further fascinating demonstrable aspect is that these people exhibit a completely unexceptional life pattern; they are not in the least "neurotic." However, when they suffer a severe loss in some essential part of the context of their lives, they may suddenly collapse in a disintegrative state. In the disabled we have been able to describe a somatization reaction. In psychosomatic patients the collapse appears as the precipitation of an actual organic disease, or, later in the course, the recrudescence of a quiescent disease.

In our experience, the lack of formal education in the disabled is associated with a specific deficit in *creative* thinking. The claimant has difficulty in adapting to changed conditions by creating a new self-concept that fits the new situation. In an often pathetic way, such a claimant says, "All I want is to be like I was before the accident and to go back to work." In Piaget's language, such an attitude shows a major lack of the ability to accommodate to changed circumstances. Because he cannot accommodate, he cannot develop new assimilative schemas. The lack of adaptation means that the disabled person seems to himself discontinuous with his former self: he says, plaintively but indirectly, that he has lost his self, that he is not the same person any more. This inability falls into both the contexts noted above. The pre-accident and post-accident selves are *not* similar, so they do not fall into the same class; while the series "me$_1$, me$_2$, me$_3$" experienced by most human beings seems to these claimants to have been interrupted. This observable is less prominent in the psychosomatic group, although Case 2 (see below) said, "I went into a kind of tailspin because, you know, with no athletics there was no *me* type of feeling." He said, "I no longer trust my body." But he also said, "I didn't think it was an emotional type thing." Persons demonstrating this "fracture" in the continuity of a life can be described in Piaget's language as unable to *conserve the self.*

In a complex civilization the self has to be learned in ways quite unknown in primitive societies. But more significantly for our purposes, in a complex society the self that is learned is very different in relation to the linguistic context in which the person lives. Those living in the context of a restricted code (Bernstein, 1964) learn a restricted self—that is, primarily a self that is context-dependent. In more highly educated persons, the context of an elaborated code allows the development of a far more context-independent self. I have elsewhere referred to the latter as a "generalized self" in noting how much an executive position in a multinational corporation requires that the person tolerate frequent moves and a generally "expatriate" status.

The most fascinating observable generally true of the psychosomatic group is a lack of development of the *affective* foundation of a self-definition in this generalized mode. This inability is shared with the disabled—but in the psychosomatic group it is possible to find many intellectually sophisticated persons who still report in very clear terms the inability to "know themselves" by feeling. In another way of putting this, the sophisticated psychosomatic patient may be an acute self-describer when the self is considered as an object. But such persons in our experience do not understand what it is to describe the self as a subject; they do not "know" subjective experience. Paradoxically, this observation can be phrased to say that this sort of person cannot "objectify his subjective feelings." He appears to have a specific problem in "intersubjectivity."

In terms used by Head, Bartlett, and Piaget, the utility of being able to describe *affective schemas* is closely related to the problem of conservation of the self. It is only possible to know oneself in totally different external contexts by knowing how one feels. If it is not possible to know "myself" from the inside out, but only from the outside in, then when the outside changes, "I" change. The problem is that of context-dependence, precisely the same as that of the child who, even while watching a liquid being poured from a vessel of one shape into a vessel of another shape, insists that the quantity must have changed: "There is more because it is taller."

This cognitive limitation is most interesting in its affective implication. The claimant says, in various ways, "I am not myself any longer; it's just not me," carrying out unavailing self-examination, as did the woman who looked closely at her injured ankle every morning for years to see whether it had gotten all right overnight. Most astonishing, however, is the consistent finding that the disabled claimant has lost his ability to enjoy all his previous activities. He shows what can be called *anhedonia*, a loss of the capacity to feel pleasure; as a dramatic example, there is a marked deficiency in or actual loss of the ability to have sexual intercourse.

In approaching these claimants with assumptions gained from working with psychotherapy patients, one is repeatedly impressed with the comprehensive lack of introspective skill or interest. The inability to conserve the self appears to be the reciprocal of the lack of a developed self-concept. The significant connection is that a limitation in a cognitive function appears to play an important part in producing a chronic disability. We believe that it is probable that this disability state is similar to that of wartime disabilities in service personnel. The inability to develop a definition to fit altered circumstances seems to lead to a loss of identity and specifically to the loss of the capacity for "enjoying oneself," with the continuation of a state of confusion. We understand the bodily complaints in such persons as a misinterpretation of input that convinces the claimant that he must have some "organic" illness. We call this condition a *somatization reaction,* one variant included in the "conversion reaction" diagnostic category.

PSYCHOSOMATIC DISORDERS

We have returned recently to review the psychosomatic problem in the light of our experience with disability. Interviews with a group of randomly referred patients are strikingly similar to others done more than twenty years ago. In reviewing material collected by other observers over a period of almost thirty years, the uniformity of report is astonishing. In 1948, Ruesch reported that in psychosomatic patients, "verbal, gestural, or other symbols are not connected with affects and feelings." In 1949, MacLean (p. 350) noted an "apparent . . . inability to verbalize . . . feelings." In the 1960s two French workers, Marty and de M'Uzan (1963) commented that psychosomatic patients do not "produce fantasies." In several papers Nemiah and Sifneos (e.g., 1970), together and singly, have pursued the same observation. They emphasize in one of their papers the frequency with which patients have more than one of these disorders, an observation suggesting that the "diathesis," or "predisposition," is more generic than specific (in sharp opposition to the once popular idea that a particular conflict had to do with a specific disease).

In a paper on "suitability for psychotherapy" published in 1958 but written several years earlier, I summarized the characteristic verbal patterns in the following categories: *unsuitable* patients (1) cannot describe feelings, (2) exhibit relations in which the human other is implicitly regarded as essential but is not "overvalued" in a romantic sense, (3) tend to use nonspecific pronouns (especially "you" for "I"), (4) make bizarre interpretations of sensations, and (5) display circumstantiality in accounting their experiences. Shortly thereafter, I wrote a paper (only now in press: Shands, 1975) in which a comparison was made between anxious college students and rheumatoid arthritic patients. In this paper it was reported that all of the characteristics of "unsuitability" were typical of the arthritic patients. What was perhaps more interesting was the "selection" test done (with serendipity) by urging psychiatric residents to work psychotherapeutically with arthritic patients. Without exception, it was impossible to persuade any resident to undertake psychotherapy with any arthritic patient, while at the same time the anxious college student was enthusiastically accepted even when the resident had to work overtime to find a place in his schedule.

Some of the experiences we had with such patients on a psychiatric ward in the fifties were interesting in relation to context-dependence. A patient who was given cortisone for rheumatoid arthritis developed a psychiatric complication and was admitted to a ward functioning as a therapeutic community. In this ward both nurses and patients wore street clothes in a major attempt to eliminate some of the traditional professional separations. The arthritic patient absolutely refused to go along with these ideas. Instead, he insisted on wearing pajamas and a bathrobe and spending most of his time in bed. He insisted that being in a hospital prescribed this kind of behavior, and nothing could persuade him to try any other.

Reverting for a moment to the disability problem (in this case related to an open heart operation), we followed and reported the case of a man who complained of severe chronic disability (Shands et al., 1973). He was offered admission to the psychiatric ward, but he dramatically refused to be admitted. In the case report the patient is quoted as saying, after being handed a form entitled "The Rights of Mental Patients," "There's nothing the matter with me. I'm not like these people here, I'll stay here only if I can be in a bed where they'll take care of me, in a real hospital." In addition, he said, "What, am I going to stay here and get like these people?" This question indicates his fear of being assimilated into the group of "crazies"; it is recurrently interesting that the person who cannot find similarities has the reciprocal difficulty, namely that he also cannot differentiate accurately. With reference to the specific problem of recovery from cardiac surgery, Willner has shown that his test of the ability to find analogies (= similarities) predicts the post-operative course: the better the analogies score, the better the prognosis.

With uneducated persons in the disability context, the lack of sophisticated ways of describing human relations and the closely connected feelings was not unexpected. In taking our understanding of the disability problem to the psychosomatic context, however, it was again —as it had been previously—astonishing to find how precise the above descriptions of the psychosomatic way of talking are. Several excerpts from the transcribed records of a series of interviews follow.

Case 1

A middle-aged black woman who had been a maid in a hotel reported that she had developed rheumatoid arthritis about ten years
before. In the course of the interview she also reported that she had
had hypertension for a long time. Asked specifically about important
changes in her life at the time of onset, she said that her husband had
died a few months before her arthritis began. Then she said that they
had been separated, as though his death were of no account to her—
but then she added that she had had to "bury him."

In the transcript, a "matter-of-fact" way of presenting herself comes
through immediately. She reports the course of her illness joint by joint
with no indication of personal (as differentiated from somatic) suffering at all. In answer to a request, "Tell me a little bit about what kind
of problem you have . . ." she said, "Well, uh, this whole problem that I
have, it swells, aches, and this is a traveling situation. It first started in
my hands and went to my shoulders, then both of my knees. Now
what's bothering me is my hand swells sometimes, fingers, the wrist,
left knee, pressure, got so bad I couldn't stand at all, I couldn't hold my
weight. Knee swoll up, had fever in it, ah, swelling. Then the right
hip has been bothering me for years and ah, so now I went to therapy,
they had gave me heat treatment on my left knee, which seemed to
help, but still very weak and sore in it." The patient interpreted the nonspecific request as a concrete indication for a "travelogue" in which she
reported the movement of the disorder from joint to joint over many
years.

In an attempt to explore the emotional connotations of the disease,
the examiner asked, "Does it bother you? How much does it . . . ?" The
patient's answer runs, "Well, ah, it's about, it about, I have stiffness, too,
you know, any position that I'm in too long there, it bothers me. If I'm
sitting, then, you know, it bothers me to get up and move around."

Still pursuing the emotional connotations, the examiner asked, "Are
there lots of things that you used to be able to do that you can't do any
more?" The patient replied, "Well, of, see, as I get . . . it seems to me
as I get older (laughs) this arthritis, ah, it bothers me more, and, ah,
I say it travels, you know, and ah, ah, being in certain joints for about
eight years, you see, it seemed better in that way, that before, I could
walk. Before then I, December I came in here for about two weeks, before then I did my own shopping. I could walk 5 or 6 blocks, back and
forth, push my cart, very active you know."

The examiner attempted to explore what it is easy to assume must be distressing feelings associated with the marked loss of mobility, asking, "And how do you feel about that, how does that make you feel?" Again the answer is quite remote from the point of view implied in the question; she said, "Well, for one thing that helped me a lot, ah, to understand my condition, understand my illness, what's happening with me, I wrote away to the Arthritis Foundation, and got a pamphlet on this thing, and I read about it, and I found that you've got to have a state of mind with it, because, ah, at first it bothered me cause I didn't understand it. I'd think I was getting better and I'd encourage myself, and I'd feel great and I'd build a big, you know, like I'm going to get well, and then the next thing you know I'm down again, and just, I have depression, I feel depressed, I got nervous, I'm upset, I cry, you know, but now that I know. . . ."

The examiner asked, looking for "inner" feelings, "When you get depressed, how does that feel inside?" The patient answers, quite characteristically, in terms of the "outside" rather than the inside, "Well, for one thing, when I get depressed is when I get, see, what depress me is to be helpless, and I've been like that, ah, I've been in the hospital with this arthritis twice, the first time was a month. But then I still didn't fully understand until lately, really, you know. . ."

The examiner begins a question, but the patient continues, "What depress you, what depress you, is that when it flares up you aching, you in pain, you can't sleep, you can't move in any position. With me, I couldn't walk I couldn't, I couldn't take the covers off me, I couldn't do anything, I couldn't move, I just lay there and ache, so I depressed, feel sick and tired, can't sleep, and, ah, you feel awful [laughs] you feel bad, that's all."

What is characteristic in this sequence is what we have called the "pronoun shift." Predictably, as soon as the psychosomatic patient begins to talk about a "sensitive" area in which one would expect a comment about "my feeling" what comes out is a comment about how "you" feel. What is most fascinating is that the shift is quite systematic: when describing action, e.g., "I couldn't move," the "I" is appropriately placed, but when it is a matter of feeling, "I" disappears and "you" appears, "You're in pain, you aching." This repetitive and predictable technique appears to have the effect of distancing the unbearable situation, of "disclaiming" its connection with "me."

Still persistent in seeking "inner" feeling, the examiner asked, "Do you have any feelings inside when you're depressed or when you feel bad and depressed like that?" The patient completely and concretely misunderstands, hearing the "inside" question as an inquiry about her digestive–excretory function, with reference to medication. "Well, ah, no, because, ah, I was aware of taking my medication, the pills I have, with milk. Right now, I'm taking Maalox so I, ah, never had no trouble, you know, with my stomach, because I always tried to—and then it's important to take your medication after eating, you know, to sort of save the stomach, like, and I take prune juice every night to keep myself open, you know, stuff like that, very important, and lately I try to cut down on my weight."

Case 2

The cultural requirement in a highly complex civilization for the internalization of the social environment is a curious circular process involving first an "externalization" of one's own behavior followed by an "internalization" of the description of that behavior associated with the perception of the internal components. A second, highly intelligent, arthritic patient described his own distaste for this process in clear fashion in the words, "On occasion people have said 'Why do you look so angry?' or 'Why do you look so glum?', and I don't feel this on my face. It's kind of unconscious. When people will say that, it's disturbing to me because I don't, I'm not that type of person who likes to be read that easily."

Further, he said, "At the moment I'm isolating myself too much, I don't know why . . . I think it's something I've always done. I mean I've always felt alone. I don't know if that's something you would understand, but I've always felt personally pretty much alone, from as far back as I can remember . . . When I was growing up I think I was very unhappy, I think I was unhappy a lot of the time. I couldn't really figure out why I was alone, it made no sense at the time. . . . I always felt different in that sense." Asked about girl friends, he said that he had a steady girl "from time to time," but when asked if that made him feel less lonesome, he answered that it made him feel "more vulnerable." In discussing what he describes as a fanatical interest in athletics prior to the onset of arthritis in adolescence, he said, "My athletics was everything to me, to me it was a tangible accomplishment and for someone who didn't know how to make friends very well, it was a very good way of, a lot of camaraderie, a sense of belonging. After that I guess I felt I didn't belong anywhere."

The importance of the externalization of himself is attested in his description of the disastrous appearance of arthritic pain: "One day I noticed that it felt like my right toe was broken . . . I felt like my whole body was falling to pieces." When asked, "How was that disturbing?" he answered, "Well, because I took a lot of pride in my body. I was lifting weights . . . As I said, athletics was my whole life . . . it was probably too much of my life . . . it got to be kind of like a fix, . . . I couldn't do without it, and I felt kind of trapped in it . . . I really was kind of going at it like a maniac . . . When I found I couldn't do it at all, I went into a kind of tailspin because, you know, with no athletics, there was no *me* type of feeling. I felt like my body was betraying me somehow, it didn't want to go along with . . . and football was what I was primarily interested in . . ." A moment later, he elaborated, "At first I didn't think it was an emotional type thing . . . I guess the feeling that sticks out in my mind primarily was 'where is it going to end?'— because I no longer trust my body . . . Along with the depression there was a kind of fear of 'Where—am I going to end up in a wheelchair?' kind of feeling."

In relation to the feeling he calls depression, the interviewer suggested the presence of "inner" feelings, saying "Did you notice anything inside when you felt depressed? in your chest? or your stomach? or . . . ?" The patient said, "I didn't have anything that I . . . you know, physically, like you just mentioned, that I associate with . . . because at first I didn't think it was an emotional type thing, I didn't think there could be any possible connection."

What is most striking from one point of view is the way in which this arthritic patient objectifies an alien body that "betrays me." He is unable to identify with his own body. In the athletic frenzy of his adolescence, he was lifting enormously heavy weights, in isolation, with no comment positive or negative from a family that apparently left him alone and expressed no interest of either an approving or a disapproving sort.

He described himself as intensely, "viciously" competitive on the football field to the extent that other players were afraid of him— but he felt no anger. His "body" comes through as a mechanical object, perhaps like the racing car of the dedicated driver—but an "object" to him with a "mind of its own." In the most peculiar fashion, when observed from the point of view of those sensitively aware of many nuances in bodily function, it is inconceivable that "the body" could be so alien an object.

In a sophisticated social system, it is necessary to develop a high level of skill in constructing a self that takes into consideration both the physiological and the social contexts, the first representing a "lower" level of integration, the other a "higher" one. The self emerges as a mediator, an "interlocutor" that "interprets" from the lower to the higher level and from the higher to the lower. To do this one has to integrate data derived from social process (primarily in linguistic terms) with data derived from "physical" or "organic" change.

Case 3

Another patient interviewed in relation to her rheumatoid arthritis, an elderly woman who had been a successful singer before her marriage, reported that she also had had hypertension for many years, with a surgical intervention in the form of a sympathectomy. This woman was pleasant, gracious, and cooperative. Her comments in relation to her human relations showed a considerable distance and a preoccupation with not getting close to others. She reported an idealized relation with her much older husband, but she could not describe any feeling of grief or sadness when he died, although in speaking of it many years later she shed a few tears in a transient episode of weeping.

She responded to a question-suggestion, "It still upsets you [to think about your husband's last illness]?" with a simple "Yes"; then, to the further probe, "Could you tell me about that? You haven't gotten over it?" she replied, "No, not quite. He was a marvellous man, and he was in a nursing home for [sighing] three years." Still pursuing the problem, the interviewer asked about her feelings at his death, and she replied, "Well, doctor, I felt I should have been strong enough physically to keep him with me, to keep him at home, but I wasn't." Here she suddenly wept, but she could not relate the weeping to any "inner" feeling.

In response to a question as to concern about being alone most of the time, the patient answered in the affirmative; then, asked "Does that bother you?" she replied, "Yes it does. I would like to do volunteer work if I were able, but with this arthritis, I can't accept something . . ." Further pursued, the patient answered in the affirmative again when asked if her limitations "got her down," but when asked, "What's that like? What does it feel like?" she replied, "Well, I'm not really a gloomy person. I do a great deal of reading. I don't know that I'd be happier if I had a lot of people around me . . . I've been a loner, I guess." She reported going out to dinner with an old friend, but "She was so gloomy, she's getting old, too, and she told me all her problems, and I wanted to get away from there."

In this excerpt, what is perhaps most noteworthy to a psychiatrist is the patient's reluctance even to hear about the feelings of other persons. The threat of "contamination" or "contagion" is apparent: if the friend talks gloomily about aging, she might make the patient feel gloomy, and it is thus easier to abandon a human relationship of long standing than it is to tolerate the possibility of being threatened with "feeling bad" in whatever way.

Case 4

A very interesting patient was seen on referral from the internist because of a previous history of psychosomatic disease. Although he has no current psychosomatic disorder, his character is consistent with the syndrome we have seen, and his method of talking about his problems is typical. This man was in "analysis" with two well-known analysts but without much benefit—and obviously without the kind of "material" usually considered essential for the analytic process. A highly intelligent and well-educated man, this patient commented that, "I was always good about keeping my appointments," but he recognized his own problem: "I would go in and just talk, constantly and unstoppably, but very superficially. It wasn't that I was holding anything back, it was just that nothing was coming out but trivia . . . and I really just couldn't even stop talking. I was sort of out of control. I talked the way a deaf person does when he doesn't want you to say anything because he'll be reminded of his deafness."

This man noted that there had been a mixup in appointments for one of these analyses, and he was perplexed for a long time about what happened. His major complaint about the analyst was that he could get no information from him about whether he had been at fault or whether the secretary had made a mistake; he thought the latter because his appointment was made by a woman he never saw again. He explained that it was vitally important to him because he thought he was going crazy; he remembered the second analyst as much more helpful because he was "giving guidance." In the contemporary relation with an internist, he complained of chest pain he feared might be cardiac in origin. The internist told him it was due to muscular tension. In explaining why he had continued to see this physician, he said, "I evidently looked very depressed."

This peculiar statement indicates that the patient "looked depressed" but did not "feel depressed." Asked about a feeling of depression, he answered, "Just very lonely and, well, sort of, I sort of say over and over to myself I'm really depressed, you know, that I wish I were dead. And it's true really I don't get much fun out of life, but I'm not really suicidal, it has nothing to do with that. In fact it's sort of an escape valve, it makes me feel much better and relaxes me." As he said this, he smiled broadly, and when the smile was brought to his attention, he said, "I smile too much . . . It's probably a way of dealing with people. I think I was told that if you smile other people will like you, you know, when I was a child."

Because of his chest pain he feared heart trouble, but at the same time he described himself objectively as "healthy." Sounding somewhat like a familiar TV commercial, he said, "I'm really in pretty good health, I'm not overweight, I don't smoke, I don't take drugs, drink too much, or anything like that. I get a reasonable amount of exercise."

About the mistake in the appointment that occurred many years before, the patient commented that he "talked elaborately about how he felt," but he showed complete incomprehension when asked about how that was in his body. He said, "I don't think it upset me physically . . . I just feel upset." Pressed, he said, "I must have felt hurt and angry . . . I really wanted to know what had happened because I couldn't evaluate my own behavior." He later described himself as "anxious and compulsive," pointing out that these traits were useful in his work—which he found "boring."

He described his relation to his five-year-old son as the one human relation of importance to him; he is "on good terms" with his divorced wife. He has (in his late 30s) no female or male sexual partner and has not had sexual relations with anyone for over three years, since his marriage broke up. He thinks he is "just too frightened to get involved at all."

Returning to the problem of feeling, the interviewer explained to the patient that many people can localize sensory experiences of bodily change in "emotional" states. This seemed a novel idea to the patient, and he went on to explain that he had had severe asthma as a child, but that it disappeared at puberty. Then he said that in his analysis he once threw a pillow at the analyst upon leaving the office. Shortly thereafter he developed a severe asthmatic attack, which lasted several hours; otherwise he had had none except during the time his marriage was breaking up and he was making some renovations around the house. He could describe significant events only from the point of view of an outside observer: to him feelings are not *felt*, they are *inferred* as a necessary extrapolation from his overt behavior.

In relation to his almost complete lack of friends or female companions, his comment on a long trip he took with his parents and brother when he was sixteen is notable: "I guess being thrown in at close quarters with them on an extended trip like that made me very nervous." He cannot, however, describe a nervous feeling: "very nervous" is an inference. He developed diarrhea and was later shown to have two small ulcers—thus a mild ulcerative colitis. He consulted a psychiatrist and saw him for several years—but "it really didn't get anywhere."

In this patient the combination of excellent appearance and intelligence, good economic situation, and good education with almost total isolation and absence of intensely pleasurable experiences was most striking. It is apparent that he avoided "entangling alliances" of any sort. His reports are full of "I must have been angry" or "I appeared depressed" or other external statements. In the situation in which he was rejected in favor of the other patient, he was not angry—his reaction was an intense need to know what had happened, because otherwise he "didn't know whether I was wrong."

The most extraordinary implication of this interview is the fluency and accuracy with which the patient presented an *objective* view of himself—without any trace of a subjective experiencing.

WHAT DOES IT MEAN?

This material demonstrates again a remarkable consistency in observation over almost thirty years in many different places by different observers. The consistency of observation, however, is associated with a considerable lack of consistency in interpretation. What I want to discuss is the degree to which interpretative efforts using psychological and semiotic systems of thought, for the most part previously ignored in clinical psychiatry, add to possible understanding. The interpretation to be presented is quite different from the usual psychiatric instance, since it ranges into the clinical implication of Piaget's work for adults.

I have not been able to find any detailed epidemiological studies of diseases of the sort in which we are particularly interested. There are, however, bits of "circumstantial" evidence that suggest a significant correlation. In a review of the problem of allergy by Holt (1967),

there is a suggestion that this general disorder is a "disease of civilization." Holt cites as a specific example that infants born to Chinese parents in the United States and those born to West Indian parents living
in London have a much higher incidence of infantile eczema than do
those born in their parents' respective homelands.

Bohrer, an American-trained radiologist, responded to Holt's article
by reporting that he had found a remarkably low incidence of allergic
reactions to materials used in pyelography and angiography in Nigeria
as compared with his expectations from working in the United States
(1967). In Nigeria he had found a low incidence of disorders in the
auto-immune class, such as thyroiditis and hemolytic anemia, as well as
of ulcerative colitis, rheumatoid arthritis, and pernicious anemia. It
was recently reported by Short (1975), a rheumatologist, that the
"modern" disease rheumatoid arthritis appeared only three hundred
years ago—although archaeological evidence shows ankylosing spon-
dylitis to be much older.

A news report quoted the director of Lincoln Hospital in New York
as saying that in the South Bronx, by general agreement the most dis-
advantaged section of the metropolis, there is an inordinately high incidence of hypertension, asthma, diabetes, and obesity. Since the population in this area is mostly black and Hispanic, the contrast to the low
incidence of a similar list of diseases in Nigeria is striking.

The suggestion emerges that diseases in this general category may
have some significant relation to progress and advances in civilization
and its complexity. Inkeles and Smith (*Becoming Modern*, 1974) report on the extensive examination of about a thousand workers in each
of six developing nations. A checklist of psychosomatic symptoms filled
out in the course of a long and complicated interview procedure showed
no increased incidence of medical complications that might be thought
related to "modernization"—but then the authors take note of the fact
that all their subjects were in the process of making a successful adap-
tion to modernity.

In our experience, the disease states of interest tend to occur differ-
entially in the *unsuccessful* members of this society. Secondly, these
disorders occur only when there is some kind of crisis in personal or
occupational status or in both. We have found very convincing indica-
tions that the problem is first one of *predisposition* then of *precipitation*
—and as in any epidemiological context, it is obvious that many are
confronted with the "stress" or the pathogen while relatively few are

significantly affected. Perhaps the clearest example of this kind of sequence is that blacks living in the ghetto have an enormously higher incidence of hypertension when compared with middle-class whites, which is often attributed to the greater amount of "stress" undergone. When the control group of whites is compared with middle-class blacks in similar adaptive context, however, the supposed ethnic difference disappears. This finding suggests that it is not the simplistic notion of "stress" that is significant as much as the matter of *relativity* of "stress" and "resistance to stress." A strong differential susceptibility appears to be concentrated in those who are poorly prepared to cope with the complexity of our society.

A most important feature of Durkheim's (1897) classic work on suicide is his description of the *anomic* state of those who had lost (or never adequately developed) a sense of their own identity so that they felt themselves to be "unnamed"—itself an interesting indication of the importance of the word-labels attached to all of us. We have found a great deal of evidence in our disabled subjects that the crucial loss for many appears to be that of the occupational context and the fellowship of co-workers. In a technological society, it appears that there is so great an erosion of the traditional modes of self-identification in context (especially in the extended family and in the pursuit of religion as a central theme in life) that the context of work takes a larger and larger place. Inkeles and Smith (1974) state that the process of modernization is most accelerated through two artificial institutional contexts, the school and the factory; they estimate that three years in a factory is the rough equivalent of a single year in school.

From a slightly different standpoint, it is clear that what is the same in both, and different in both from the background of the preliterate person, is that these are artificial institutional contexts of a highly formal type. Both the school and the factory require a rapid, intensive process of socialization to a completely different set of norms and forms. The not uncommon occurrence of school phobias in children and the notorious "resistance" of ghetto children to the socialization involved in school work in modern urban centers speak to the same point. The first consideration in the school and in the factory is the development of what can be called in psychoanalytic terms a "transference to the institution," along with the development of a preference for the society of those already acculturated. There is thus required both an institutional and a new form of group transference in this somewhat extended use of the term. The school and the factory become "homes away from home," in a movement often fostered and intensified by the provision of recreational activities as a function of both school and factory—for the greater development of "school spirit."

SOME CONTRASTS

Carothers (1959) has given a description of preliterate Africans with reference to social context and to some of the implications of that context. He points to the "embedded" status of the human being in a preliterate culture.

> A man comes to regard himself as a rather insignificant part of a much larger organism—the family and clan—and not as an independent, self-reliant unit; personal initiative and ambition are permitted little outlet; and a meaningful integration of a man's experience on individual, personal lines is not achieved. By contrast to the constriction at the intellectual level, great freedom is allowed for at the temperamental level, and a man is expected to live very much in the "here and now," to be highly extroverted, and to give very free expression to his feelings.

Here I would stop for a moment to take issue with the term "expression of feelings." What the author is talking about is significant *action*—but I know of no evidence that freedom of action is correlated with the *inner* perception we call "feeling" or "affect"; instead, there is a great deal of evidence that strongly suggests that only when *action is internalized* is it possible to speak of "feelings." This is implied every time a psychoanalyst talks about either "acting-out" or about "delay of gratification": it is the internalization of significant action that appears as feeling—and it appears as feeling only when it *cannot be* exhibited as action. Anger is internalized attack, appetite is internalized eating, passion is internalized sex—all predictive of possible outcomes of some current situation in which direct action is impossible, inhibited, or blocked. Sexual intercourse is very different from romantic love—although it is not infrequently the outcome of a period of romantic love, just as eating is often subsequent to the experience of appetite. But the act of intercourse involves "feeling" in quite a different sense from that in which one can (if he knows how) *describe feeling* in a psychiatric interview.

The problem of the highly civilized person in a developed social system is the reverse of those items cited by Carothers. He has to learn

to think of himself as an independent, self-reliant unit; he has to learn
how to differentiate, and tolerate differentiation, in the self-family context; he has to abandon primary identification in terms of his clan; he
has to learn to live in the future (and the past), not in the here and
now; and he has to learn to inhibit "free" action and to show highly
structured and secondary skilled action.

Carothers describes the context of control in the preliterate:

> Behavior is minutely governed from childhood on in a host of particular,
> concrete situations by meticulous rules and taboos, and not on the basis
> of a few broad principles which require personal decisions for their ap-
> plication. These rules acquire much of their force from the fact that they
> are sanctified by tradition and reinforced by supernatural "powers," and
> so may not be questioned. Explanations of events are given to children
> on magical and animistic lines, which are far too facile and too final, and
> effectively suppress childish curiosity and suppress the urge to speculate.
> . . . The African child receives . . . an education which depends much
> more on the spoken word and which is relatively highly charged with
> drama and emotion.

IIere again it is necessary to introduce a *caveat.* In the above sentence, *drama* and *emotion* refer to the situation "in the real," not in the
formal, sense. In the formal sense *drama* connotes an elaborate illusional
system like that of grand opera, and the eliciting of an *emotion* requires
great ability to sit still, look first, and listen second, and experience
emotion not in dancing, yelling, fighting, sex, and the like, but as a
purely "inner" experience that can only be "externalized" by retrospective appraisal of "how moved I felt when. . . ."

In the preliterate society, every individual plant has a name and
a use, and there are hundreds of them. On the other hand, the preliterate person is "embedded" in the clan or family and so is not "a
particular" to himself. In the complex society in which "a few broad
principles" govern social conduct, Einstein characterized the ideal of
scientific problem solving as the pursuit of just those few broad principles. Einstein (1949:17) writes (in an "autobiographical note"), "I soon
learned to scent out that which was able to lead to fundamentals and to
turn aside from everything else, from the multitude of things which clutter up the mind and divert it from the essential."

The contrast is one between particularity of "objects" associated with
"embeddedness" of persons in a preliterate society vs. departiculariza-
tion of objects into categories and classes that constitute scientific "fun-

damentals" in a complex society. Generalization according to "simple principles" is carried out by an "individual" person; in Einstein's case, there is much to suggest that he could tolerate, to a remarkable degree, being alone—"an individual." The mutually inverse relation is similar to that of the private who lives in general quarters and the general who lives in private quarters.

CONCRETE–ABSTRACT

What is embedded in this discussion is the precise distinction between "concrete" and "abstract" in terms of thinking. Lévi-Strauss (1966) emphasizes that the savage who knows particular plants is a "scientist of the concrete"—a term that contradicts Einstein's assertion that the scientist learns to avoid "the multitude of things that clutter the mind." The "concrete savage" is characterized by a cluttered mind: Bartlett (1932) points out that the Swazi have an extraordinary memory for each cow, calf, or bull that was bought or sold and remember details of coloring, price, and the like from unimportant auctions years ago. On the other hand, the principle of special relativity is (in something of an oversimplification) an exploration of the implications of the fact that the speed of light is finite, one overwhelmingly important "fundamental."

When we see the contrast between two such polar extremes, it becomes more reasonable that the "savage" should react or act in the immediate, concrete, particular present, exhibiting his behavioral responses here and now under the control of particular rules his associates take as absolute and which they are highly interested in enforcing at every moment. He is "embedded" in his group, and he *does not need* internalized thoughts or feelings. Malinowski (1923) notes that the savage never considers language in terms of reflection, only in terms of action: speaking words is like paddling a boat. Only when it becomes possible to use a written symbolism is it possible to begin to imagine that the universe is "reflected in" verbal sequences, to use the metaphor of a mirroring technology, and thus to approach "reflective thinking."

At the opposite pole from the preliterate savage, we find "modern man," in Inkeles and Smith (1974), quoting Moore: "The traditional kinship structure provides a barrier to industrial development, since it encourages reliance of the individual upon its security rather than upon his own devices"—the implication is clearly that of "his [individual] devices" (p.74). They point to the emergence of women's rights (defining women as individuals, that is) as characteristic of modern societies, and to the use of birth control as a function of the same kind of "motivation." They go on to say, "Religion ranks with the extended family as the institution most often identified both as an obstacle to economic development and as a victim of the same process." Parrinder is quoted, "African society has traditionally been permeated with religion. But the ancient religious beliefs cannot stand the strain of modern urban and industrial life." Still further, "It is widely believed that . . . an almost inevitable tendency of modernization is to erode respect for the aged, and to foster a youth culture in which old age is viewed . . . as a dreadful condition to be approached with reluctance, even horror."

In summarizing these contrasts, it becomes apparent that "modern man" is *abstracted* man, *disembedded* man, who lives not in a world of immediate meaningful sensory experiences but in a world of remote indirect conceptual structures. Much of the history of contemporary rebellion against what is now the dominant theme of science and technology in the United States has to do with a disenchantment with the general and a reappraisal of the particular; with the task of the artisan rather than with that of the intellectual, especially the intellectual specialist; with feeling instead of with thinking; with "consciousness expansion" rather than with the development of analytic precision.

With this background, if we look again at the self-description given by the relatively young man in Case 4, we find a departicularized person. He insists that there is "nothing physical" about his actions, even when he seems to have been intensely "moved." He cannot stand the long continued presence of even his immediate family on a pleasure trip and develops ulcerative colitis in that context. His job is one of editing and preparing manuscripts, at which he is very good—but which he finds boring. He stays by himself except for seeing his small son. He thinks of himself as "healthy" because he does not smoke, is not overweight, and takes exercise—but at the same time he develops hypochondriacal fears. When the physician tells him that he *looks* "extremely depressed," he takes the physician's word for it—even though he can find no "depressed feelings" in himself. Instead, he says to himself, "I wish I were dead," without suicidal affect—and even with "relief." This man has a graduate degree from a first-class American university, he is solvent, obviously highly intelligent—and almost totally isolated and without feeling. A tragic "accident" of modernization.

To cope with life in a developed society one must develop "inner resources," significant *personal* relations based on personal preference, which in turn means selection based on *feeling*. "I" do not automatically associate primarily with an extended family, "I" select those I find "in harmony," those with similar "attitudes" and "interests." Instead of inheriting an extended family, "I" select a corporation, a psychoanalytic institute, a university department. In all of these "I" have to deal with the fact that membership is purely contingent and continuously dependent upon the acceptance of "me" by the other members of that group, whatever it may be.

The problem of "finding my way about" in so ambiguous a context is one of "consulting entrails," but in a somewhat different sense than does the haruspex. "I" have to know primarily from the inside out, what "turns me on" if "I" am to be turned on. It is not routine to live in a complex society, it is a constant struggle not only to survive economically but to continue to live in supporting social context. At the same time, in a big city, almost every trend works toward separating, isolating, differentiating citizens from each other.

The educational problem confronted by a member of a complex civilization is dual. In the first place, he has to learn intellectual schemas in the context of formal education, which for the most part are based upon and presuppose intensive training in the technology of literacy. On the other hand, and almost "covertly," he has to learn affective schemas that can serve as programmatic elements in his human relations. Scheflen (pers. comm.) has emphasized how large a part *courtship* patterns play in these affective schemas; in the cases cited above, each one shows a significant lack of success in making and maintaining satisfactory sexual relations. Where divorce is instantly and easily available, the maintenance of a marriage is a constant struggle rather than a matter "taken for granted."

What we have been working with in the above inquiry is the range *within* the human condition, in relation to the problem of *relative* describability. The disabled person who cannot "see" what may appear to be obvious categorical similarities (apple and banana, table and chair) may nevertheless have been a satisfactory member of his group and a satisfactory industrial worker until he became "other than himself" or "not me" through the complex processes of accident and bureaucratic processing of the implications of that accident. The disabled claimant appears to be in Humpty Dumpty's condition: he "had a great

fall" and nobody (not the compensation board, the psychiatrist, the re-
habilitation worker, etc.) was able to "put him together again." The
situation demonstrates the *brittleness* of personality integration in a
cognitively unsophisticated member of a complex industrial society.

In terms used by Bernstein (1964) in referring to the implications
of a *restricted* code, we find again the basic problem of "consciousness":
"Where meanings are context-independent and so universalistic, then
principles may be made verbally explicit and elaborated, whereas where
meanings are context dependent and so particularistic, principles will be
relatively implicit, or, as in regulative context, simply announced." The
process of becoming "context-independent" is closely related to the
process of *abstraction* as implied in the notion of "taking away from" a
particular situation into a general context. In our observations, this
problem is demonstrated again and again in the assumption that "my
feelings" are the same as those of "everyone" and therefore need not
be described or abstracted; in answer to the question "How did you
feel?" the claimant says, "How would anybody feel if . . .". With this
undeveloped describability, the person cannot know that his inner feeling may join two contexts in both of which he feels angry or anxious;
instead, the two situations are unintegrated, and he cannot "separate
himself" from the context to understand that both context A and context
B induce "the same" inner feeling.

CONCLUSION

I have attempted to summarize some new ways of looking at old
problems inherent in a semiotic point of view. When we speak of a
basic science, we usually ignore the fact that the most basic study of all
is the study of the way sciences are formulated. That is, before we can
"know" a thing, we have to have a description of it and its name, with
the definition forming the reciprocal of the name. Then when we begin
to study studying, we find that the preliterate "savage," a scientist of
the concrete in Lévi-Strauss's paradoxical term, knows an enormous
variety of useful plants and animals as separate items. A true abstract
science appears at the moment when, by keeping records of the various
items, significant similarities to distant and past forms can be established. Then and only then does it become possible to construct categories and families of relata, and from this construction to set up hierarchies in various methods of comparing developments.

We can conclude that mentational progress depends not only upon man's inherent neural data-processing apparatus but also upon the technological adjuvants that appear in their own line of evolution. Until and unless human beings find a written technology, it is impossible to perform certain intellectual operations—although, on the other hand, once the implications of the written technology are developed and internalized, it becomes possible to carry out many intellectual operations "in the head" (i.e., in the "imagination" through projecting internal images). A truly transactional process appears, in which "projection" and "introjection" necessarily participate. What we first formulate "out there" is later discoverable "in here." Very interesting examples of this reciprocal "innering" and "outering" are to be found in the many analogues between the brain and electronic data processing.

At the abstract level, it is continuously fascinating, as the various components appear, to see the basic similarity between cybernetic and linguistic technologies and those discovered in neural methods. When Boole invented the binary code, he did not know that in its long-distance operations the nervous system uses the "all or none" principle represented by the 0,1 that is the core of binary codes. Influenced by "standing waves" in the electrical context and by the humoral "field" in the hormonal context, the nervous system shows many of the characteristics of the "more-or-less" pattern of the analogue computer. The leitmotif of all knowing is the similar in the apparently different and the different in the apparently similar—the construction of categories and the discovery of *anomalies*, a term used by Kuhn, meaning "un-named."

The process by which a human being learns how to split himself so as to become his own primary respondent is best described as one of *inner speech*, in which "I" talk (as it were) to "me"; then, suddenly shifting places, often quite without realizing that the "subject" is now different (both the subject matter and the subject-speaker), a different "I" hears a different message. It is only when such a system has been developed that it becomes possible to speak of a "self-concept," that is, of a definition of "me" by "myself." With a well-developed self-concept, a long step toward becoming an "independent individual" has taken place.

The peculiar operations included under "psychoanalysis" and "insight psychotherapy" using some variant of "free association" are all based upon the possibility of the externalization of inner speech in the presence of another who is thereby made privy to what most of us keep secret (often keep secret from ourselves!). The implication of this exposure of privacy is that the other who may do little or nothing except be there with an occasional explanatory comment becomes a highly significant other. Because this other knows "all my secrets" he becomes powerful enough to alter the internal conversation. Through projection, the other is identified with all those who in previous contexts "knew what I am thinking"—but as the therapist becomes powerful by projection, he also comes to have access to the program by introjective identification—so that in principle it is possible to change the program of control and thus change the "patient's" behavioral patterning. Obviously the process is only occasionally and partially effective—but in principle, it is overwhelmingly fascinating.

We have come to realize with an increasing sense of wonder and excitement that we have another comprehensive example of the same basic pattern noted above. The human being's *program* in a static description is the reciprocal of a complex set of programmings throughout his whole life history. What we know as a "personality" is the reciprocal of the "history" of his experience, a history more unconscious and indescribable than it is conscious and describable. The "elements" of the "program" are the assimilative schemata controlling behavior that have been learned through accommodation in "outer-oriented" behaviors.

In the latest development in this series it is possible for the human being, in Bartlett's (1932:206) imaginative phrase, to "turn round upon his schemata" and to learn how to describe his own behavior and, more important, his own implicit or inhibited behavior. These appear as significant "feelings." Human beings know how to describe actions in others by observing the others from the outside. Ultimately the human being, by "othering" himself in association with a preceptor (cf. Mead, 1934) comes to be able to describe himself *from inside*. We call this process by the everyday expression "knowing one's feelings," in a context in which *feeling* is primarily a descriptive term applied to affective schemata that include muscular, visceral, and glandular potentialities.

We have spoken of the goal of this development as the human being's arrival at the *conservation of the self*. As far as we can tell only the very highly educated person is able to know his own patterns and potentialities in terms of his feelings—so that he is able to be social or solitary depending upon the context in which he finds or places himself. In our experience, one gets to this point by paradoxically accepting the impossibility of freedom as the basic condition of *relative* freedom *within* some system in the construction of which one has at best only a very minor and unimportant part to play.

REFERENCES

Bartlett, F. C. 1932. *Remembering.* London: Cambridge University Press.

Bernstein, Basil. 1964. "Social Class, Speech Systems and Psychotherapy." *Brit. Jour. Socio.* 15:54–64.

Bohrer, Stanley P. 1967. Letter to the Editor, "Allergy in Ibadan." *N. Eng. J. Med.* 277:766.

Carothers, J. C. 1959. "Culture, Psychiatry, and the Written Word." *Psychiatry* 22:307–20.

Durkheim, Emile. 1897. *Suicide.* Glencoe, Ill.: Free Press, 1951.

Einstein, Albert. 1949. In *Albert Einstein: Philosopher-Scientist*, Paul Schlipp, ed. New York: Harper Torch Books, 1959.

Holt, Emmet L., Jr. 1967. "A Nonallergist Looks at Allergy." *N. Eng. J. Med.* 276:1449–54.

Inkeles, Alex, and Smith, David H. 1974. *Becoming Modern.* Cambridge: Harvard University Press.

Lévi-Strauss, Claude. 1966. *The Savage Mind.* Chicago: University of Chicago Press.

MacLean, Paul D. 1949. "Psychosomatic Disease and the 'Visceral Brain'." *Psychosomatic Medicine* 11:338.

Malinowski, B. 1923. "The Problem of Meaning in Primitive Languages." In *The Meaning of Meaning*, C. K. Ogden and I. A. Richards, eds. New York: Harcourt.

Marty, P., and de M'Uzan, M. 1963. "La Pensée Operatoire." *Revue Française de Psychanalyse* 27:345–56.

Mead, George H. 1934. *Mind, Self and Society.* Chicago: University of Chicago.

Moore, Wilbert E. 1965. *Industrialization and Labor: Social Aspects of Economic Development.* New York: Russell and Russell.

Nemiah, J. C., and Sifneos, P. E. 1970. "Psychosomatic Illness: A Problem in Communication." *Psychotherapy and Psychosomatics* 18:154–60.

Piaget, Jean. 1950. *The Psychology of Intelligence.* New York: Harcourt.

Ruesch, Jurgen. 1948. "The Infantile Personality: The Case Problem of Psychosomatic Medicine." *Psychosomatic Medicine* 10:134.

Shands, Harley C. 1954. "Problems of Separation in the Etiology of Psychosomatic Disease." *Bulletin of the Muscogee County Medical Society* 1:9–19.

———. 1975. "How are 'Psychosomatic' Patients Different from 'Psychoneurotic' Patients?" *Psychotherapy and Psychosomatics*, in press.

Shands, Harley C.; Lipner, Joan; Harris, Paul; Katz, Steven; Meltzer, James D. 1973. "Hospital Management of Heroin Addicts Undergoing Cardiac Surgery: A Team Approach." *Brit. J. of Addiction* 68:373–76.

Shands, Harley C., and Meltzer, James D. 1973. *Language and Psychiatry*. The Hague: Mouton.

———. 1977. "Unexpected Semiotic Implications of Medical Inquiry." In *A Perfusion of Signs*, T. A. Sebeok, ed. Bloomington: Indiana University Press.

Short, Charles L. 1975. Quoted in *MGH NEWS* 34, #2 (March).

Sifneos, Peter E. 1967. "Clinical Observations on Some Patients Suffering from a Variety of Psychosomatic Diseases." *ACTA Medica Psychosomatica*: 3–10.

Skinner, B. F. 1963. "Behaviorism at Fifty." *Science* 140:951–58.

For a Semiotic Anthropology

Milton Singer

CULTURE THEORY TILTS
TO SEMIOTICS

During the 1960s and early 1970s, discussions of culture theory
showed a preoccupation with the idea that cultures are systems of symbols and meanings. At the least, this preoccupation seems to be creating
a new subfield of cultural anthropology; it is probably also transforming
the aims, methods, and subject matters of cultural anthropology and its
relations to other disciplines. Leading anthropologists who have articulated this symbolic conception of culture have given different names to
the emerging field or subfield. Lévi-Strauss calls it "structural anthropology" and "semiology"; Geertz, extending Weber, Dilthey, and Schutz,
refers to it as "interpretative anthropology"; Schneider simply calls it
"a cultural account." In a recently published book, Peacock notes that
he and several colleagues introduced the designation "symbolic anthropology" for the new field, while Victor Turner prefers "comparative

I am indebted to Professor Thomas A. Sebeok for the opportunity to present a
shorter version of this paper at Bloomington in March 1976. The paper also draws
on material from my course on Semiotic Anthropology at the University of Chicago
and from my forthcoming book, *Man's Glassy Essence: Explorations in Semiotic
Anthropology*, to be published by Indiana University Press. I am grateful to Michael
Silverstein, Victor Turner, and Paul Friedrich for helpful comments on the paper
and to Benjamin Lee for assistance in my course in 1975 and 1976.

symbology" as a wider designation to take account of the symbolic genres of advanced civilizations as well as of the ethnographic materials of nonliterate cultures. Turner has also emphasized the need for a processual analysis of symbols in the concrete contexts of social life, in contrast to the formal analysis of symbols as algebraic, logical, or cognitive systems, which Turner regards as characteristic of semiology, semiotics, and linguistics.

Other anthropologists who have contributed to these recent developments of culture theory have not introduced any special designation for the field, but have either aligned themselves with one of the named approaches—Leach, e.g., with Lévi-Strauss's "structural anthropology" and "semiology," Mary Douglas with Victor Turner's "symbology," Margaret Mead with "semiotics,"—or, as in Firth's book on *Symbols*, have adopted an eclectic attitude toward the different approaches.

In this paper I should like to consider two problems that these recent developments in culture theory pose: (1) Why does the tilt of culture theory to semiotics occur just when it does, in the 1960s and early 1970s? and, (2) What kind of general theory of signs and symbols is likely to prove most fruitful and adequate for a general theory of culture?

The answer to the first question will be found, I believe, both in the preceding developments within anthropological theory and in what was going on outside of anthropology. It is perhaps premature to predict the answer to the second question, but an analysis of some of the issues in dispute between the semiotic and semiological theories of signs should enable us to state a case for a *semiotic anthropology* and to prefigure some of its contours.

CULTURE AND SOCIETY AS COMPLEMENTARY CONCEPTS

In trying to sort out and understand the recent proliferation of symbolic theories of culture, it is tempting to see in them different expressions of national character or at least of different national traditions in anthropological thought and research. In their joint introduction to the symposium *African Systems of Thought*, Meyer Fortes and Germaine Dieterlen, the British and the French co-editors, agreed on two major propositions: (1) That there were two broadly contrastive approaches in the symposium papers to the description and analysis of African religious systems. The one approach, characteristic of French ethnogra-

phy, starts with the total body of knowledge—(the "connaissance")—
"expressed in a people's mythology and in the symbolism of their ritual,
reflected in their conceptions of man and of the universe, and embodied
in their categories of thought, their forms of social organization and their
technology, and constituting a coherent logical system." The other approach, characteristic of British social anthropology, "starts from the
social and political relations in the context of which ritual, myth, and
belief are found to be operative." It "links the body of knowledge and
beliefs of a people with the actualities of their social organization and
daily life." (2) A second proposition accepted by the British and the
French co-editors is that the two approaches are not antithetical but
deal with complementary aspects of African religious and ritual institutions. The question then arises as to how these two aspects of African
religious systems are interconnected. The editors reported that in the
symposium discussion, evidence emerged very clearly "for the way in
which myth, ritual, concepts of personality, and cosmological ideas penetrate the social organization of a people and are in turn shaped by the
latter" (Fortes and Dieterlen, 1965:4).*

Audrey Richards, in a review of *African Systems of Thought* (1967),
sought to pinpoint the social and institutional reasons for the difference
between the French and the British approaches. French anthropologists,
she pointed out, tend to do their field observations in their brief vaca-
tion periods extended over many years, while British anthropologists do
theirs in an intensive year or two of fieldwork. These differences in the
ways of doing fieldwork, she suggested, helped to explain the French
and British contrastive approaches to African religious systems. The
French get to know individual informants and their belief systems,
while the British concentrate on the functional connections between
social actions and institutions.

In his recent book, *Symbolism Reconsidered*, Dan Sperber also in-
vokes a national character kind of explanation for the French semiological approach: "The Frenchman lives in a universe where everything
means something, where every correlation is a relation of meaning,
where the cause is the sign of its effect and the effect, a sign of its cause.
By a singular inversion, only real signs—words, texts—are said, sometimes, to mean nothing at all" (Sperber, 1974:83).

---

* The explicit characterization of the difference between the British and the
French approaches to the study of ritual and symbolism was introduced and elaborated by Victor Turner (Fortes and Dieterlen, 1965:9–15).

Claiming that "semiologism" is an essential aspect of French culture and ideology but not necessarily of all cultures, Sperber argues that "Lévi-Strauss has demonstrated the opposite of what he asserts, and myths do not constitute a language."

"All these learned terms—signifier and signified, paradigm and syntagm, code, mytheme, will not for long hide the following paradox: that if Lévi-Strauss thought of myths as a semiological system, the myths thought themselves in him, and without his knowledge, as a cognitive system" (Sperber, 1974:84).

Before we become involved in the debate over whether "semiologism" is a French disease, or a British or American disease, a Russian, Polish, or Italian disease, it would be advisable to review the historical and analytic aspects of the *culture* concept. Such a review, I believe, would also help to clarify Sperber's distinction between semiological and cognitive systems, as well as illuminate the recent tilt of culture theory to semiotics.

In historical perspective, the two contrastive approaches to African religions identified by Fortes and Dieterlen represent a specialized application and transformation of the contrast between *society* and *culture* as global, inclusive concepts. The national affiliations of the two concepts, however, have undergone a sea change. The British anthropologist, Edward Tylor, was one of the first to formulate a global concept of culture in his famous definition: "Culture or civilization, taken in its wide ethnographic sense, is that complex whole which includes knowledge, belief, art, morals, law, custom, and any other capabilities and habits acquired by man as a member of society" (Tylor, 1871).

The inclusive conception of society as a social system and synchronic structure, which became a trademark of British social anthropology, derives from Durkheim, Comte, and Montesquieu, as well as Spencer, and the American anthropologist Morgan (Singer, 1968).

The later vicissitudes of these concepts are equally unrespectful of national boundaries: Tylor's culture concept was miniaturized and pluralized by Malinowski in England and by Boas and his students in the United States. As such, it first guided the study of "primitive" and "tribal cultures" and later of "peasant," "urban," "ethnic" and all sorts of "subcultures." The French sociological tradition, on the other hand, not only led to the concepts of social system and social structure in British social anthropology, but also influenced American sociology decisively.

In "The Concepts of Culture and of Social System" (*American Sociological Review*, 1958), Alfred Kroeber and Talcott Parsons proposed "a truce to quarrelling over whether culture is best understood from the perspective of society or society from that of culture." The historical significance of this proposal is that it marks a public and professional recognition of the shift from the global and intellectually imperialistic concepts of culture and social system to an analytical distinction between the two concepts as quasi-independent, complementary, and interrelated: "We suggest that it is useful to define the concept of *culture* for most usages more narrowly than has been done in most American anthropological tradition and have it refer to transmitted and created content and patterns of values, ideas, and other symbolical-meaningful systems as factors in the shaping of human behavior and the artifacts produced through behavior. On the other hand, we suggest that the term *society*—or more generally, *social system* —be used to designate the specifically relational system of interaction among individuals and collectivities."

By 1958 when the Kroeber–Parsons article appeared, the proposed condominious merger of anthropological and sociological concepts of culture and society was beginning to occur in the work of Raymond Firth (1951), Fred Eggan (1955), and Robert Redfield (1955), among others. In fact, Kroeber himself, who was one of the leading exponents of a global concept of culture that encompassed social relations and social organization, had started to think about a narrower and more differentiated culture concept as early as 1909. As a result of an extended debate with Rivers and then with Radcliffe-Brown over their "sociological" interpretation of classificatory kinship terminologies, Kroeber crystallized a conception of kinship terms as little systems of semantic logic. Almost fifty years after Kroeber made this suggestion, Lounsbury and Goodenough both returned to it in 1956, and developed the method of "kinship semantics," a method from which Goodenough and others extrapolated a general theory of culture as "ethnosemantics" or "ethnoscience" (Singer, 1968; Schneider, 1968).

Rivers and Radcliffe-Brown were similarly stimulated by the debate with Kroeber and with each other to crystallize a conception of kinship systems as social systems that included as components kinship terms and categories, kinship behavior and norms, rights and obligations, as well as rules of marriage and descent. For Radcliffe-Brown this conception of kinship system became an exemplary paradigm for his broader concepts of social system and social structure.

The place of the *culture* concept in this paradigm remained somewhat ambiguous for Radcliffe-Brown. He was critical of the survival in American anthropology of Tylor's global culture concept and referred to it as "a vague abstraction." He preferred to eliminate that concept altogether. On the other hand, Radcliffe-Brown began to construct a fairly precise concept of cultural system complementary to his concept of social structure as early as his 1937 lectures on "A Natural Science of Society." In the published version of the lectures (1957) he analyzed the concept of culture into three aspects: (1) A set of rules of behavior "which exists in the minds of a certain number of people owing to the fact that they recognize it as the proper procedure," and carry it out in behavior, or "social usages." (2) The existence of certain common symbols and common meanings attached to those symbols—words, gestures, works of art, rituals, and myths are symbols which provide the means of communication between individuals. (3) Common ways of feeling or sentiments and common ways of thinking or beliefs shared by a majority of the people in a society—Durkheim's "collective representations."

These three aspects of culture together make possible a "standardization," or "system," of behavior, sentiment, and belief of individuals in a society. In fact, Radcliffe-Brown uses the term "culture" to refer to just such a standardized *system*, not to the individual acts of behavior or even to a *class* of such acts. But Radcliffe-Brown insists that there can be no independent, autonomous science of cultural systems, for the standardization of behavior, sentiments, and beliefs implies a set of relations between persons, or a social structure. "Neither social structure nor culture can be scientifically dealt with in isolation from one another. . . . You can study culture only as a characteristic of a social system" (Radcliffe-Brown, 1957:106–107).

One can read many of Radcliffe-Brown's ethnographic papers—e.g., on joking relations, totemism, the mother's brother and other kinship studies, religion and society, taboo, etc.—as attempts to explore the "functional" connections between culture as collective representations, cultural symbols, rules of behavior, and social usages, on the one hand; and social structures as networks of actual social relations, on the other. In the 1930s, when he was at the University of Chicago, and in the years immediately following at Oxford, Radcliffe-Brown became sufficiently convinced of the fruitfulness and validity of this approach to attempt an explicit general formulation of it in the lectures on a natural science of society and on social anthropology, and in papers on the concepts of function, social structure, kinship systems, the comparative method in anthropology.

For American anthropologists, Radcliffe-Brown's methodological views and their ethnographic exemplifications offered a needed alternative to the Boasian eclectic "descriptive integrations" of observed facts and historical reconstructions. As Redfield pointed out in his 1937 introduction to the volume in honor of Radcliffe-Brown prepared by some of his American students, the alternative provided by Radcliffe-Brown consisted not so much in the formulation or discovery of general social laws, as in providing a guide to research: the formulation of general concepts, classification of problems, explicit statement of general postulates and propositions. "The propositions are not to be treated as final but are to be challenged, revised, or abandoned as the investigation into special fact guided by them proceeds" (Redfield in Eggan, 1955:xiii).

Redfield's description of Radcliffe-Brown's American contributions to social anthropology as a generalizing science is both confirmed and extended by his own study of *The Folk Culture of Yucatan*. And nowhere is Radcliffe-Brown's influence more explicit and striking than in the definitions of culture and society as complementary concepts, which Redfield uses in that study. Redfield had in fact formulated explicit definitions of "culture," "society," and "community" as complementary concepts as early as 1941 (in *The Folk Culture of Yucatan*, pp.14–15). His definition of culture as "an organization of conventional understandings expressed in act and artifact" extends some of Sapir's ideas from his 1931 articles on "symbolism" and "communication," as well as Tylor's charter definition. The definitions of "society" and "community," however, were very close to those of Radcliffe-Brown and show the influence of the latter's presence in the Chicago department from 1931 to 1937. Redfield defined "society" as a network of social relations, and "community" as the territorial group that is characterized by a given culture and society.

While these early formulations of Redfield's formed an integral part of the conceptual framework of *The Folk Culture of Yucatan* and of his more special concept of "folk" culture and "folk" society, they did not become at that time a stimulus for developing a semiotic theory of culture either in Redfield's thinking or in that of other anthropologists. The interest instead turned to processes of acculturation and other forms of culture change generated by the contact of "folk" cultures and societies with modern, Western urban societies and cultures.

After the Second World War, when Redfield became interested in studying and comparing the "great traditions" of living civilizations, he saw a greater need for anthropologists to work with the humanists on their left than with the natural scientists on their right. What is of special interest for the present story, however, is that in developing a "social anthropology of civilizations," Redfield did not abandon the complementary concepts of culture, social structure, and community or the conception of culture as a system of meanings and values. Rather, he enlarged the scope of their application, and modified their definitions to take account of history, high cultures, and large organized states. He defined a civilization as consisting of a *societal structure* of communities of differing size, complexity, and interrelations and of a *cultural structure* of little and great traditions in reciprocal interaction. Such complex structures were not simply conceived as *synchronic* structures, but were to be traced through their persistences and changes as *historic structures*. And just as Firth and V. Turner, among others, studied specific social structures through their *social organizations* in particular places and times, so the societal and cultural structures of civilizations could be studied in the *social organization of their cultural traditions* in particular centers and networks. The formation, maintenance, and transmission of these cultural traditions were not only "organizations of conventional understandings expressed in act and artifact," but also bodies of knowledge, "more or less pyramidal, more or less multilineal," embodying distinctive world views and value systems, cosmologies and religions. The cultivation and understanding of these bodies of knowledge are socially organized in schools, in churches and sects, in towns and cities, by cultural specialists, literati, and intelligentsia. The French conceptions of culture and civilization as organized knowledge and the British conceptions of society as social structure and social organization found their synthesis in Redfield's conception of civilizations as social organizations of great and little traditions, and of great and little communities (Singer, 1976).

The Kroeber–Parsons article on culture and social system and Redfield's conceptions of the cultural and societal structures of civilizations indicate that by 1958 culture theory, in the United States, at least, had reached a phase of explicit formulation that emphasized the structural, symbolic, and cognitive aspects of the culture concept, and its complementarity with the concept of social structure.

It is noteworthy that Lévi-Strauss, whose work in the 1950s and 1960s was to make anthropology famous for two new *isms*—"structuralism" and "semiologism"—recognized theoretical affinities with some of his predecessors, whom, in other respects, he characterized as practitioners of a natural science model of empiricism, functionalism, and naturalism. He found such affinities, for example, in Radcliffe-Brown's 1951 paper on totemism and wondered if Radcliffe-Brown realized how radical a departure he had made from his own previous functionalism in developing a theory of totemism that explained the selection of totemic species because they were good to think, not because they were good to eat. Lévi-Strauss even suggested that this out-of-character paper of Radcliffe-Brown's may have been influenced by the development of structural linguistics and structural anthropology in the previous decade, 1940–1950 (Lévi-Strauss, *Totemism*, pp.89–90).

Meyer Fortes ignored Lévi-Strauss's suggestion; Radcliffe-Brown's 1951 paper on totemism, Fortes (1967) said, covered ground so familiar to his students and colleagues, that its publication caused no stir whatever among them. While Fortes may have underestimated some of the novel features of Radcliffe-Brown's structuralism and of Lévi-Strauss's, I believe that for both, the roots of a structural and symbolic theory of culture, and of society, can be found in the preceding fifty years' development of culture theory, which was sketched in the preceding section. The formulation of such a theory was started by Radcliffe-Brown as early as 1937 and by Redfield in 1941. Elsewhere I have tried to show that both of these anthropologists, and Lévi-Strauss, as well, did not so much abandon the natural science model as they extended and modified it. Humanism did not replace science in the development of a structural and symbolic theory of culture and society; it was incorporated into a transformed philosophy and method of science. That transformation began about 1900 with new developments in the foundations of mathematics, symbolic logic, theoretical physics, and the mathematical theory of communication. Structural linguistics and structural anthropology participated in this transformation, as did social and cultural anthropology (Singer, 1968, 1973, 1976; Jakobson, 1961).

> Where ordinary logic talks of classes the logic of relatives talks of *systems*. A *system* is a set of objects comprising all that stand to one another in a group of connected relations. Induction according to ordinary logic rises from the contemplation of a sample of a class to that of the whole class; but according to the logic of relatives it rises from the contemplation of a fragment of a system to the envisagement of the complete system." [Peirce 4.5]

SEMIOTICS AND SEMIOLOGY: A
COMPARISON AND A CONTRAST

In his Inaugural Address at the Collège de France in 1960, Lévi-Strauss proposed that anthropology devote itself to the study of signs and symbols, to the science that Saussure called "semiologie." In this address Lévi-Strauss conceives of anthropology as a branch of *semiology*, "the occupant in good faith of that domain of semiology which linguistics has not already claimed for its own, pending the time when for at least certain sections of this domain, special sciences are set up within anthropology" (*Current Anthropology* [1966]:114).

Within Saussure's conception of semiology as the study of "the life of signs at the heart of social life," Lévi-Strauss claims for anthropology some of the sign systems mentioned by Saussure—e.g., symbolic forms of politeness, military signals, as well as many others: "mythic language, the oral and gestural signs of ritual, marriage rules, kinship systems, customary laws, certain conditions of economic exchange."

The enumeration is not intended to be exhaustive and, indeed, cannot be in view of Lévi-Strauss's broad perspective on man and anthropology: "Men communicate by means of symbols and signs; for anthropology, which is a conversation of man with man, everything is symbol and sign, when it acts as intermediary between two subjects."

Even stone axes, techniques, and modes of production and consumption, Lévi-Strauss suggests, can be seen as signs, "according to Peirce's celebrated definition, that which replaces something for someone." A certain type of stone axe is a sign because it replaces another tool that another society uses for the same purpose.

Clearly such a semiotic theory of culture implies, and perhaps presupposes, a philosophical anthropology about the nature of man, and an epistemology about how we can know that nature, which are not made entirely explicit in the writings of Lévi-Strauss. The closest he comes to explicit revelation of his position is in the autobiographical travelogue, *Tristes Tropiques*, in which it turns out that the Western anthropologist's vision quest for "true savages" finds only men—conversing with men. When conversation fails, because men do not know one another's language, there can only be a dumb silence. When conversation across cultures occurs, it does not matter whether we see the flow of communication as going from us to them or in the reverse direction. In this perspective structuralism and structural anthropology provide a method for the analysis of human communication, which Lévi-

Strauss suggests can be analyzed into a unified theory of the exchange of words, of women, and of goods and services.*

Two years after Lévi-Strauss's Inaugural Address, Margaret Mead, at the Indiana University Conference on Paralinguistics and Kinesics, having listened to the papers and discussions, tried to describe what the conference was about and to suggest a name for the field, "which in time will include the study of all patterned communication in all modalities, of which linguistics is the most technically advanced. If we had a word for patterned communication in all modalities, it would be useful. I am not enough of a specialist in this field to know what word to use, but many people here, who have looked as if they were on opposite sides of the fence have used the word 'semiotics.' It seems to me the one word, in some form or other, that has been used by people arguing from quite different positions."

Despite some expressed preferences for the word *communication* and some argument about whether *semiotics* should be restricted to the non-linguistic aspects of communication, the organizers of the conference and the editors of its proceedings adopted Margaret Mead's suggestion and incorporated it in the title of the conference proceedings as *Approaches to Semiotics*. In addition, one of the organizers and editors, Thomas A. Sebeok, took this same title for a series of volumes published under his editorship by Mouton from 1969 to 1976. In 1976 he started another series, *Advances in Semiotics*, published by Indiana University Press.†

Semiotics is a plural formed by analogy from *semiotic*, Peirce's designation for a general theory of the nature and different kinds of signs. Whether, in adopting *semiotics* as the designation for the study of culturally patterned communication in all modalities, Sebeok and his co-editors were endorsing Peirce's *semiotic* rather than Saussure's *semiology* is not certain. Nevertheless, the apparent convergence between Lévi-Strauss's and Margaret Mead's proposals to bring anthropology within a broader interdisciplinary study of patterned communication is striking both in timing and in content. In view of such consensus it may seem like quibbling to raise the question whether the new field should

---

* Levi-Strauss's application of Peirce's definition of a sign to tools and exchange is consistent with Peirce's teleological logic of Semiosis. Also see Sahlins (1976), Firth (1973).

† For a historical review of the terms *semiotics* and *semiology* see Sebeok (1976), Jakobson (1975).

be called *semiology* or *semiotics*. Indeed some scholars have been using the terms interchangeably, while others have tried to synthesize the pioneering insights of Peirce and Saussure into a comprehensive and integrated point of view (Eco, 1976; Jakobson, 1967; Sebeok, 1975). Yet there are many issues in dispute between *semiotic* and *semiological* theories of signs that need to be clarified at the present time. In culture theory, particularly, the differences between Radcliffe-Brown and Lévi-Strauss, between Geertz and Lévi-Strauss, between Victor Turner and Leach, between Goodenough and Schneider, for example, are not just the expression of personal or national prejudices but spring from differences in underlying conceptions of cultures and societies as systems of symbols and meanings. It would help to sharpen and clarify these differences, I believe, if the two most influential theories of signs, Peirce's *semiotic* and Saussure's *semiology*, were contrasted as well as compared with respect to some features that are especially relevant for culture theory. Such a comparison and contrast between *semiology* and *semiotic* need not be based on a comprehensive and historically detailed study of all writers who have used these terms. For purposes of the present discussion it is sufficient to construct an ideal typical comparison based on Peirce and Saussure and on some of their leading descendants.

Underlying similarities between Peircean *semiotic* and Saussurean *semiology* are important and have been recognized. Both regarded themselves as pioneers opening up a new field, both aimed at a general theory of signs that would deal with all kinds of signs and symbol-systems, and both analyzed the nature of signs in relational and structural terms rather than as "substances" and "things." Both also regarded linguistic signs as "arbitrary" in the sense that the meanings of such signs generally depend on social conventions and usages rather than on any "natural" connections between the signs and the objects they denote.

The major items in the comparison and the contrast between semiotic and semiology are summarized in Table 1.

The differences between semiotic and semiology are equally important and not so frequently recognized.

In spite of the shared aim of both semiotic and semiology to become general theories of all kinds of sign systems, in actual practice the two theories differ in subject matter and method, in specific concepts and "laws," as well as in epistemology and ontology.

The subject matter of semiology tends to fall in the domains of

Table 1

	Semiotic (Peirce)	*Semiology* (Saussure)
1. Aims at a general theory of signs.	Philosophical and normative, but observational.	A descriptive, generalized linguistics.
2. Frequent subject matter domains.	Logic, mathematics, sciences, colloquial English (logic-centered).	Natural languages, literature, legends, myths (language-centered).
3. Signs are relations, not "things."	A sign is a triadic relation of sign, object, and interpretant.	A sign of diadic relation between signifier and signified.
4. Linguistic signs are "arbitrary"	but also include "natural signs."	but appear "necessary" for speakers of the language (Benveniste).
5. Ontology of "objects" of signs.	Existence pre-supposed by signs.	Not "given," but determined by the linguistic relations.
6. Epistemology of empirical ego or subject.	Included in semiotic analysis.	Presupposed by but not included in semiological analysis.

natural languages, literature, myths and legends, and folk classifications. Semiotic, on the other hand, tends to concentrate on the domains of the formalized languages of mathematics, logic, and the natural sciences; on colloquial speech; and on nonverbal communication, human and animal.

Peirce conceived of semiotic as an "observational science," dependent on the observations and experience of everyday life. In this respect it was a philosophical and normative science, a branch of logic in fact, in contrast to the special sciences, both physical and psychical, which depend for their observations on travel, special instruments, and training. Linguistics, ethnology, psychology, and sociology he classified as special psychical sciences, to which semiotic as "a quasi-necessary" doctrine of signs can be applied (*Collected Papers* 3.427–30).

Saussurean semiology also makes use of logical analysis, but since its subject matter consists of natural languages, its methods are descriptive and empirical rather than purely theoretical and analytic. In Peirce's classification, semiology could be a special science, a kind of generalized linguistics, dependent on special observation and comparison, rather than a philosophical science like semiotic.

These differences in subject matter and method between semiology and semiotic can be summarized in terms of a third important difference: that semiology is language-centered, while semiotic is interested in the process of communication by signs of all kinds—a process Peirce named *semiosis*.

The language-centeredness of semiology is based on three assumptions: (1) That language is the most important of all sign systems. (2) That all other sign systems presuppose or imply the use of language. (3) That linguistics, as the scientific study of language, offers the best model for the study of all other sign systems (Barthes, 1963; Hymes, 1971; Jakobson, 1971; Lévi-Strauss, 1963).

If these three assumptions are accepted, then a language-centered semiology becomes as broad in scope as Peirce's logic-centered general semiotic, since any kind of sign system, including culture, would then be studied as modeled on language. While this linguistic interpretation of semiology has been seriously proposed by Barthes, among others, the assumptions on which it is based are not self-evident. They need to be taken as hypotheses for discussion and testing, as does the linguistic interpretation of culture.

In one of his letters to Lady Welby, Peirce told her that her concentration on language and on English words was far narrower than his own studies, which "must extend over the whole of general semiotic": "I think that perhaps you are in danger of falling into some error in consequence of limiting your studies so much to language, and among languages to one very peculiar language, as all Aryan languages are; and within that language so much to words" (Welby, *Other Dimensions*, p.312).

Peirce added that there were only three classes of English words with which he had "a decent acquaintance": "the words of the vernacular of the class of society in which I am placed, the words of philosophical and mathematical terminology," and chemical words—"which can hardly be said to be English or any other Aryan speech, being of a synthetic structure much like those of the tribes of our own brown 'red Indians'" (*Other Dimensions*, p.313).

In contrast to such a narrow concentration on the meaning of words in one language, Peirce urged a broader science of semiotic that will also study all kinds of signs—including icons, indices, and symbols—and their relations to their objects as well as to their interpretants. Peirce brought the comparative study of linguistic signs in different languages and of equations, graphs, and diagrams within the scope of his general semiotic, but he regarded the different linguistic forms by which a concept was signified, or an object designated, as "inessential accidents" like the skins of an onion. What was essential was that a thought have some possible expression for some possible interpreter (*Collected Papers* 4.6).

The semiological and the semiotic analyses of signs are both relational and structural. This is quite explicit in both Saussure and in Peirce.

In his search for the basic data for linguistic analysis, Saussure rejected the position that there are given "objects," "things," or "substances" that could serve as the point of departure for linguistics. He insisted instead on the importance of the point of view from which the subject was studied and, in particular, on giving priority to relations: "The more one delves into the material proposed for linguistic study, the more one becomes convinced of this truth, which most particularly— it would be useless to conceal it—makes one pause: that the bond established amongst things is preexistent, in this one area, *to the things themselves*, and serves to determine them" (quoted in Benveniste, 1971, "Saussure after Half a Century"—italics in the original).

Saussure applied this relational point of view to the analysis of the linguistic sign, which he defined as a relation between an acoustic image and a concept, or, more generally, as a relation between a *signifier* and a *signified* (Saussure, *Course*, part I, chap. 1).

In Peirce's semiotic theory a sign is also defined in relational terms but as a triadic relation rather than a diadic relation, and the definition is intended for any kind of sign, not just for linguistic signs. Peirce's triadic definition of a sign is well known. One version that seems to me especially lucid and succinct is the following: "A sign is in a conjoint relation to the thing denoted and to the mind. If this triple relation is not of a degenerate species, the sign is related to its object only in consequence of a mental association, and depends upon habit. Such signs are always abstract and general, because habits are general rules to which the organism has become subjected. They are, for the most part, conventional or arbitrary. They include all general words, the main body of speech, and any mode of conveying a judgment" (*Collected Papers* 3.360).

Peirce called such signs "symbols" to distinguish them from signs whose relation to their objects were of a direct nature and did not depend on a mental association. If the sign signifies its object solely by virtue of being really connected with it, as with physical symptoms, meteorological signs, and a pointing finger, Peirce calls such a sign an *index*. A sign which stands for something merely because it resembles it Peirce called an *icon*. Geometrical diagrams, maps, paintings, are in this sense icons although they may also have conventional and indexical features as well.

The difference between a diadic and a triadic definition of the sign leads to other important differences. Benveniste has pointed out some confusions in Saussure's conception of the arbitrary nature of the linguistic sign because his concentration on the relation between significr and signified slighted the object denoted, although in reality, "Saussure was always thinking of the representation of the *real object* (although he spoke of the 'idea') and of the evidently unnecessary and unmotivated character of the bond which united the sign to the *thing* signified" (Benveniste, 1971, "The Nature of the Linguistic Sign").

Eco, and others, have explained Saussure's slighting of the object as springing from his giving primacy to the study of codes, of *langue*, over the study of the messages or *parole* (Eco, 1976:60). It is also possible that Saussure's emphasis on "objects," "things," and "substances" as determined by relations rather than regarding them as preexisting "givens" influenced his attitude towards naming and denotation.

In any case, Peirce, who was a major contributor to the development of a logic of relations, felt no compulsion to omit objects from his definition of a sign. On the contrary, "objects" enter essentially into his definition of a sign and into many of his classifications of signs. "A *Sign* or *Representamen*, is a First which stands in such a genuine triadic relation to a Second, called its *Object*, as to be capable of determining a Third, called its *Interpretant* to assume the same triadic relation to its Object in which it stands itself to the same Object" (Peirce [Buchler] 1955:100).

I would suggest that Peirce was able to include objects in his relational analysis of signs and sign processes or semiosis because in his logic of relations, or relatives, he regarded objects as whatever was denoted by the subject of a relational statement. If such a statement contained two subjects, the relation was dyadic; if three subjects, then the relation was triadic, if *n* subjects, then the relation was *n*-adic.

From Peirce's logical point of view, the ontological status of the "objects" denoted by the subjects of the statement is the same whatever their number.

Peirce's ontology of "objects" is not, however, simply one of logical or conceivable "objects"—although these are included. His ontology contains as well the "real" objects of the external world in two senses: (1) That such objects are indicated or denoted by the subjects of the statements as indexical signs. Without the indices we would not know what we are talking about, no matter how detailed our verbal descriptions or graphic our maps and diagrams. A proposition would then become a predicate with blanks for subjects. The object of a sign is "that with which (the sign presupposes) an acquaintance in order to convey some further information concerning it" (Peirce [Buchler] 1955:100; *Collected Papers* 3.414–24). (2) Peirce distinguishes between the "immediate object" of a sign and its "dynamical object." The latter is the object as it will eventually be determined by a community of scientific investigators, while the "immediate object" is the object that an index calls to the immediate attention of an interpreter. "Look, it's raining!" would usually send the listener to the window to see the immediate object of the statement, while meteorologists' reports would be concerned with the dynamical object (Peirce, ibid.).

The epistemological differences between semiology and semiotic are as striking as their differences with respect to the ontology of "objects." I shall confine my comments on these to the roles of the empirical ego or subject in both theories.

Lévi-Strauss has accepted Ricoeur's characterization of structuralism as "Kantism without a transcendental subject," but neither he nor Ricoeur have indicated the role of the empirical subject. Although Lévi-Strauss declared in his 1960 Inaugural Address that anthropology is "a conversation of man with man," he has been accused of neglecting just those face-to-face interactions considered essential for fieldwork by many social anthropologists (e.g., Geertz, 1973, "The Cerebral Savage").

Some of Lévi-Strauss's formulations frequently seem to justify such charges. If "the myths think themselves in me" and I do not think them, then there is "decentering" of the empirical ego in structural and semiological anthropology in favor of a centering on signs and symbols.

Fortes (1967) has suggested an interesting interpretation of the difference between Lévi-Strauss and Radcliffe-Brown that bears on this epistemological point. Lévi-Strauss's structural analysis, Fortes says, is "message-oriented" while Radcliffe-Brown's, and that of British social anthropology, is "actor-oriented."

Fortes attributes the source of the general distinction between "message-oriented" and "action-oriented" analysis to an article of Ja-kobson's. Drawing on Bohr's complementarity principle, and on Ruesch, MacKay, Cherry, and others, Jakobson distinguishes between two kinds of observers; the first of these is outside the system, "the most detached and external onlooker," and having no knowledge of the code, acts as a cryptoanalyst and attempts to break the code through a scrutiny of the messages in Sherlock Holmes fashion.

In linguistics Jakobson regards cryptoanalysis as "merely a prelim-inary stage toward (the second, which is) an internal approach to the language studies, when the observer becomes adjusted to the native speakers and decodes messages in their mother tongue through the medium of its code" (Jakobson, 1971:575). Such an observer becomes a "participant observer" who is placed within the system.

Fortes undoubtedly saw in the two kinds of observers, the crypto-analyst and the participant observer, the difference between Lévi-Strauss and Radcliffe-Brown, respectively, and possibly that between French and British anthropology in general. Jakobson does not him-self make such an application of the distinction, although some well-known criticism of Lévi-Strauss as a poor fieldworker (e.g., by Maybury-Lewis) and Lévi-Strauss's description of his dramatic silent encounter with the Mundé in *Tristes Tropiques* would seem to lend plausibility to such criticism.

The dismissal of Lévi-Strauss as a poor fieldworker is much too easy a polemical tactic, as it was when used against Radcliffe-Brown by Firth, Needham, and others. Functionalist social anthropology and participant observation in face-to-face interactions are accepted by Lévi-Strauss, especially as practiced by Mauss and the British school of social anthropology (Lévi-Strauss, 1960). That, however, is for him only the foundation on which to erect a structural and semiological an-thropology. Fieldwork provides the empirical data—including native terminologies and texts—from which structural and semiological analy-sis constructs the unconscious categories and structures behind the level of observed facts. In these constructions the existence of subjects and their face-to face interactions with one another and the anthropolo-gist are presupposed, but are abstracted from in structural analysis.

In a metaphor reminiscent of Kroeber, Lévi-Strauss calls structural anthropology the astronomy of the social sciences, since it studies soci-eties and cultures at a distance through the telescope, rather than with microscopic observation of face-to-face community studies. In Lévi-

Strauss's semiological telescope everything looks like sign and symbol, whose hidden meanings, however, are not observable through a telescope or a microscope. They must be deciphered by the French Sherlock Holmes from the fragmentary empirical clues he finds in primitive myths, masks, and marriage practices.

In Peircean semiotic there is no transcendental ego but there is an empirical ego. Peirce's critique of the prevailing Cartesianism of modern philosophy denied that we have the powers of introspection and intuition, of thinking without signs, of universal doubt. One's self is not a thinking substance whose existence is guaranteed by thinking—*Je pense, donc je suis*. All knowledge of the internal world is derived from hypothetic inferences from knowledge of external facts. "What passes within we only know as it is mirrored in external objects" ("Pearson's Grammar of Science," Peirce [Buchler], 1955).

Becoming aware of an inner world is a developmental process deriving from observation and experience of the external world and of other people. "We first see blue and red things. It is quite a discovery when we find the eye has anything to do with them, and a discovery still more recondite when we learn that there is an *ego* behind the eye, to which these qualities belong" (Peirce [Buchler], 1955:308).

The *ego* exists in and is formed from these interactions with the external world and with other people. It is a phase in the dialogue with others and with oneself. "A person is not absolutely an individual. His thoughts are what he is 'saying to himself,' that is, saying to that other self that is just coming to life in the flow of time. When one reasons, it is that critical self that one is trying to persuade; and all thought whatever is a sign, and is mostly of the nature of language" ("The Essentials of Pragmatism," Peirce [Buchler], 1955:258).

Eco quotes from one of Peirce's early lectures a passage in a somewhat similar vein to support the thesis that semiotics either defines subjects of semiotic acts in terms of semiotic structures or cannot deal with the empirical subjects at all (Eco, 1976:316). This is an unwarranted conclusion to draw from the Peirce passage as well as from Eco's own preceding acceptance of a Peircean semiotic. Empirical subjects are included in Eco's definition of the field of semiotics and of the subject matter of his book: "In this book semiotics has been provided with a paramount subject matter, *semiosis*. Semiosis is the process by which empirical subjects communicate, communication processes being made possible by the organization of signification systems" (ibid.).

Why, given such a definition of semiosis, Eco should place the empirical subject beyond the semiotic threshold is puzzling. By accepting this limit, Eco seems to think that semiotics "fully avoids any risk of idealism" (ibid., p.317).

Peirce did not exclude the empirical subject from his doctrine of semiotic and yet he avoided an idealistic conception of the self. By locating the existence and development of the empirical ego within the process of communication, external and internal, he laid the foundations for a social theory of language, mind, and self, which was developed by William James, John Dewey, G. H. Mead, C. H. Cooley, J. M. Baldwin, Jean Piaget, Charles Morris, and came to be known as "symbolic interactionism" (Parsons, 1968).

Peirce would probably have accepted a good deal of this theory, for he regarded the dictum of the old psychology "which identified the soul with the ego, declared its absolute simplicity, and held that its faculties were names for logical divisions of human activity" as "all unadulterated fancy." He looked instead to a new psychology whose observation of facts "has now taught us that the ego is a mere wave of the soul, a superficial and small feature, that the soul may contain several personalities and is as complex as the brain itself, and that the faculties, while not exactly definable and not absolutely fixed, are as real as are the different convolutions of the cortex" (Peirce [Buchler] 1955:52).

FOR A SEMIOTIC ANTHROPOLOGY

In retrospect the tilt of culture theory to semiotics and semiology in the 1960s was no accident. It was a logical next step that followed important developments in anthropological theory as well as in other disciplines. By the 1950s some anthropologists and sociologists had recognized and explicitly formulated the concepts of culture and society as complementary, quasi-independent and interconnected systems. This formulation represented a contraction of the long-standing definitions of culture and society as all-inclusive and rival concepts. The more restricted formulations tended to define "culture" as some kind of symbol system, and "society" as sets of social relations among individual actors or among groups of actors. The specification of what kinds of symbols systems cultures were made of and how these were related to social action, to individual personalities, and to ecological conditions began to be explored in the 1960s and 1970s in the work of Lévi-Strauss, Geertz, Schneider, Leach, and Victor Turner, among others. These explorations in culture theory coincide with and draw upon a veritable explosion in the general theories of signs and symbols, and particularly in the *semiology* of Saussure and in Peirce's *semiotic*, both of which have become international and interdisciplinary movements.

Lévi-Strauss has acknowledged Saussure as a source for his semiology and structural anthropology, and he also acknowledges Jakobson and Trubetzkoy, structural linguistics generally, nonmetrical mathematics, cybernetics, and the theory of games and much else. The Indiana University Conference on Paralinguistics and Kinesics encompassed a similar sweep of disciplines and specialized developments in psychology, medicine, philosophy of language, ethnology, literary and art criticism, and other fields. This interdisciplinary scope of discussion was also characteristic of the 1960s conferences and publications on semiotics and semiology in the Soviet Union, Poland, France, Italy, Israel, the United States, and elsewhere (Sebeok, 1975).

As a result of these developments culture theory now confronts two major options—whether to become a branch of *semiology*, as Lévi-Strauss, Barthes, and Leach have proposed, or to follow a Peircean *semiotics*, as Margaret Mead, Sebeok, and Geertz have done to some extent. The choice between these options, and the consequences of each choice, can be clarified by an ideal-typical comparison of semiology and semiotics as general theories of signs, as well as through a historical study of their associations with culture theory.

The publication of some of Peirce's letters to Lady Welby and other selections from his writings in the appendixes to Ogden and Richards's *Meaning of Meaning* brought his semiotic theory to the notice of anthropologists as early as 1923. Malinowski, e.g., whose essay on "The Problem of Meaning in Primitive Languages" was also included as an appendix to the Ogden and Richards volume, adapted the use of Ogden and Richards's semantic triangle, which was a simplified version of Peirce's semiotic triad. Lloyd Warner in turn extended the triangle to his analysis of Murngin totemism (1937) and then to his study of Yankee City memorial and tercentenary ceremonies (1959).

Semiotic tends to develop a theory of signs that is philosophical and normative ("quasi-necessary"), takes as its primary subject matter the formalized languages of logic, mathematics, and the special sciences, with some illustrations from the vernacular. It defines the nature of signs and sign processes in terms of an irreducible triadic relation of *sign–object–interpretant*, and it includes within this analysis externally real objects as well as empirical subjects or egos. Peirce has made his definitions of the sign and of semiosis sufficiently abstract and general to apply to cases of nonhuman semiosis, if there should be such, as well as to mixed cases of "natural signs" of weather, diseases, etc., where there are no utterers.

At the opposite pole, semiology develops a general theory of signs that tends to be a descriptive and comparative study of "natural languages" and their literatures, oral and written. Defining the linguistic sign in terms of a dyadic relation between signifier and signified, it can find no place within its analysis for either externally given objects or for empirical subjects, although the existence of both empirical objects and egos are presupposed.

Lévi-Strauss's structural analyses of South and North American Indian myths and legends showed the possibilities of a semiological anthropology. He has also proposed application of the approach to other culture domains—kinship and marriage, ritual, economic exchange, cuisine—within a unified theory of communication. Jakobson (1971), who approves of that proposal, also points out that it requires different levels of analysis for different cultural domains. Boon and Schneider (1976) have shown how these different levels operate in Lévi-Strauss's treatments of myth and kinship.

Barthes (1963), Leach (1976), and others have interpreted semiology as a generalized linguistics and have suggested how it can be applied to food, clothes, furniture, architecture, traffic signals, as "languages" and "codes."

Without wishing to deny the fruitful ingenuity of a semiological analysis of culture, or accepting Sperber's criticisms of Lévi-Strauss as a semiologist, I would urge the application of Peircean semiotic to the problems of culture theory. In keeping with Peirce's ethics of terminology, I suggest that we call such explorations "semiotic anthropology." In one important respect, at least, a semiotic theory of signs has a distinct advantage over a semiological theory: it can deal with some of the difficult problems generated by acceptance of the complementarity of cultural and social systems. Because semiology limits itself to a theory of signification and linguistic codes, it cannot deal with the problems of how the different cultural "languages" are related to empirical objects and egos, to individual actors and groups. The existence of such extra-linguistic relations is, of course, recognized by semiologists, but the study of them is relegated to other disciplines—psychology, sociology, economics, geography, and history. They do not enter directly and essentially into a semiological analysis.

In a semiotic anthropology, on the contrary, it is possible to deal with such extralinguistic relations within the framework of semiotic theory, because *a semiotic anthropology is a pragmatic anthropology*. It contains a theory of how systems of signs are related to their meanings as well as to the objects designated and to the experience and behavior of the sign users.

Peircean semiotic is a "pragmatic semiotic," as Morris aptly calls it (1970: chap. II). Morris refers particularly to the important point that "pragmatism, more than any other philosophy, has embedded semiotic in a theory of action or behavior. The relation of a sign to what it signifies always involves the mediation of an interpretant, and an interpretant is an action or tendency to action of an organism" (1970: p.40).

This formulation of the pragmatic aspect of semiotic reflects the extensions added by James, Dewey, Mead, C. I. Lewis, and Morris himself. It has, however, a foundation in Peirce's formulation of the fundamental maxim of pragmatism: "The most perfect account of a concept that words can convey will consist in a description of the habit which that concept is calculated to produce. But how otherwise can a habit be described than by a description of the kind of action to which it gives rise, with the specification of the conditions and of the motive?" (in Morris, 1970:24).

This particular formulation of the pragmatic maxim, as Morris notes, coincides with Peirce's definition of the *final interpretant* of intellectual concepts and is therefore an essential component of his semiotic. Peirce also distinguishes two other kinds of interpretants, the *emotional interpretant*, which is a kind of first impression created by the sign in the mind of the interpreter, and the *energetic interpretant*, which is an interpreter's direct reaction to a sign, expressed in verbal or nonverbal behavior.

There are two other pragmatic features implied by Peirce's semiotic theory of signs: the very definition of a sign in terms of a triadic relation of sign, object, and interpretant includes an essential reference to the sign user. Similarly Peirce's conception of sign processes (semiosis) as a process of growth and development of signs from other signs depends on the persuasive force of signs in the mind of the interpreter.

"Pragmatics" has gotten a bad name in contrast to the more rigorous "syntactics" and "semantics" because it has not until recently been greatly formalized and also because it has been regarded as a vague residual category. As a result, there have emerged two counter tendencies aiming to redefine "pragmatics": (1) as a study of indexical signs

(Jakobson, 1971; Silverstein, 1976), (2) as a formalization of a theory of indexical signs (Montague, 1974). It is to be hoped that these useful recent developments will not lead us to abandon Peirce's broader conception of a pragmatic semiotic or discourage its application to the problems of a semiotic anthropology. For as the reclusive Yankee Yogi explained to Lady Welby, a new scientific field, such as the study of signs, can be best delimited in terms of a community of scholars prepared to devote themselves to that field.

"I smiled at your speaking of my having been 'kindly interested' in your work, as if it were a divergence—I should say a deviation—from my ordinary line of attention. . . . It has never been in my power to study anything—mathematics, ethics, metaphysics, gravitation, thermodynamics, optics, chemistry, comparative anatomy, astronomy, psychology, phonetics, economics, the history of science, whist, men and women, wine, meteorology, except as a study of semiotic. . . . How . . . rarely I have met any who cares to understand my studies, I need not tell you. . ." (Welby, *Other Dimensions*, pp.304–305).

"I am satisfied that in the present state of the subject, there is but one general science of the nature of Signs. If we were to separate it into two,—then according to my idea that a 'science'—as scientific men use the word, implies a social group of devotees, we should be in imminent danger of erecting two groups of one member each! Whereas if you and I stick together, we are, at least, two of us. . . . We shall have to try to seduce one of the linguists to our more fundamental study" (Peirce, *Collected Papers* 8.378).

In the 65 or more years since Peirce wrote these words, the "dialogical" community of scholars devoting themselves to semiotic studies has multiplied many-fold. There are many signs that some members of this community are prepared to explore the application of Peirce's quasi-necessary doctrine of signs to the problems of anthropology.

REFERENCES AND BIBLIOGRAPHY

I.   RECENT SYMBOLIC THEORIES OF CULTURE AND SOCIETY

Bateson, G. 1972. *Steps to an Ecology of Mind.* New York: Ballantine Books.
———. 1958[1936]. *Naven.* Stanford: Stanford University Press.
Cohen, A. 1974. *Two Dimensional Man.* Berkeley: University of California Press.

Douglas, M. 1970. *Natural Symbols.* New York: Pantheon Books.

Firth, R. 1973. *Symbols: Public and Private.* Ithaca: Cornell University Press.

Geertz, C. 1973. *The Interpretation of Cultures.* New York: Basic Books.

Goodenough, W. H. 1974[1971]. "Culture, Language, and Society." Reading, Mass.: Addison-Wesley. Module in Anthropology, no.7.

Hymes, D. 1971. "Sociolinguistics and the Ethnography of Speaking." In *Social Anthropology and Language*, E. Ardener, ed. London: Tavistock.

Keesing, R. M. 1974. "Theories of Culture." In *Annual Review of Anthropology*, vol.3, B. J. Siegel et al., eds.

Leach, E. 1970. *Claude Lévi-Strauss.* New York: The Viking Press.

————. 1976. *Culture and Communication.* London: Cambridge University Press.

Lévi-Strauss, C. 1963, 1976. *Structural Anthropology*, vols. I and II. New York: Basic Books.

————. 1966. "The Scope of Anthropology." *Current Anthropology* 7, no.2 (April).

McQuown, N. A. 1972. "The Nature of Culture." In *Studies in Linguistics in Honor of George L. Trager*, M. E. Smith, ed. The Hague: Mouton.

Munn, N. 1974. *Walbiri Iconography.* Ithaca: Cornell University Press.

Peacock, J. 1975. *Consciousness and Change.* New York: John Wiley.

Piaget, J. 1971. *Structuralism.* New York: Harper and Row.

Schneider, D. M. 1968. *American Kinship: A Cultural Account.* Englewood Cliffs, N.J.: Prentice-Hall.

————. 1976. "Notes Toward a Theory of Culture." In *Meaning in Anthropology*, K. Basso and H. Selby, eds. Albuquerque: University of New Mexico Press.

Sebeok, T. A.; Hayes, A. S.; and Bateson, M. C.; eds. 1964. *Approaches to Semiotics.* The Hague: Mouton.

Spencer, R. F., ed. 1969. "Forms of Symbolic Action." In *Proceedings of the American Ethnological Society.* Seattle: University of Washington Press.

Sperber, D. 1974. *Rethinking Symbolism.* London: Cambridge University Press.

Turner, V. 1968. "Myths and Symbols." *IESS.*

————. 1974. *Dramas, Fields, and Metaphors.* Ithaca: Cornell University Press.

————. 1974. "Liminal to Liminoid, in Play, Flow, and Ritual." *Rice University Studies.*

————. 1975. "Symbolic Studies." In *Annual Review of Anthropology*, vol.4, B. J. Siegel et al., eds. Pp.145–61.

Tyler, S., ed. 1969. *Cognitive Anthropology.* New York: Holt, Rinehart and Winston.

II.   Culture and Society as Complementary Concepts

Eggan, F. 1974. "Among the Anthropologists." In *Annual Review of Anthropology*, vol.3, B. J. Siegel et al., eds.

————, ed. 1955[1937]. *Social Anthropology of North American Tribes.* Chicago: University of Chicago Press.

Firth, R. 1951. *Elements of Social Organization.* London: Watts.

Fortes, M., and Dieterlen, G., eds. 1965. *African Systems of Thought.* London: Oxford University Press.

Geertz, C. 1973. "The Impact of the Concept of Culture on the Concept of Man." In *The Interpretation of Cultures.* New York: Basic Books.

Kroeber, A. L. 1952. *The Nature of Culture.* Chicago: University of Chicago Press.

Kroeber, A. L., and Kluckhohn, C. 1963. *Culture: A Critical Review of Concepts and Definitions.* New York: Vintage.

Kroeber, A. L., and Parsons, T. 1958. "The Concepts of Culture and of Social System." *American Sociological Review* 23:582–83.

Lévi-Strauss, C. 1963[1962]. *Totemism.* Boston: Beacon Press.

Murdock, G. P. 1971. "Anthropology's Mythology." Huxley Memorial Lecture. *Proc. RAI.*

Parsons, T. 1972. "Culture and Social System Revisited." *Social Science Quarterly* 53:253–66.

Radcliffe-Brown, A. R. 1952. "Introduction" to *Structure and Function in Primitive Society.* London: Cohen and West.

————. 1957. *A Natural Science of Society.* New York: The Free Press.

————. 1958. *Method in Social Anthropology,* M. N. Srinivas, ed. Chicago: University of Chicago Press.

Redfield, R. 1941. *The Folk Culture of Yucatan.* Chicago: University of Chicago Press.

————. 1962. "Anthropological Understanding of Man" and "Societies and Cultures as Natural Systems." In *Human Nature and Society,* M. P. Redfield, ed. Chicago: University of Chicago Press.

Richards, A. I. 1967. "African Systems of Thought: An Anglo-French Dialogue." *Man, the Journal of the Royal Anthropological Institute,* n.s. vol.2, no.2.

Schneider, D. M. 1968. "Rivers and Kroeber in the Study of Kinship." In *Kinship and Social Organization,* W. H. R. Rivers, ed. New York: Humanities Press.

Schneider, L., and Bonjean, C., eds. 1973. *The Idea of Culture in the Social Sciences.* London: Cambridge University Press.

Singer, M. 1960. "A Survey of Personality and Culture Theory and Research." In *Studying Personality Cross-Culturally,* B. Kaplan, ed. New York: Harper and Row.

————. 1968. "Culture." *International Encyclopedia of the Social Sciences.*

————. 1972. *When a Great Tradition Modernizes.* New York: Praeger.

————. 1973. "A Neglected Source of Structuralism: Radcliffe-Brown, Whitehead and Russell." Paper prepared for A.S.A. Colloquium, Oxford.

————. 1976. "Robert Redfield's Development of a Social Anthropology of Civilizations." In *American Anthropology. The Early Years,* J. Murra, ed. St. Paul, Minn.: West Publishing Co.

Srinivas, M. N. 1952. *Religion and Society among the Coorgs of South India*. London and New York: Oxford University Press.

Stocking, G. W., Jr. 1968. "Matthew Arnold, E. B. Tylor, and the Uses of Invention" and "Franz Boas and the Culture Concept in Historical Perspective." In *Race, Culture, and Evolution*. New York: The Free Press.

White, L., and Dillingham, B. 1973. *The Concept of Culture*. Minneapolis: Burgess.

Wolf, E. R. 1974[1964]. *Anthropology*. New York: W. W. Norton.

III.   THE GENERAL THEORY OF SIGNS: PEIRCE'S
SEMIOTIC AND SAUSSURE'S SEMIOLOGY

1. Philosophical Theories

Carnap, R. 1955[1938]. "Foundations of Logic and Mathematics." *International Encyclopedia of Unified Science*. Chicago.

————. 1956[1947]. *Meaning and Necessity, A Study in Semantics and Modal Logic*. Chicago: University of Chicago Press.

Cassirer, E. 1953. *Philosophy of Symbolic Forms*, 3 vols. New Haven: Yale University Press.

Cherry, C. 1968. *On Human Communication*. Cambridge: MIT Press.

Davidson, D., and Harman, G., eds. 1972. *Semantics of Natural Language*. New York: Humanities Press.

Derrida, J. 1973. *Speech and Phenomena and Other Essays on Husserl's Theory of Signs*. Evanston: Northwestern University Press.

Dewey, J. 1930. *Human Nature and Conduct*. New York: Modern Library.

Eco, U. 1976. *A Theory of Semiotics*. Bloomington: Indiana University Press.

Gallie, W. B. 1966. *Peirce and Pragmatism*. New York: Dover.

Greenberg, J. H. 1957. "Language as a Sign System." In *Essays in Linguistics*. Chicago: University of Chicago Press.

Habermas, J. 1971. *Knowledge and Human Interests*. Boston: Beacon Press.

Lacan, J. 1968. *Language of the Self*. Baltimore: Johns Hopkins University Press.

Langer, S. 1942. *Philosophy in a New Key*. Cambridge: Harvard University Press.

Mead, G. H. 1924–25. "The Genesis of the Self and Social Control." *Int. J. Ethics*, XXXV:251–77.

————. 1927. "A Behavioristic Account of the Significant Symbol." *J. Phil.* 19:157–63.

Merleau-Ponty, M. 1964. *Signs*. Evanston: Northwestern University Press.

Miller, D. L. 1973. *George Herbert Mead: Self, Language and the World*. Austin: University of Texas Press.

Morris, C. W. 1971. *Writings on the General Theory of Signs*. The Hague: Mouton.

————. 1970. *The Pragmatic Movement in American Philosophy*. New York: Braziller.

Natanson, M. 1956. *The Social Dynamics of George Herbert Mead*. Washington, D.C.: Public Affairs Press.

Ogden, C. K., and Richards, I. A. 1923. *The Meaning of Meaning*. New York: Harcourt, Brace.

Parsons, T. 1968. "Social Interaction." In *International Encyclopedia of Social Sciences* 7:429–41.

Peirce, C. S. 1931ff. *Collected Papers*, 8 vols. Cambridge: Harvard University Press.

———. 1955. *Philosophical Writings of Peirce*, J. Buchler, ed. New York: Dover.

Quine, W. 1960. *Word and Object*. Cambridge: MIT Press.

———. 1973. *The Roots of Reference*. La Salle, Ill.: Open Court.

Ricoeur, P. 1970. "The Model of the Text: Meaningful Action Considered as a Text." *Social Research* 1970:529–62.

Russell, B. 1940. *An Inquiry into Meaning and Truth*. New York: Humanities Press.

Searle, J., ed. 1971. *The Philosophy of Language*. London: Oxford University Press.

Sebeok, T. A. 1974. "Semiotics: A Survey of the State of the Art." In *Current Trends in Linguistics*. The Hague: Mouton.

———. 1975. "The Semiotic Web: A Chronicle of Prejudices." *Bulletin of Literary Semiotics* 2:1–63.

———. 1976. " 'Semiotics' and Its Congeners." In *Contributions to the Doctrine of Signs*. Bloomington, Ind.: Research Center for Language and Semiotic Studies.

Tarski, A. 1956. "The Establishment of Scientific Semantics" and "The Concept of Truth in Formalized Languages." In *Logic, Semantics, and Metamathematics*. London: Oxford University Press.

Thompson, M. 1953. *The Pragmatic Philosophy of C. S. Peirce*. Chicago: University of Chicago Press.

Welby, V. 1903. *What Is Meaning?* London: Macmillan and Co., Ltd.

———. 1903, 1911. *Significs and Language*. London: Macmillan and Co., Ltd.

———. 1931. *Other Dimensions*. London: Jonathan Cape.

Whitehead, A. N. 1959. *Symbolism: Its Meaning and Effect*. New York: Putnam.

Wittgenstein, L. 1958. *Philosophical Investigations*. New York: Macmillan Co.

2. *The General Theory of Signs: Linguistic and Literary Theories*

Barthes, R. 1970[1963]. *Elements of Semiology*. Boston: Beacon Press.

Benveniste, E. 1971. *Problems in General Linguistics*. Coral Gables, Fla.: University of Miami Press.

Boas, F. 1911. "Introduction" to *Handbook of American Indian Languages*, Pt. I. B.A.E. Bull. 40. Washington, D.C.: Government Printing Office.

Boon, J. 1972. *From Symbolism to Structuralism*. New York: Harper and Row.

Burke, K. 1966. *Language as Symbolic Action*. Berkeley: University of California Press.

Carroll, J. B., ed. 1956. *Language, Thought, and Reality: Selected Writings of Benjamin Lee Whorf*. Cambridge: MIT Press.

Chomsky, N. 1968. *Language and Mind*. New York: Harcourt, Brace.

Friedrich, P. 1975. "The Lexical Symbol and Its Relative Non-arbitrariness." In *Linguistics and Anthropology: In Honor of C. F. Voegelin*, M. Dale Kinkade, Kenneth L. Hale, and Oswald Werner, eds. Lisse: Peter de Ridder Press. Pp.199–247.

Greenberg, J. H. 1957. *Essays in Linguistics*. Chicago: University of Chicago Press.

————, ed. 1963. *Universals in Language*. Cambridge: MIT Press.

Greimas, A., ed. 1970. *Sign, Language, Culture*. The Hague: Janua Linguam Ser., Maior 1.

Hoijer, H., ed. 1954. *Language in Culture*. Chicago: University of Chicago Press.

Jakobson, R. 1975. "Coup d'oeil sur le développement de la semiotique." Bloomington, Ind.: Research Center for Language and Semiotic Studies.

Kristeva, J.; Rey-Debove, J.; and Umiker, D. J. 1971. *Essays in Semiotics*. The Hague: Mouton.

Lyons, J. 1968. *Introduction to Theoretical Linguistics*. London: Cambridge University Press.

Macksey, R., and Donato, E. 1970. *The Languages of Criticism and the Sciences of Man: The Structuralism Controversy*. Baltimore: Johns Hopkins University Press.

Sapir, E. 1949. *Selected Writings in Language, Culture, and Personality*. Berkeley: University of California Press.

Saussure, F. 1954. *Course in General Linguistics*. New York: Philosophical Library.

Sebeok, T. A., ed. 1960. *Style in Language*. Cambridge: MIT Press.

Segre, C. 1973. *Semiotics and Literary Criticism*. The Hague: Mouton.

Silverstein, M. 1972. "Linguistic Theory: Syntax, Semantics, Pragmatics." In *Annual Review of Anthropology*, vol. 1, B. J. Siegel, et al., eds. Pp.349–82.

————, ed. 1971. *Whitney on Language*. Cambridge: MIT Press.

Weinreich, U. 1968. "Semantics and Semiotics." In *International Encyclopedia of Social Sciences* 14:164–69.

Wells, R. 1967. "Distinctively Human Semiotic." *Social Science Information* 6:103–24.

IV.   FOR A SEMIOTIC ANTHROPOLOGY

Firth, R. 1973. *Symbols: Public and Private*. Ithaca: Cornell University Press.

Fortes, M. 1966. "Totem and Taboo." *Proceedings of the RAI*.

Geertz, C. 1973. *The Interpretation of Cultures*. New York: Basic Books.

————. 1974. "From the Natives' Point of View: On the Nature of Anthropological Understanding." *Bull. Amer. Acad. of Arts and Sciences*, Oct.

Hymes, D., and Gumperz, J. J., eds. 1970. *Directions in Sociolinguistics: The Ethnography of Speaking*. New York: Holt, Rinehart and Winston.

Jakobson, R. 1971. *Selected Writings II*. The Hague: Mouton. Especially "Linguistics and Communication Theory" (1961), "Linguistics in Relation to Other Sciences" (1967), and "Language in Relation to Other Communication Systems" (1968).

Lévi-Strauss, C. 1963, 1976. *Structural Anthropology*, vols. I and II. New York: Basic Books.

Malinowski, B. 1923. "The Problem of Meaning in Primitive Languages." In *The Meaning of Meaning*, C. K. Ogden and I. A. Richards, eds. New York: Harcourt, Brace.

Montague, R. 1974. *Formal Philosophy*. New Haven: Yale University Press.

Morris, C. W. 1955. *Signs, Language and Behavior*. New York: Braziller.

————. 1970. *The Pragmatic Movement in American Philosophy*. New York: Braziller.

Munn, N. 1974. *Walbiri Iconography*. Ithaca: Cornell University Press.

Peacock, J. 1975. *Consciousness and Society*. New York: Wiley and Sons.

Sahlins, M. 1976. *Culture and Practical Reason*. Chicago: University of Chicago Press.

Schneider, D. M. 1968. "Rivers and Kroeber in the Study of Kinship." In *Kinship and Social Organization*, W. H. R. Rivers, ed. New York: Humanities Press.

————. 1976. "Notes Toward a Theory of Culture." In *Meaning in Anthropology*, K. Basso and H. Selby, eds. Albuquerque: University of New Mexico Press.

Sebeok, T. A. 1972. *Perspectives in Zoosemiotics*. The Hague: Mouton.

Silverstein, M. 1976. "Shifters, Linguistic Categories, and Cultural Description." In *Meaning in Anthropology*, K. Basso and H. Selby, eds. Albuquerque: University of New Mexico Press.

Singer, M. 1972. *When a Great Tradition Modernizes*. New York: Praeger. Especially "Text and Context in the Study of Hinduism" and "Search for a Great Tradition in Cultural Performances."

————. 1978. "The Symbolic and Historic Structure of an American Identity." *Ethos*. In press.

Sperber, D. 1974. *Symbolism Reconsidered*. London: Cambridge University Press.

Spiro, M. E. 1970. *Buddhism and Society: A Great Tradition and Its Burmese Vicissitudes*. New York: Harper and Row.

Staal, J. F. 1971. "What Was Left of Pragmatics in Jerusalem." *Language Sciences* 14:29–32.

Turner, T. S. 1976. "Narrative Structure and Mythopoesis." Ms.

Wallis, M. 1975. *Arts and Signs*. Bloomington, Ind.: Research Center for Language and Semiotic Studies.

Warner, W. L. 1958[1937]. *A Black Civilization*. New York: Harper and Row.

————. 1959. *The Living and the Dead: A Study of the Symbolic Life of Americans*. New Haven: Yale University Press.

A Semiotic Approach to Religion

Boris Ogibenin

Much has been said about religion, and this may be attributed to the fact that religion offers an explanation for the mental life of man. Indeed, quite frequently, such an explanation takes on as much importance as existence itself. For if we only had accurate and full descriptions of the religious systems of the many societies, ancient and modern, we might be able to trace both their cultural and their extra-cultural histories. It is taken for granted here that: (1) Religion is an all-encompassing system through which the manifold semantics of human culture and man's experiences can be comprehended. Hence, any religious system tends to be fully comprehending and its categories are those of human experience. (2) Religion is a modeling system; thus, there is no direct correspondence between it and categories of human experience since modeling does not imply mere reflection.

Melford E. Spiro has defined religion in such a way that leaves many questions open for the semiotician: "I shall define 'religion' as an 'institution consisting of culturally patterned interaction with culturally postulated superhuman beings'" (1969:96). It should be noted,

The first draft of this article was delivered as a lecture at the Research Center of King's College, University of Cambridge; the final version was completed at Indiana University, Bloomington, for the Pilot Program in Semiotics in March 1976. I would like to thank Professor Edmund R. Leach and Thomas A. Sebeok for the opportunity of staying at these two universities.

however, that although Spiro proceeds to briefly explain what is meant by *interaction, institution,* and *superhuman beings* on a universal level, he presents them in a manner that is predominantly Christian. Unfortunately, it seems to be a general rule that anything that we try to explain is assigned to the concepts that we already have. Thus, unavoidably, our explanations appear to be the intersections of our conceptualizations with those of another.

Piatigorsky has written a remarkable passage on this problem, in trying to explain what a strange world Buddhism is to one not acquainted with it.

It seems to me that there are at least two possibilities of getting comfortable in an absolutely new house you are invited in. The first possibility is to try the language . . . of this house, that is, to try to translate the strange words of this language into those of one's own, i.e., in seeking and finding equivalents, analogies and parallels in one's own house in order to become accustomed to the new one. The second possibility is to try to understand *anew* the words of one's own language, i.e., first of all to understand some words which were not understood before, but seemed to be, and only after that to try simply living in the new house with a new understanding of one's old. I think that the stranger and newer [a] thing is, the less must be the importance of translating and the greater of understanding it. Buddhist philosophy is really one of the strangest things ever to happen in time and space. Therefore, in my opinion at least, it requires of a person an absolutely new mode of thinking about things which are old, common, and even truistic. In other words, one has to try philosophizing in a strange way long before being admitted (by oneself, of course) into the strange *system* of Buddhist philosophy (first step), then one has to try systematizing one's philosophizing, i.e., to create some metatheory (concerning the real existing Buddhist theory), and only after that can one live (wrongly or rightly, properly or improperly) in the new house (world) of Buddhist words and notions. [Piatigorsky, 1975:2]

The approach explicated by Piatigorsky seems to be the only realistic one. Sociologists and, in particular, those studying religion rightly complain that the interaction of both observer and observed—in this case, society or religious categories—presents an uneasy situation (Goody, 1961:156–57; Goody even reports P. Winch's opinion that "all sociology is impossible since the observer can never get outside the conceptual apparatus of his own society nor, conversely, inside that of any other"). It follows, then, that if we succeed in creating a metatheory of religious thinking and put as a first step the questions of a particular religion, such an approach may help in developing a further synthesis. Creating a metatheory within semiotic vistas accentuates not so much what we should understand in a religion (Spiro, 1969:92–94, may be right when he insists that superhuman beings are accounted for even in Theravada Buddhism, where, unlike ordinary human beings, Buddha acquires the power of attaining Enlightenment) but what the particular religion we are studying communicates either to its practitioners or to us. A semiotic metatheory does not include discussions of whether—to take a most controversial issue—the sacred or the profane is present and, if so, in what forms; rather, it examines which features and which categories are structurally relevant within a religion, which of them signify and what they signify within that religion. Religion is treated, then, as a self-sufficient system for interpreting man and his world within a socio-communicative matrix. Adding the dimension of communication does not change our understanding of religious phenomena. The theoretical framework proposed by Clifford Geertz is, after all, very close to the semiotic conception of religion and culture—so much so that he defines culture as "a system of inherited conceptions by means of which men communicate, perpetuate, and develop their knowledge about and attitudes toward life" (Geertz, 1969:3). Geertz, then, has cast his definition of religion in accordance with this conception of culture:

> religion is (1) a system of symbols which acts to (2) establish powerful, pervasive, and long-lasting moods and motivations in men by (3) formulating conceptions of a general order of existence and (4) clothing these conceptions with such an aura of factuality that (5) the moods and motivations seem uniquely realistic. [Geertz, 1969:4]

I will comment, below, on this conception, which is a succinct formulation of some fundamental principles—although I do not find all the implications that Geertz discusses acceptable.

First, let us look at the concept of motivation. Motivations for Geertz are of two kinds: motives and moods. The formal difference between them is that moods (for example, a 'reverential', 'solemn', or 'worshipful' mood) occur under particular circumstances; they are 'made meaningful' with reference to the conditions from which they are thought to spring. Motives are vectorial qualities described as liabilities that perform particular classes of act or have particular classes of feeling; they are 'made meaningful' with regard to the ends toward which they are thought to conduce (Geertz, 1969:11–12). Motivations are to my mind the essential operations that man performs across the continuum of meaning—i.e., the perceptible universe on which he tries to apply the matrix of order. That religious problems are always problems of meaning, as postulated by Weber, is quite true, but semioticians approach meaning in a more technical sense by looking for meaningful operations over a semanticized universe. The universe itself is, as it were, felt and perceived as coextensive and commensurable to the human discourse on it. Universe *is* discourse. Again, it may be said that this discourse does not need to be specifically religious since there are many varieties of discourse on man's universe; as Geertz points out, scientific, esthetic, or just commonsensical discourse challenges religious discourse. Rather than try to define what distinguishes religious discourse from other types of discourse, I will analyze one aspect of religious discourse —that of motivational patterns as complexes of semantic rules and operations over a meaningful whole.

One may wonder why this particular aspect of religious discourse is singled out for analysis. It is an area proper for semiotic analysis since such an analysis would insist on the manipulation of meanings by a religious subject, on the techniques of performing operations, and on the types of operations fulfilled. It seems to me that by emphasizing this point, one approaches more the essence of individual involvement in the religious understanding of the universe, since meaningful operations not only have their own meaning but also provide us with a knowledge of what a person wants when he or she faces the choice of being religious. What I have in mind is that accounting for religious experiences implies more of subjective psychology than of dealing with cultural patterns that are necessarily highly socialized and, as the semiotic approach deems it, quite mandatory. This generalization, of course, may appear questionable; its immediate justification is that I will try to delineate the most general features common to religions in societies where all of its members are involved in religious life and in those in which one can choose whether to become involved in religion or not.

One important feature of religion is that it not operate directly with worldly matters—although it was noted above that the entire universe is permeated with religious discourse. Another proper feature of religious discourse is that it coexist with mythological discourse; in fact, it may be difficult to separate the two. It is therefore advanced here that religious discourse contains a set of semantic rules and operations to be performed on mythological discourse. Looking at the relationship of these two types of discourse, one can find characteristics of both the rules and their operations. Mythological discourse intercedes between worldly discourse—that is, if it can be assumed that the world communicates with us—and religious discourse.

If one compares the meaning of operations produced within a religion and within a mythology, these two complexes of organized, patterned meaning would be defined as having somewhat different relations with each other than what Geertz, for one, postulates for religion and ritual performance. Ritual performance often tends to be considered as an illustration of religious principles, belonging more to the domain of mythology than of religion; this is especially so since religion appears to be more abstract than either mythology or ritual. It is obvious that the three are somehow related, but can we say, with Geertz, that "by inducing a set of moods and motivations—an ethos—and defining an image of cosmic order—a world-view—by means of a single set of symbols, the performance makes the model *for* and model *of* aspects of religious belief mere transpositions of one another" (Geertz, 1969:34)? Here I maintain that mere transposition or, in other terms, transcoding, is not the case universally and cannot be viewed as a permanent, inherent feature of the interrelation between religion and the two domains.

Thus coming back to motivational patterns and to the question of their working within both mythology and religion, we will now give some examples from which we will later draw conclusions.

As far as scholars have been able to reconstruct, Vedic religion is not identical with Vedic mythology; however, it can be stated that the motivational patterns within both are similar. This means that what is induced, advised, or recommended by the religious ideology as taught by Vedic seers is what mythology—which *in this particular case* is shaped by religion—enhances and intensifies. If Vedic religion is predominantly a cosmogony (Kuiper, 1975:107; Ogibenin, 1973) and a cosmogonical conception of all-pervading character, it may be said that the operations supposedly carried within such a conceptual framework have been the very ones that are fulfilled the moment that religious understanding of phenomena is abandoned and their mythological interpretation is taken up. Motivation in Vedic religion, if concisely formulated for the present purposes, consists of stressing the overall importance of two essential and opposite poles, which have been expressed in a multitude of ways—now as "the being, that which is" (*sat*) *vs.* "the non-being" (*asat*), "gods" *vs.* "demons" (*asuras*), "Order (*Ṛta*) *vs.* "chaos" (*anṛta*), and so on. The whole series of bipolar concepts is valued according to the elementary binary design in which a positive term is opposed to its corresponding negative term. This patterning is, however, intermediary between the concept that the universe was first undifferentiated and the notion of *Ṛta*, the "Order" and "Truth" on which the welfare of the world depends. The basic philosophy reflected in these concepts is followed by the mythology of the Vedic texts, which, in fact, is ruled by them. It may appear quite trivial that a mythology that operates with less abstract material is modeled on the premises of a set of more abstract ideas. It is, however, valuable to take advantage of this in order to see the basic congruence between religious presuppositions and assumptions and the body of mythological signs.

Vedic mythology makes extensive use of the same patterning of motivations that is most probably clothed in a series of binary oppositions that are structurally similar to those that have been mentioned above. A created universe is thus valued positively as against an uncreated one, i.e., the realm of chaos. The Vedic universe is in fact considered to be the universe in which normal human existence can be carried on, while the non-Vedic universe—the realm of the foes of the Vedic man—is doomed. Vedic man's microcosm is opposed to non-Vedic man's microcosm. As in religious thinking, mythological patterning includes the concept of an all-encompassing totality: in fact, the god Viṣṇu appears throughout the Vedic texts as one who transcends the cosmic antithesis in which *sat* and *asat* have been reconciled in the synthesis of an all-embracing entity (Kuiper, 1975:118). In some respects, if viewed in their roles as cosmogonic agents, all the other Vedic deities only reiterate the deeds that are supposed to lead to the establishment of a livable world—although these deeds are presented in various forms corresponding to aspects that are necessary for producing such a world. The main hypothesis that is being formulated here is that Vedic poets, authors of the mythological hymns, conspicuously attack the problems of environment and its conceptualization in a one-sided manner: they elaborately treat the world which they desire while the one which they reject and which would be that of their god's enemies is either given little note or not described at all. All we can know of this adversary world is that it is the inverse of, and opposed to, the Vedic world. It could be, as U. Masing (1973) suggested, that such dichotomies were only the mode of description used by the Vedic authors and that their adepts were aware of such a model and deliberately arranged their ideas on those levels. Masing (1973:18) admits though that even if "they could express their thoughts by means of some other sublanguage also, the structure of their system would . . . remain the same." The principle of bipolarity *is* pervasive, leading one to infer that here the laws of Vedic religious thinking were also determinant. As in the case of reiterating the basic structural oppositions that have been instrumental for the conception of the world, the principle has been used anew for discriminating the actions of the gods within the descriptions of Vedic man's existence; here, only one pole has been evaluated while the value of the other pole had to be *automatically inferred*.

The mythology of evil in the Veda is not as abundantly elaborated upon as in Tantric mythology or in Dante's *Inferno*. Again, all that we are allowed to know about evil is that it had to be defeated by Vedic deities so that the desired goods could be obtained within the Vedic universe. If, then, one admits that this one-sided extolling of the Vedic universe may have originated at the very outset of Vedic religious thinking and mythological speculation (since the initial dichotomizing seems to be a product of the imposition of a matrix of ordering in contradistinction to that of disordering), it may help explain why Viṣṇu, for one, has been chosen to impersonate the concept of totality. This totality, referred to also as a "third heaven" or the "highest heaven" in the *Ṛgveda*, encompasses not only chaos but also ordered cosmos; not only gods as positive agents but also, at the same time, the potential gods— the Asuras—who have been discarded to the netherworld (Kuiper, 1975:114–18). If Kuiper's explanation of the basic concept of Vedic religion is accepted, it is worthwhile to ask why it is not the god Varuṇa, the former Asura, who still preserves his connections with the *asuras* since he is their jailer, as *Mahābhārata* narrates it, and who accordingly is an ambiguous figure. One may think that, in accordance with the dominant semantic operation, Vedic religion prescribes the promotion of only a positively evaluated personage of the mythology to the rank of a symbol of totality, even though an ambiguous personage possesses all the requisite qualities when viewed from the standpoint of their significant values within the structure of the mythology.

This semantic operation may be considered dominant, thereby commanding other structurally relevant operations within the mythology. Dichotomizing and positively valuing one element of the dichotomy

are most likely to be connected with the fact that whatever was subjected to this operation was designed to saturate the meaningful field
of mythology. In other words, once positive meanings were proclaimed
as valued, the sets of meaningful elements in general increased. Non-
positive meanings were not described at all; rather, as mentioned
above, they have been designated as functions of positive meanings,
i.e., brought within the signified and sensible field through the operation of relating them to the set of positive meanings.

Mythology is always concrete. If the religious system is really one
that provides rules for handling the meanings and values within a
mythology, this should hold even in the case of a more complex mythology. It is not implied here that Vedic mythology is a simple system;
we only mean that the rules and the structures on which these rules
operate are more conspicuous than in, say, Purāṇic mythology. It is still
possible, however, to elicit some overtly formulated rules and operations by comparing the doctrinal teachings of the Purāṇas with their
mythological presentation.

It is known that in such religious works as the *Bhāgavata Purāṇa* the
most important tenet that is taught and preached is *bhakti*, the devotion
to the Lord Kṛṣṇa or Viṣṇu. The purpose of *bhakti* is to destroy man's
attachment to worldly values; *bhakti* alone is likely to bring salvation to
an individual, but such salvation is mainly understood to be total concentration on the person of Bhagavān (The Blessed Lord). As the texts
assembled by Thomas J. Hopkins (1971; Hopkins's article also interprets
other aspects of the same teachings) show, the doctrine makes constant
use of two levels and two sets of meaningful elements. The two sets
obviously correspond to the levels in such a way that the level of selfless
devotion to the Lord reworks the elements of secular life and transforms
them into the elements of devotional and religious life. It is explicitly
demonstrated that attachment may be of two kinds: attachment to the
world of senses, and attachment and devotion to Bhagavān. Uncon-
trolled thinking is conducive to increasing one's attachment to the
world, whereas thinking under the control of *bhaktiyoga* helps one to
concentrate on Bhagavān. Moreover, almost any human act that is felt
to be alien to the ritualism of the true devotee of Kṛṣṇa—even those
that are accomplished as religious acts within Vedic ritualism—can be
classified in view of its value toward increasing devotion to Bhagavān.
As written in the *Bhāgavata Purāṇa*:

What [is accomplished] by what is heard (i.e., the Vedas) or by religious austerity, by commands or the activities of thought? What by skilled intellect, strength, or the power of senses?

Wandering in the Veda, which is difficult to get through and is extremely extensive, and worshipping intermittently with ceremonies having the sacred texts as their characteristic feature, they have not known the Highest.

When Bhagavān, self-created, favors a person, that person lays aside thought that is thoroughly dependent on the world and on the Vedas. [*Bhāgavata Purāṇa* IV. 31.11–12 and IV. 29.44–47; translated by Hopkins, 1971:12]

In a more sophisticated manner, the same *Purāṇa* rejects acts that are not aimed at Bhagavān's devotion even though Bhagavān himself is embodied in everything, including human acts:

Thus having heard Bhagavān's request, they whose desires were mean, whose acts were many, fools whose pride was great, did not listen.

Because of seeing [Him as] human, these stupid mortals did not honor Bhagavān Adhokṣaja, that highest Brahman in person,
Of Whom consist place, time, various articles, prayers, Tantras, priests, fires, divinity, sacrificing, worship and *dharma*. [*Bhāgavata Purāṇa* X.23.9–11; translated by Hopkins, 1971:13]

It appears that there are unmarked acts *vs.* marked ones. The former belong to the level of worldly life, where devotion to Bhagavān is not practiced, while the latter are the same elements of worldly life (which include rituals of Vedic origin) that are introduced within the realm of devotional life. The category of the Lord Bhagavān, if seen as a unit of religious structure, appears to be a cover category in which both marked and unmarked acts and elements merge. Mythology may well distinguish between both: *bhakti*, treated as an imperative goal within such a system of values and goals, may thus eliminate minute distinctions.

Religious doctrine may also formulate principles that can be illustratively revealed by specially arranged texts that portray these abstract principles. These texts may, however, contradict or use a given technique that responds to the doctrine. This is perhaps where the elegant ingenuity of Buddhist parables lies. Let us look now at two such parables.

When King Milinda asked the Reverend Nāgasena to explain one of the subtle problems of Buddhist doctrine—that of the discontinuity of personal identity, which is based on the negation of the self—the monk answered by telling two famous parables, "Embryo and child" and "Lamp and flame." The former illustrates the absence of continuity in the development of a human being, which takes place regardless of prevailing conditions; the latter describes the continually changing nature of a flame. The account that is offered is as follows.

Seen as a short narrative, the first parable relates that (I) the king's development from a being "once young, tender, weak, lying on . . . back" to an adult proves that the king could not always have been the same person. This is further confirmed by the king himself: "He that was young, tender, weak, lying on his back, was one person; I, big as I am now, am a different person" (quoted from Burlingame, 1922:204–205); (II) as Nāgasena suggests, the corollary is that the king never had a mother, a father, or a teacher, that he never acquired knowledge of the arts and crafts, and so forth. This last point is illustrated by another parable inserted within the first; this second parable relates that (a) it is possibly true that (i) the mother of a fetus in the first stage of development is one person; that (ii) the mother of the fetus in the second stage is another; and so forth. (b) It ends by asking whether the mother of the little child is one person, and the mother of a grown man is another person. The next point is (III) of the first parable; here analogous questions are asked—whether the person who is learning the arts and crafts is different from a person who has already acquired them, and whether the person who performs evil deeds is different from a person whose hands and feet are cut off. (IV) The king reverses the question; Nāgasena answers that he himself is obviously not the same person now that he is an adult, as compared to when he "was once young, tender, weak, lying . . . back," since only the dependence on his body would explain that all these states are embraced in one. Nāgasena thus reiterates point (I) of the story.

In the second story, questions are again asked in an analogous manner: (I) Is the flame that (i) burns in the first watch the same as (ii) the flame that burns in the middle watch; and (iii) is the flame that burns in the middle watch the same as (iv) the flame that burns in the last watch? (II) Since the lamp remains the same during all three watches, it is (III) stated that the lamp was only the cause of the flame that burned all night.

It should be noted that both parables are coupled in the collection

"Milindapañha" because of their overt structural similarity. Moreover, the common summary given to these two parables by Nāgasena emphasizes the doctrinal point that they illustrate: "there is an uninterrupted succession of mental and physical states. One state ceases to exist and another comes to exist. The succession is such that there is, as it were, none that precedes, none that follows. Thus it is neither that same person nor yet a different person which goes to the final summation of consciousness" (Burlingame, 1922:205).

The structuring of both parables is purposely analytic; this is shown by the segmentation indicated by the Roman numerals and the small Latin letters. The analytic nature of the exposition is shaped after the model of discontinuous reality in which everything is subjected to momentary changes. Remarkably, the parable "Embryo and child"—after stating that the king never had a mother, a father, or a teacher; that he never acquired the arts and crafts; and so forth—draws explicitly only on the example of the mother denied. Other items (father, teacher, acquisition of arts and crafts, etc.) are left for the attentive listener to analyze, and this is encouraged by both the topic under discussion and by the structuring of the parable.

It can be said that the narrative code of the parables corresponds to the dominant philosophic categories of Buddhist doctrine and, at the same time, disavows it. Its correspondence—which is in fact the correspondence of the narrative metalanguage to the semantic system of Buddhist religion—is shown by the emphasis of the iconic, which dissects the items that Nāgasena calls forth; its contradiction seems to follow from the special attitude of Buddhism toward word and sign. The discussion of this problem by Piatigorsky proves quite clearly that in Buddhism words like *I, you, person* may have been used only very carefully, as purely objectified signs (or in linguistic terminology, as "markers") of the precarious and ever changing because of the nature of the states of the speakers (Piatigorsky, 1975:9–13ff.). Nāgasena could only be too well aware of the basically approximate character of his demonstration.

We have shown here that fundamental semantic properties and characteristics that can be called the "semantic dominants" of religious thinking determine the operations that are produced on the level of mythological structure. In fact, motivations—the motives and moods of Geertz—may be either identical or dissimilar in both frameworks. It is, however, very likely that the system of religious thought precedes that of mythology with regard to the hierarchy of operations fulfilled.

The other implications that Geertz raises are beyond the scope of this paper. I was particularly interested by his "powerful, pervasive, and long-lasting moods and motivations in men," the properties of which appear to fluctuate the most.

REFERENCES

Burlingame, E. W. 1922. *Buddhist Parables*. New Haven: Yale University Press.

Geertz, C. 1969. "Religion as a Cultural System." In *Anthropological Approaches to the Study of Religion*, M. Banton, ed. London: Tavistock.

Goody, J. 1961. "Religion and Ritual: The Definition Problem." *British Journal of Sociology* 12.

Hopkins, T. J. 1971. "The Social Teaching of the *Bhāgavata Purāṇa*." In *Krishna: Myths, Rites, and Attitudes*, M. Singer, ed. Chicago and London: University of Chicago Press.

Kuiper, F. B. J. 1975. "The Basic Concept of Vedic Religion." *History of Religions* 15(2).

Masing, U. 1973. "De hermeneutica." *Communio Viatorum* 1–2.

Ogibenin, B. L. 1973. *Structure d'un mythe védique*. Paris and The Hague: Mouton.

Piatigorsky, A. 1975. "The Attitude of Buddhism Towards Word and Sign." Paper prepared in advance for participants of the Burg Wartenstein Symposium no.66, "Semiotics of Culture and Language." New York: Wenner-Gren Foundation for Anthropological Research.

Spiro, M. E. 1969. "Religion: Problems of Definition and Explanation." In *Anthropological Approaches to the Study of Religion*, M. Banton, ed. London: Tavistock.

A Semiotic Approach to Nonsense: Clowns and Limericks

Paul Bouissac

There exist, in our cultural environment, some "objects" that are commonly characterized as being nonsensical, such as clowns and limericks. Even though they are referred to as nonsense, they obviously play an important part in our sociocultural life, where they are particularly popular. It would be difficult indeed to find anybody, within the culture considered, for whom the words *clowns* and *limericks* would not trigger some mental associations and evoke some memories. It is true enough that they prosper in a state of semi-marginality and even semi-rejection, but, at the same time, they show a remarkable vitality and sophistication. One can wonder how it is possible that these forms of nonsensical patterned behavior not only exist but also are "cultivated," so to speak, with such great care. Limericks indeed involve complex poetic and semantic rules. They are nevertheless so popular that one could claim that they are one of the rare poetic genres that are really alive although the situations they describe are usually absurd with respect to physiological possibilities or social norms. The existence of clowns is equally puzzling; their performances comprise manipulation of special artifacts, stereotyped "illogical" behavior, distinctive garments

The research for this paper was supported by a J. S. Guggenheim Fellowship in 1973–74. I am indebted to Professors John A. McClelland, Eric G. Schwimmer, Ivan Karp, and Paul Perron for helpful comments and criticisms. However I am solely responsible for the interpretation presented.

and make-up, and dialogues that are spoken or mimed. Their tradition is transmitted mainly through observational learning, either in a family context or by individual apprenticeship, or even in official institutions such as the Clown College set up by Ringling Brothers Barnum and Bailey circus in Venice, Florida, or the State School for circus performers in the Soviet Union. All this collective training and the individual efforts put into their acts by the performers are curiously aimed at producing displays of apparently inadequate conduct, intellectual or physical shortcomings, impossible situations, and irrational artifacts.

But as both clowns and limericks generally trigger elation and laughter, they obviously convey some sort of meaning; they are a form of semiosis. Their nonsensical character is more than the result of haphazard combinations of words or sequences of behavior. On the contrary, they are produced by strict rules, which are not explicitly formalized but can nevertheless be negatively experienced whenever they are not strictly followed. To coin a "good" limerick is often a painstaking effort because both poetic and semantic constraints have to be obeyed; similarly, every clown knows that to make people laugh is not an easy task. These remarks, by alluding to the contextual features of the performances, point to the fact that clown antics and limericks are instances of communication and can be adequately described as messages; they therefore involve rules, codes, contextual competence, etc. They are indeed made up of signs, and, as such, they qualify as objects of semiotic analysis, although it might seem paradoxical to claim that nonsensicalness can be an essential property of some kinds of sign systems.

The purpose of this paper is not to expound a formal semiotic theory of nonsense, but rather to analyze two examples from which I will outline a tentative hypothesis regarding the semiotics of nonsense. But before introducing the examples it is necessary to sketch the background considerations that led me to formulate the problems in this manner.

One can indeed hypothesize that if clown performances and limericks are at one and the same time *nonsensical* and *noncontingential* (i.e., they are not random phenomena but culturally bound phenomena governed by rules), it is because they are meta-cultural, or meta-semiotic, messages. By this I mean that they refer to, or denote, the semiotic systems which constitute our culture. Such an operation (denoting our own cultural system by enumerating the specific rules it includes) cannot be performed if one stays within the semiotic system to which one wants to refer. Therefore if one has to consider from '"outside" the rules that

condition the meaningfulness of *normal* cultural behavior, one is bound
to produce messages that are, *in certain aspects*, meaningless with respect to these rules without being irrelevant.

To summarize this approach (which incidentally was inspired by
a remark made by A. J. Greimas[1]): the only way to "speak" meaning-
fully about meaning is to use a meaningless "language." Of course this
tentative view needs to be qualified and confronted with actual instances of nonsensical culturally bound behavior. In particular these
meta-semiotic discourses cannot be described or assessed independently
of the institutions through which they are produced and the strict conditions that regulate their performances. The reason for their existence
may be that they make some semiotic systems (more) manifest without
exposing or questioning their arbitrariness. They might also be the only
possible intellectual freedom with respect to the cultural constraints
that can be pleasurably exercised without jeopardizing the consistency
of those systems. In any case, whenever we are confronted with an instance of institutionalized nonsense, the semiotic question is: What does
that stand for with respect to our cultural norms? What kind of operations are effectuated upon these rules, which pattern our "normal"
behavior? The answer is rarely easy to give because it is altogether too
tempting to take for granted that the apparent content is the actual content of the operations considered. "Concrete" individual signs are signs
only inasmuch as they play their part in mutually definable sets of signs,
and the nature of the relationships posited and transformed may refer
to another system than the one to which the "objects" involved belong.
I have shown elsewhere that sequences of clown performances that include musical instruments and food items deal in fact exclusively with
the classification of sounds in their contextual culture.[2] Codes are commonly translated one into another as it is obvious in the metaphorical
process. It might even be hypothesized that a condition for engaging in
meta-semiotic discourses is such a translation. If this is the case it cannot be assumed, for example, that an obscene limerick, even if it has been
laundered, articulates a sexual content. This will be my working hypothesis for this paper.

I

The first example is the initial sequence of a clown act performed
by Pierre Etaix and Annie Fratellini in a French context.[3] It follows a

traditional pattern according to which a very elegant and extremely articulate character—usually referred to as the "white clown" because of the color of his make-up—successfully performs tricks of magic or plays musical instruments, but is soon interrupted again and again by another character, who disrupts him and interferes with his schemes. The second clown epitomizes the exact opposite of all the qualities displayed by the first one; indeed, he exhibits an awkward gait, ridiculous garments and make-up, and nonsensical behavior. I have shown in another paper that these two types of characters can be viewed as embodiments —or signs—of the categories of nature vs. culture.[4] In fact the attributes that characterize them are signs mutually defined by a systematic inversion of their components. Not only are these two clowns passive displays of those signs, but also they engage in complex social interactions and manipulations of artifacts—i.e., in semiotic operations—such as the ones that will be described now.

The white clown (Pierre Etaix) performs some tricks of magic with scarves of various colors. Then he announces that he will pour a pitcher of milk into a top hat and that the milk will completely disappear. At this precise moment, the other clown (Annie Fratellini) enters the ring, walks comically along the side until he arrives near his partner, pretends that there is a door between them, rings an imaginary bell (which actually produces a sound), looks through an imaginary keyhole, then opens the invisible door and enters the nonexistent room where the act of magic was going to take place. He rushes to the pitcher of milk and empties it in an imaginary glass from which he drinks,—i.e., he mimes the act of drinking. Once there is no milk left in the pitcher, he quietly exits from the ring, leaving his puzzled partner alone. Of course the apparent emptying of the pitcher is an illusionary effect, but this paper is not concerned with the technological aspects of the act.

Because the milk has disappeared, the white clown cannot perform his intended magic trick. He tosses the top hat on a chair before starting another manipulation, one that involves cutting a rope into pieces and restoring it to its previous integrity by sleight of hand. The second clown enters the ring again, carrying a box—something like a guitar case or a large briefcase—but built in the shape of a dog. He borrows the rope from his puzzled partner, opens the case, and puts "the leash" on an invisible dog, which seems to be pulling the rope until it becomes straight. The built-in device that makes the trick possible does not concern us here. After a brief walk with the dog, the clown takes the top hat, which had been left on the chair, and puts it on the ground. He shows the dog that it must urinate in the hat. He does this by miming a urinating male dog and pointing to the hat at the same time, while addressing the invisible animal. Then he pretends that he is watching the dog performing its act of urination until it is finished. He walks in the direction of the exit, but halfway there he hesitates, comes back to the hat, and empties it ostentatiously. Actually there was some liquid inside, which is spilled on the ground. Finally, he leaves the ring at a fast pace.

Some obvious formal features permit considering these two successive sequences as a whole. First, they show the same pattern of action: (1) interruption of a magic act, (2) appropriation by the intruder of an element of the act, (3) completion by the intruder of a different magic act involving a nonsensical element. Second, they both include a hat and some liquid in a symmetrical relationship :(1) a visible liquid, which was supposed to disappear into a visible hat, disappears into an invisible object (the imaginary glass); (2) an invisible object (the imaginary dog) produced a visible liquid in the hat in which the liquid appears. This involves two material transformations: (1) the liquid in the first sequence is milk and in the second one it is animal urine, (2) the liquid reappears in the very object (the hat) into which it was supposed to disappear but, in the process, it has been transformed as stated in (1).

Bearing this in mind, we can make some further remarks on other aspects of the act. First the initial action of the second clown was to stop in front of an invisible door (or threshold) and to apply a visible "normal" procedure for passing through it, i.e., ringing the bell, looking through the keyhole, opening the door. Remembering that the other features that characterize this type of clown are symmetrical inversions of the ones that define the "hypercultural" clown, we can hypothesize that "not to transgress an invisible (nonexistent?) boundary" is the equivalent of "to transgress a visible (existent?) one," and "to observe normal cultural procedure in the absence of cultural artifacts" is somewhat like "not to observe those normal procedures in the presence of these artifacts." This can suggest therefore that the first actions of the intruding clown qualify him as a transgressor, or at least as a semiotic manipulator.

Second, all the gestural items that are mimed during the two sequences are performed in relationship with actual (visible) artifacts and as such are not of the same kind as the one mentioned above in the initial action. Two typical behaviors are mimed: (1) drinking, i.e., ingestion of a liquid; (2) urinating, i.e., excretion of a liquid. The latter differs sensibly from the former because it consists of an "imitation performed as an invitation to perform" and is followed by the invisible action supposedly performed by the invisible dog with an actual result. However, as nothing is said to be closer to a man than his pet dog and as the act of urinating (although in the manner of a dog) is actually mimed by the man, it is possible to say that the liquid produced is the same as the liquid absorbed after it has been digested. Such a displacement can be explained by the fact that, contrarily to the crudeness of ancient circus clowns, contemporary clowns apply to their acts a certain voluntary censorship. The presence of the invisible dog is also necessary for reasons of formal symmetry. The dog case and leash and the clown's body occupy the central position. The two sequences can be read as diagrammed in Fig. 1. The mirror symmetry construction raises the

1	2	3	4	4	3	2	1
visible	visible	invisible	visible	visible	invisible	visible	visible
container	liquid	container	container	container	container	liquid	container
(pitcher)	(milk)	(glass)	(clown)	(case)	(dog)	(urine)	(hat)

Fig. 1

question of the formal (poetic) principles at work in circus acts, which I have developed in my book *Circus and Culture*.[5]

Third, this obvious syntactic ordering does not apply to empty forms but articulates a semantic content. By juxtaposing in succession milk and urine, the sequence exhibits the normal process of transformation through digestion of a nutrient liquid into excretion. An immediate interpretation of this operation could be that the strong disjunction between ingestion and secretion that governs our cultural behavior with respect to "natural functions" is exposed by means of its transgression. This is undoubtedly the case, but such an interpretation would be drastically reductive because it does not account for the presence of the other objects, whose selection can be assumed to be logically motivated. The top hat, for example, is a powerful sign in our society—both as a symbol of social formality and as a traditional crucible for the magician, who makes all sorts of animals and objects appear from it, disappear into it, or become transformed within it. A top hat, by itself, could suffice to signify highly elaborate forms of culture, in the cultural context of the place where this clown act was observed. Connecting it immediately (as container and content) with a "call of nature" constitutes a very strong statement. It is similar to a familiar trick sometimes performed by circus-trained chimpanzees in which one of the animals signals to the trainer that it has an emergency "call of nature," and after using the chamber pot brought to it in a hurry, the animal puts it on its head as if it were a hat.

Other elements are also culturally relevant. Milk, a powerful sign, is a product of nature—even of "Mother Nature"—which does not require (at least in theory) any transformation before it can be consumed, or rather it is a natural product that is already processed. It is therefore similar to honey and can be interpreted—as far as mythical constructs are concerned—in the light of Lévi-Strauss's views regarding honey in its relationship to tobacco.[6] These remarks allow a reformulation of the act's sequence: the white clown, a hypercultural figure, wants to make some milk disappear into a top hat, an emphatic symbol of culture. Therefore, the intended action can be considered as a negation of nature and an overaffirmation of culture. The other clown, who embodies all the reverse of his partner, disrupts the intended "statement" by introducing into the operation the natural process of digestion, which had been overlooked and eventually produces a counterstatement. The transformation of the top hat into a dog's chamber pot brings forth with maximal effect the "rights of nature." The semiotic operation of the clown act enunciates negatively the fragile balance of culture always threatened on the one end by the seduction of nature and on the other end by its own excesses. Something can be overdone to the extent that it disappears; this, in turn, can disrupt the system to the extent that the most basic cultural categories are overturned.

It is therefore suggested by this tentative analysis that the kind of "nonsensical" patterned behavior directed to an audience, which signals its understanding by laughing, is in fact "meta-sensical." The expression *nonsense* can be accounted for by taking into consideration that if we are dealing with the class of sensical items or instances that our experience comprises, whatever is situated outside this class is experienced as being nonsensical, but the class of nonsense may include both randomly disorganized behaviors and meta-semiotic operations. The problem of the conjunction of nonsense, humor, and laughter has been and still is a controversial issue, which has produced an abundant and frustrating literature during the last hundred years. My ambition is not to solve it but to focus on actual situations in which collective laughter takes place and to attempt a semiotic description of such events.

II

A semiotic description consists essentially, in my opinion, of translating messages from one code into another or, even better, into several codes successively. This is indeed the only way to set forth intelligible relationships that thus replace the mere juxtaposition of terms confronting us when we attempt to understand why and how any instance of symbolic interaction makes sense. In so doing, a meta-language is being developed. This does not mean necessarily that the ultimate goal of such an undertaking is to arrive at a final relationship endowed with absolute explanatory value. The reliance on mutually definable concepts such as Nature and Culture is a notational convenience, a sort of algebraic expedient that makes possible some groupings for the purpose of simpler formulations; the Nature vs. Culture relationship is definitely not an ultimate interpretant. The result of systematic translations is to elicit networks of relationships through which the "stuff" from which meaningful reality is made, is "woven." It should be pointed out also that a meta-semiotic operation is not necessarily expressed through natural or artificial languages but can develop itself through means such as the complex multimedia "discourse" of a clown act. The immediate understanding (i.e., laughter) of the sequence that has been described earlier shows that the successive operations effectuated upon the relationship initially posited at the beginning of the act are decoded by the audience at a cognitive level that does not seem to involve any linguistic mediations but presupposes a cultural competence. This is true of all purely visual jokes. In the above example, the act performed undoubtedly would have been less effective if a neutral container had been used instead of a top hat and if the liquids used had not been qualified in the same manner. It is likely that it would have made some sense, but somewhat like an abstract formula "correctly" written, i.e., according to some formal rules. It is likely also that other contents could be semiotically manipulated through this formula with interesting impacts.

The analysis of a series of limericks in view of this general hypothesis will now provide some further instances of what I consider to be meta-semiotic discourse. As I am not a native speaker of English and only partially competent with respect to North American culture, I benefit from the point of view of an outsider to whom limericks are not familiar, i.e., they have no taboo value whatsoever. For the student of semiotics, limericks are indeed fascinating cultural items.

A sequence of twenty-eight stanzas published in G. Legman's collection, *The Limerick*,[7] will serve as an example for this tentative approach. I am aware that limericks usually come as individual, self-contained units of five lines, not as long narrative sequences. However, "The Misfortunes of Fyfe" (stanzas 835–62 in Legman's book) by the compilers of "Lapses in Limerick,"[8] can reasonably be considered as an enlarged version of a single stanza, developing through the import of other classical limericks some details of the situation that is described. The resulting redundancy makes the analysis of this series somewhat easier than that of a tightly condensed stanza. Moreover, limericks tend to expand their narrative properties, first through infinite variations, second through narrative complementarity.

"The Misfortunes of Fyfe" can be summarized as follows: A man, named Fyfe, marries a virgin and gets ready for the honeymoon. His wife remains a virgin in spite of all his attempts to perforate her hymen. It is made clear that this unfortunate turn of events does not come from any inability or impotency on the part of the man. Fyfe tries several methods to palliate his misfortune: substitutive behavior, reliance on prostitutes, calls to other men for doing the job on his wife, etc., but everything fails either to relieve his tension or to perforate her resisting membrane. As she is becoming neurotic, he tells her: "You would jump at a pin." This expression gives her the idea of relying on "synthetic conception" in order to bear a child, and the action is done with a bodkin. She becomes pregnant. Fyfe takes advantage of her physiological modification and tries again and again to penetrate her, thinking that her resistance might have been weakened, but he fails to the extent that he loses his own body's integrity ("and scraped off a square inch of skin" from his penis). Eventually he dies of exertion at the very moment she gives birth to a son. Each of the twenty-eight stanzas provides either a comment about the situation or some information pertaining to the progress of the narrative. The abstract development of the story is logical but its content is largely nonsensical if the narrated events are taken literally. Provided that the tale can be contemplated from a certain cultural distance, it possesses a "mythical flavor." My hypothesis is that the meaning of this nonsense has its source in some other problematic situation, relevant to the contextual culture, than the one which is explicated, i.e., something else is coded in sexual terms. The task of this semiotic investigation is to uncover this "something else," to set forth the relationships that account for the cognitive value of "The Misfortunes of Fyfe."

A few salient aspects of the text might catch the reader's attention and be given an immediate interpretation; for instance, the violation of the taboo regarding intercourse during pregnancy might be considered crucial for the deep understanding of the tale. But this would entail that stanzas 1 to 24 be only little more than mere preparation for the relevant situation. Moreover, the assumed transgression is rather an intention, an attempt to transgress, as Fyfe dies of exertion before having succeeded. One might also be sensitive to the familiar Oedipus triangle that seems to underly the narrative, but, in my opinion, this is a fallacy because there are too many inconsistencies with respect to such an interpretation that would have to be overlooked. For example, nowhere in the limerick is it said that Fyfe's semen is responsible for his wife's pregnancy; the expression used is "synthetic conception." It is also obvious that since the father dies as the son is being born there is very little room indeed for psychological interaction. Interpretations of this sort isolate a few elements that can be satisfactorily combined at the cost of leaving most of the material unaccounted for. The basic structure of a narrative such as this one can be elicited by eliminating the redundancies, not the semiotic information.

Once the painstaking work of analyzing the text word by word, according to some tentative directions, has been done, a hypothesis can be formulated. Without trying to reconstruct the underlying heuristic process, I will now present my interpretation of "The Misfortunes of Fyfe," and give some evidence to support it. My hypothesis is that these limericks deal with the culinary system of their contextual culture through a translation of the problems involved into the sexual code. In addition, it seems that the acoustic code plays an intermediary part in the process. To be more explicit, this narrative refers to the introduction of canned food in the culinary system of the industrialized age. This will be considered the crucial problem that is mythically solved through the tale of Fyfe. The "myth" indeed describes a pathological state, which eventually comes to an end. If we accept the idea that the expressed pathological state—an imperforatable virgin—stands for a difficulty that occurs on the level of the mythical conceptualizations of the extant culinary system, then this myth is a way to conceptualize a crucial semiotic change introduced into the system.

There is ample evidence that virginity can be equated with raw food. In colloquial French *faire passer à la casserole* (to fry in the pan) can mean "to deflorate a virgin." There are equivalents of this metaphor in other languages. A striking example of this semiotic value of raw meat can be found in an Irish legend in which uncooked meat is used as a message of chastity: "A man conducting a woman leaves uncooked meat behind each night of the journey as a sign to the husband following that she has not been touched."[9] Conversely, it is possible to consider virginity as a sign of "uncookedness." In the limerick, Fyfe's wife is, by her obstinate state, a sign of an emphatic resistance of nature to being cooked. This can be verified in all the various ways in which she is qualified. In stanza 3, she appears as a nondeciduous tree. This is congruent, in the botanic code, with her basic value in the myth, since a nondeciduous tree is an evergreen, which resists the transformations caused by the seasons and is not defoliated in the winter. In stanza 5, she is said to be "hoarding her deep nest of honey." The fact that honey can have a sexual meaning in colloquial American English does not motivate the whole expression. The use of the verb "to hoard" stresses her obstinate position on the side of nature. After Lévi-Strauss's analyses of the myths dealing with honey, it is not necessary to expand this point. It suffices to point out that honey is a ready-made food provided by nature. Another metaphorical expression, "clam," refers also to food that can be consumed unprocessed, although this is not the obvious point made in stanza 7.

If this is correct, Fyfe plays the part of an unfortunate cook confronted with an uncookable meat that even manages to "uncook" him (cf. stanza 28, "he was undone"). Therefore he symbolizes culture in crisis, culture negated. Nevertheless, a son is born, and succeeds in his own way to bring to an end the pathological resistance of the woman. To simplify, the birth of the son expresses the advent of a new type of culture that cancels the one it replaces. In other words, a culinary system (i.e., what is referred to now as traditional cooking and honored in a quasiritualistic manner) is being replaced by another system (i.e., the ready-made frozen or canned food, which is still viewed by some people both as a sign of a "barbaric" way of feeding and as a fascinating way of life). Indeed, the introduction of a processed food, available for consumption without the time-consuming and painstaking efforts of gathering, preparing, cooking, etc., but in a way reminiscent of the instant gratification of a ripe fruit picked from a tree, can only have shattered the collective conceptualization through which the previous culinary code had taken shape.

There is also at play in "The Misfortunes of Fyfe" an acoustic system that is easily identifiable and that possibly serves as a mediator between the culinary and the sexual codes. In colloquial American English a female whose hymen is comparatively tough is said to be "tight as a drum." On the other hand, the well-known association of "fife and drum" as a symbol of military music, specially in the American tradition, may function as a determining formula in the general organization of the myth. The pathological situation, without which there would not be a narrative, is precisely the impossibility of producing any significant "music," i.e., the harmony of nature and culture is destroyed. This is all the more striking if one takes into consideration that the etymology of *fife* is the same as for *pipe* and that drums and honey are congruent in the myths analyzed by Lévi-Strauss. This makes it possible therefore to identify the opposition *honey/tobacco* as one of the organizing principles of this tale.

In the way myths speak (of) culture and attempt to solve contradictions arising from the experience of the environment (natural and/or technological), this sequence of limericks appears to deal with the ever-present problem of cultural changes for which it tries to account through the model of natural generation as a conceptual basis, modified according to the problems involved. The meta-cultural discourse of the historians and theorists of cultures often do exactly the same thing when they use concepts such as growth, maturity, decline, and death. In our example, the negation of a culinary system is expressed at the same time by an affirmation of nature that implies negation of culture and by the affirmation of the replacing culinary system. The passage from one system to another is expressed—in the language of the myth—by the negation of the first one in the form of an affirmation of its contradictory term. Note, for instance, that in the last stanza Fyfe is both "undone" and "done in." But, this pathological affirmation of nature is only a logical condition for its new negation in the form of a new culture, because after all Fyfe's wife became pregnant, even though it was through "synthetic conception." This may explain why we learn, even before conception took place, that there was a son to be born, i.e., an equivalent of the negated term.

If the hypothesis I have outlined in this paper is correct—the evidence presented above seems to be convergent—it would account at the same time for the ambiguous attitudes met by both clowns and limericks in our society. They are indeed dealing with very sensitive areas, not in the sense that they would touch upon taboo topics but to the extent that they manipulate delicate logical constructs that are the very foundations of our sense of rational reality. By necessity, any meta-discourse entails the relativization of its object. When this object is the "essence" of a culture, only the violation of the strongest taboos can adequately serve as metaphors for such operations to be acceptable. Discourses of this kind can only be experienced as nonsense by the members of the culture in which they take place, but, as I have tried to show, these nonsensical instances are highly meaningful meta-discourses.

REFERENCES

1. A. J. Greimas, *Du Sens* (Paris: Le Seuil, 1970), p.70.
2. P. Bouissac, "Clown Performances as Meta-semiotic Texts," *Language Sciences* 19 (1972):1–7.
3. This act was observed and recorded in Paris and in Monaco during the winter of 1975.
4. P. Bouissac, "Pour une analyse ethnologique des entrées de clowns," *Revue d'Ethnologie Française* vol.I, 3–4 (1972):7–18.
5. P. Bouissac, *Circus and Culture: A Semiotic Approach* (Bloomington: Indiana University Press, 1976).
6. C. Lévi-Strauss, *From Honey to Ashes* (New York: Harper and Row, 1973; English translation by J. and D. Weightman).
7. G. Legman, *The Limerick* (New York: Brandywine Press, 1970).
8. "Lapses in Limerick," MS., oral collection (Ann Arbor, Mich., 1938–41).
9. S. Thompson, *Motif Index of Folk Literature* (Bloomington: Indiana University Press, 1957), vol.5, T386.

APPENDIX

As a result of the discussions that followed this lecture, Professor Ivan Karp of the Department of Anthropology at Indiana University formulated his own interpretation of "The Misfortunes of Fyfe." I am pleased to reproduce here, with his kind permission, the text he wrote as a contribution to the issue of the semiotics of nonsense.

"SMART FISHERMEN TAKE CARE OF THEIR RODS"*

An Analysis of Kinship in "The Misfortunes of Fyfe"
Ivan Karp

The inspiration for this analysis derives from three sources. The first is Bouissac's skillful demonstration of the existence of a metaphor derived from a distinction between Nature and Culture to be found in the imagery of the limerick "The Misfortunes of Fyfe." The second is an intriguing essay by Barnes (1973), "Genetrix: Genitor: Nature: Culture?" in which he argues that a major puzzle with which kinship systems deal is the connection between paternity and gestation. This is in contrast to the relationship between maternity and gestation, which is "natural" in the sense that the connection is discoverable through data that come from immediate sense impressions, much as the connection between heat and fire is one that arises from immediate experiences. The third source of inspiration is Schneider's (1968) account of American Kinship, in which it is shown that the American Kinship system is organized in terms of a distinction between relationships of law and relationships of natural substance. It was on the basis of this ethnography and theory that I was able to discern a kinship code in the sexual imagery and narrative progression of the limerick.

Bouissac has already demonstrated that the sexual imagery in the limerick is derived from two opposed domains. The male sexual organ is characterized by objects derived from the domain of culture, such as knife, gimlet, pencil, cork, pin, and so on. On the other hand, Fyfe's wife's sexual organ is characterized solely in terms of natural imagery. Her vagina is tight as a clam, a nest of honey, like a mole's hole, or a dense growth of hair.

A few further comments need to be made about this nature–culture opposition before I move on to kin and familial relations. First, I think that it is significant that the two major protagonists are named and unnamed. Fyfe has a named identity; while his wife, as is befitting a natural creature, as opposed to a cultural being, remains unnamed except for her identity as the wife of Fyfe. There are two factors involved here. Traditionally, women have had no identity of their own in the

---

* Bumper sticker on a car in Tulip Tree House Parking Lot, Indiana University.

wider society. They were jural minors under the authority of their fathers and husbands. Certainly in our Judeo-Christian heritage, marriage was a transfer of rights over a woman from her father to her husband. She remained a jural minor in the eyes of the law. One of the major social developments of the modern industrial era has been the gradual emergence of women as legal persons. Hence the characterization of Fyfe's wife as a socially differentiated being only with respect to her husband reflects a long-standing tradition that has come increasingly into conflict with changing social conditions. This conflict is one that is acute in familial situations, particularly in the conflict between the image and obligations of woman as wife and mother and as jural and economic actor in her own right. A restatement of the differences between men and women that stresses traditional roles and identity attributes is singularly appropriate for limericks, whose normal context is exclusively male domains such as high school toilets and locker rooms.

The other aspect of the Nature–Culture imagery that deserves comment lies in the type of object that typifies the sexual parts of the male and female actors. The objects that provide the images for Fyfe and his friends' penises are not only cultural objects in the sense that they are manufactured. They are also cultural objects in a stricter sense. As pins, pencils, corks, gimlets, and weapons, men's penises are all instruments; that is, objects used to achieve some goal. They stand in stark contrast to the imagery for women's vaginas. A nest of honey, a mole's hole, a clam, and a wound are all found objects, which may or may not please the finder. The paradox, of course, is that the vagina, the found sexual object of the limerick, is the instrument of birth. It is precisely this paradox that forms the center of the narrative progression of the limerick and the thinking about kinship in it.

In the first stanza of "Fyfe," a kinship relation based on law is established. Fyfe marries his wife. Schneider has pointed out that marriage is symbolized by sexual intercourse and involves a legally regulated sexual relationship. Sexual intercourse, however, is a natural phenomenon, especially when undertaken for its own sake and not for procreation. This is particularly well illustrated by stanzas 14 and 15, where Fyfe goes walking in the woods in the spring and finds couples copulating. Presumably these acts of intercourse take place outside the marriage relationship. These naturally occurring acts are consummated much more easily than the sexual difficulties Fyfe is experiencing in marriage.

Fyfe's difficulties lead him to try to have his wife penetrated by a series of cultural objects in stanzas 9 through 14. All to no avail. Culture is defeated by Nature. In stanzas 14 and 15, the copulation in the woods episode, Fyfe's cultural frustration in the face of nature is highlighted. In stanzas 16 through 23, Fyfe's wife gets herself penetrated and artificially inseminated by a pin or needle and a syringe. We might interpret this as the triumph of Culture over Nature. The act of penetration is accomplished not by a penis, which is after all a natural object even if it is metaphorically classified as a cultural thing. It is accomplished instead by a pin and a syringe. Here we have an actual instrument being used to achieve what penises could not. A real cultural object, a syringe, effects what a penis described metaphorically as cultural object could not. In this sense, what man has wrought appears to be more successful than what nature has given men.

This triumph of Culture over Nature is short-lived, however. The final stanzas, 24 through 28, entail the reversal of the cultural triumph of the preceding eight stanzas. In these stanzas Fyfe appears at first to be able to penetrate his wife as a result of her artificial insemination. In stanza 25, he begins to enter. However, he encounters another source of resistance. The baby in his wife's womb, of whose existence he was unaware, is about to be born. His penis is forced out as a result of the birth of the baby, and he ejaculates and "a few minutes later" expires. In stanza 28 we are given his tombstone epitaph, "Shed a tear for poor Fyfe,/ His imperforate wife/ Did him in with the aid of their son."

Fyfe and his wife constitute a legal pair, a husband and a wife. Fyfe is destroyed by a natural pair, a mother and her son. Hence the relationship of law (and culture) that is marriage is overcome by a natural relationship between mother and son that is established by the act of birth. Note that it is the very act of birth itself that destroys Fyfe. The narrative progression of this limerick goes from the establishment of a cultural relationship of kinship, marriage, to its destruction by a natural kinship relationship, birth and the mother–child bond. The triumph of culture through marriage or artificial insemination is short-lived in the face of the facts of nature that culture cannot overcome. The conflict between natural kinship, based on shared common substance through birth and the immediately observable facts of gestation, and cultural kinship as a system of the distribution of legal rights is not resolved but simply restated at a non-empirical level. This conclusion is not entirely without its own paradox. Fyfe's epitaph says that he was done in "with the aid of *their* son [emphasis mine]." Nowhere in the limerick is there any indication that the semen used by Fyfe's wife in her act of artificial insemination was Fyfe's. In fact it is hardly credible that the semen could have been his since he was still unaware of the child in his wife's womb. Fyfe's son is his only in a legal sense. A marriage establishes legal paternity over a child no matter who the physiological father is. The limerick ends with an assertion of a right derived from a legal relationship in conjunction with a right derived from a relationship of shared natural substance. Perhaps this indicates an interdependence of cultural and natural kinship. From Fyfe's perspective, however, it is a very costly sort of interdependence.

REFERENCES

Barnes, J. A. 1973. "Genetrix: Genitor: Nature: Culture?" In *The Character of Kinship*, J. Goody, ed. London: Cambridge University Press.

Schneider, D. M. 1968. *American Kinship: A Cultural Account*. Englewood Cliffs, N.J.: Prentice-Hall.

THE MISFORTUNES OF FYFE

1. There was a young fellow named Fyfe
   Who married the pride of his life,
      But imagine his pain
      When he struggled in vain,
   And just couldn't get into his wife.

2. Now the trouble was not with our hero,
   Who, though no match for Epstein or Nero,
      Had a good little dong
      That was five inches long,
   And as stiff as a parsnip at zero.

3. But his efforts to poke her, assiduous,
   Met a dense growth of hair most prodiguous.
      Well, he thought he might dint her
      By waiting till winter,
   But he found that she wasn't deciduous.

4. Now here was this fellow named Fyfe,
   Unable to diddle his wife—
      Which fact, sad but true,
      Left him nothing to do
   But bugger the girl all his life.

Reprinted from *The Limerick*, G. Legman, ed. (New York: Brandywine Press, 1970).

5.   For diversion this might have been funny,
And of course it *did* save him some money,
    But it angered our Fyfey
    To think that his wifey
Was hoarding her deep nest of honey.

6.   He went whoring to find satisfaction,
But with whores, though accomplished in action,
    He never could capture
    That fine fucking rapture,
For the thought of his wife was distraction.

7.   So here was our fellow named Fyfe
With a truly impervious wife.
    She was not worth a damn,
    Being close as a clam—
Why, he couldn't get in with a knife!

8.   The problem that harassed his soul
Was: what kept him out of her hole?
    Was her hymen too tough?
    Was she stuffed up with fluff?
Was her coosie the home of a mole?

9.   This was just what poor Fyfe couldn't tell,
For her prow was as sound as a bell.
    He'd have needed a gimlet
    To get into her quimlet,
And it made the poor guy mad as hell.

10.   He applied to that fellow from Strensall
For help from his long, pointed pencil,
    But Strensy's tool now
    Was as blunt as the prow
Of a tug—he'd have needed a stencil.

11.   Fyfe searched for the chap from New York
Who had punctured the hymen like cork,
    But *he* was quite coy
    For he now loved a boy,
And refused to help Fyfe with the stork.

12.   Fyfe asked Durand how much he'd charge
(The fellow whose cock could contract or enlarge)
    To drill his way in
    With his prick like a pin,
And there make it slowly enlarge.

13. But Durand—though he'd fuck with no urgin'—
    Warned, "Apart from the risk that she'll burgeon,
        Your pride must be low
        If you'll meekly forego
    A crack at a genuine virgin."

14. In the spring in the woods Fyfe did wander late,
    And saw couples preparing to copulate,
        But he could not abide
        The gay sight, and he cried
    At the thought that the pigfuckers penetrate!

15. One couple he foolishly leapt on,
    To examine the wound and the weapon.
        One was rigid, one deep—
        The snug fit made him weep,
    And in shame and contrition he crept on.

16. In the meantime, Fyfe's wife, who had wed
    With *some* thought to the pleasures of bed,
        Was becoming depressed,
        In fact damn near obsessed
    By her terribly tough maidenhead.

17. She remarked, "When all joking is done,
    What I honestly want is a son.
        I would like impregnation
        If not copulation—
    But to wed and have neither's no fun."

18. She grew worried and nervous and thin,
    Till Fyfe said, "You would jump at a pin!"
        And these words, though unkind,
        Put the thought in her mind
    That a pin-point *perhaps* might get in.

19. Thus she thought of synthetic conception,
    Which at first seemed like basest deception,
        But her cunt was so sore
        From Fyfe's trying to bore,
    That she gave the thought better reception.

20. And indeed, though it's sad to relate it,
    Her first fuck was so sadly belated,
        That a poke by a pin,
        Though ever so thin,
    Was a prospect that made her elated.

21. To be brief, the great action was done:
    There was artfully planted, a son,

Through a bodkin that filled her,
And wonderfully thrilled her—
More fun than a son of a gun!

22. This syringe, which was long but quite thin,
Left a hole that Fyfe coudn't get in,
But he kept right on busting
And jousting and thrusting,
On account of his excess of vim.

23. While she mused on this synthetic screw,
The sperm got well-planted, and grew,
And the great day approached
When her breech would be broached,
But Fyfe, the poor wretch, never knew.

24. One night, while in sheer desperation
He prodded and poked like tarnation,
His wife groaned with pain—
She gave way!! Would he gain
The goal of three years' contemplation?

25. The head of his dingus went in!
He felt sure he was going to win!
He thrust like a demon,
He spilt all his semen,
And scraped off a square inch of skin.

26. But despite all his trying, he found
He was losing, not gaining, his ground.
Though he clung to her thighs
While he tried for the prize,
Each push *in* caused a greater rebound.

27. The harder the poor fellow tried,
The more her hold filled, from inside,
Till he fell back quite spent,
His prick battered and bent,
And a few minutes later—he died.

28. As he passed, a new life was begun,
And his tomb tells how he was undone:
"Shed a tear for poor Fyfe,
His imperforate wife
Did him in with the aid of their son."

1938–1941.

On Semiotic Aspect
of Translations

Bogusław P. Lawendowski

A bundle of processes subsumed under the heading *Translation* is inherent to human and animal existence. Such an assumption can be substantiated only if the traditional concepts and units of translation are temporarily set aside in order to give room to a semiotic framework for the processes. To make the following exposition clear it seems necessary, however, to recapitulate as concisely as possible the past and the present developments in the theory of translation, and to indicate unambiguously what notions are to be set aside.

One of the signals of the growing immensity of the body of writings on translation is the fact that authors of major works in the field decide to list only a few scores of bibliographical entries they deem essential to the study of the field, leaving it to the student to discover other related materials for himself (cf. Steiner, 1975). Only a little more than ten years ago one of the most significant publications in the field listed more than 2,000 entries ranging from one-page articles to vast treatises (Nida, 1964).

Let us imagine a determined and diligent analyst ready to read his way through the enormous pile of texts in search of some unequivocal

This chapter was written while the author was an American Council of Learned Societies Fellow for 1975–76 affiliated with the Research Center for Language and Semiotic Studies at Indiana University, Bloomington, Indiana.

account of the translation processes. The task upon its completion will not leave him empty-handed, to be sure, yet he may be confused by the cornucopia of attitudes, definitions, beliefs, theories, opinions, and more or less relevant comments. It will transpire from the readings that the multitude of authors agree, as it were, to disagree.

What are the reasons for this perhaps unhappy state of affairs? An answer to the question lies within the area of interaction between different anthroposemiotic systems as well as the interface between the anthropo- and zoosemiotic systems. The latter ones go beyond the scope of the present paper but will eventually be included in other writings on the semiotic framework of translation. The reader is kindly referred to the extensive treatment of zoosemiotics in the works of Thomas A. Sebeok, and also to Sebeok (1975), in particular, since it presents a very lucid taxonomy of the six species of signs.

The whole field of translation viewed in retrospect presents itself first of all as a number of activities based on *empeiria*. In the chronologically initial period *theōria* of translation did not exist. The impact of this historical development cannot be overestimated, regardless of the fact that it was the way it was with the origins of all the essential building blocks of the human world.

What differentiates human communication from other human endeavors is its enormously dynamic and heuristic nature. This, in turn, creates a formidable obstacle on the way to an ultimate end: an adequate and universal register of units and their interaction within the communication processes used by man. The rift seen today between the empirists and the theorists of translation is due to ages of an absence of a unifying theory of communication and to the lack of tangible effects of linguistic theories of the past (as regards translation, of course). As a matter of fact, translations continue to be produced by experienced practitioners, or it would be better to say, are assigned to persons with generally greater empirical than theoretical backgrounds. Numerous instances of the real-life situations confirm the fact that even the most impressive theoretical apparatus at hand is a poor substitute for several years of intensive practice in the field. The situation is likely to prevail in years to come, and the former flood tide of interest in machine translation has ebbed considerably, indicating that in this particular contest between man and computer it is man who comes out a winner, at least in certain types of translation. Now, obviously the last comment could easily take us into another, long discussion of what computers are and are not able to perform. Since it is not the basic subject here let us only repeat that the problem in machine translation lies with software rather than with hardware, which is to say that we need not worry what the machine can do for us but what we can do for the machine.

It is not our intention to call for a fast change in the field in favor of practice more solidly based on theory. The purpose of the paper is to draw attention to the underlying aspect of all translation processes— *semiotics*: "the exchange of any messages whatever and of the systems of signs which underlie them" (Sebeok, 1975). The establishing of a semiotic framework for subsequent discussions of the translation processes may help to show them as operations infinitely more complex than the traditional linguistic, literary, philosophical, logical, or mathematical propositions are ready to admit. The semiotic framework may help to bring together the efforts of those analyzing and describing translation only within the confines of their own disciplines.

Unrewarding as they are, speculations and statements concerning the origins of language are continuously elaborated. Lieberman (1975) puts emphasis on the evolution of the human supralaryngeal vocal apparatus, unique among primates, which produced the particular form of human language. Hence, vocal signs seem to be of primary importance in the development of human culture. The same author points out, however, that "one of the great 'mysteries' of human evolution is the sudden acceleration in the rate of change of human culture that occurred between 40,000 and 30,000 years ago" (1975:180), evidenced in diversification of tools, appearance of new technological materials and techniques, as well as the coming of art. Accompanying the art is the first body of engravings, which indicates "the use of technology to expand human cognitive abilities. Orthographic systems can be viewed as devices that overcome the limits of human memory, whether the orthography is numerical, alphabetic, or syllabic." Lieberman refers to a recent work (Marshack, 1972) that reveals the existence of intricate notational systems well into the pre-history of man. He admits that "the exact nature of what was being recorded is not always clear. However, the startling thing is that notational systems were in use 30,000 years ago. *Human morphology, cognitive ability, and language probably were fully evolved* [italics mine]" (Lieberman, 1975:181).

This and similar statements point to the existence of diverse sign systems in some of the earliest stages of human culture. Each of the sign systems must have been born out of the need to communicate, thus the skill of either producing or interpreting signs is as old as the sign systems themselves. The production and the interpreting were, or, put better, have always been taking place at several levels: (1) Personal; (2) Interpersonal, which falls into (2a) Intra-tribal or Intra-societal and (2b) Inter-tribal or Inter-societal. A parallel set of terms could be (3a) Intra-cultural and (3b) Inter-cultural.

The evolution of the orthographic systems provided a dual system of language signs, which stratified the society into illiterates and literates, that is to say, a group of individuals able to exchange messages only by means of a single sign system in language—speech (plus some 'non-verbal codes'), and a group able to use freely the two linguistic sign systems. Social, cultural, political, and other implications of this stratification need not be elaborated here; suffice it to mention the role of the orthographic systems in religion. Versatility and economy of the writing systems (though, as we know, some are more economical than others) account for their dominance among other anthroposemiotic systems used in the signaling behavior of man. The position of the linguistic sign systems is unchallenged and will remain so, no doubt. But at the same time it is worth pointing out that the importance of language overwhelmed if not stifled attempts to consider communication as a result of messages being exchanged via several channels simultaneously, which eventually led to the establishing of the term *translation* as representing the transfer of 'meaning' from one set of language signs to another set of language signs at what we call here the 'inter-societal' (2b) level. In other words, *translation* could mean only one thing, as Catford (1965) put it: "an operation performed on languages: a process of substituting a text in one language for a text in another." (It is interesting to note that Catford refers to Roman Jakobson in a single footnote on p.74 of his work but passes in silence over Jakobson's famous article on linguistic aspects of translation [Jakobson, 1959], which should be regarded as the first step toward a semiotic concept of translation.)

Jakobsonian 'intralingual', 'interlingual', and 'intersemiotic' translation processes bring us back again to the developments in the past history of translation. But first it seems in order to discuss briefly the two terms *interpreter* and *translator*. Both persons are engaged in the exchange of messages by means of transferring 'meaning' from one set of language signs (Source Language: SL) to another set of language signs (Target Language: TL). The interpreter, however, works with speech units while the translator does it with units of the writing systems. The enormous body of writings on translation is primarily concerned with the translator and the written texts. To be sure, all available translation theories deal exclusively with written languages, while interpreting is usually mentioned as a 'very difficult type of oral translation', better left to practitioners only. On the other hand, to do justice to the handful of authors solely concerned with interpreting, we must say that since World War II a few books as well as a number of technical articles have been published, as, for example, Cary (1956), Min'iar-Beloruchev (1969), Herbert (1965), Seleskovitch (1968), and others. The growing interest in interpreting, techniques of which are discussed later in the paper, stems from the development of highly advanced electronic devices; for example, one enables a group of 1,200 people to communicate simultaneously in six, seven, or more languages.

Chronologically, the interlingual interpreter came first, and in all likelihood, when acting at some inter-tribal contacts he had to be familiar with or take quick guesses at signals from the opposite party, which belonged to what semiotic literature calls 'non-verbal codes': gestures, clothes, symbolic gifts, and others. He had to have sufficient knowledge to distinguish between *signals, symptoms, icons, indexes, symbols,* and *names* (cf. Sebeok, 1975), as different signs, although the knowledge must have been intuitive and confirmed only empirically. Consequently, the interpreter combined in his act information conveyed to him through a whole array of channels. This process continues today in almost the same way on such occasions as diplomatic visits. It is of considerable assistance to the interpreter that he is receiving information in forms other than a string of spoken words. That helps him do a better job of exchanging the messages, but his work is affected by the need to act fast.

The translator, on the other hand, has a lot of time to think over the text in SL, consult reference books, specialists, etc., but no other channel of information other than the written or printed text is available to him (unless there is a direct contact between the translator and the author of the text, in which case the translation may be done more accurately). The total effect of his work depends basically on his command of the SL and the TL, which implies mastery of both cultures.

The entire body of texts on translation, enormous as it is and largely concerned with the work of the interlingual translator, can be roughly divided into three categories: *rhapsodic, technical,* and *theoretical.* The rhapsodic writings embrace a considerable part of texts concerned with translation of the literary materials: prose, poetry, drama. A typical piece from this category lays stress on the difficulty of performing an act of literary translation by reiterating statements about the elusiveness of the language of belles lettres versus the simplicity and unambiguity of the language of science and engineering. Either bluntly or in a disguise of a more or less effective figure of speech the message that comes across from the author of such a piece is that the language of literary arts does not lend itself to systematic examinations, consequently only the gifted have the right to talk about it; *implicite,* he is one of the chosen few. Often texts of this kind are sprinkled with verbal flowers of praise for colleagues working in the same field. A common feature is a series of quotations from the translations, yet only some authors carry out a step-by-step analysis of the features that make a given translation good or bad. Most often the quotations are there for the friendly reader to admire, contemplate, and draw conclusions for himself. This category includes critical reviews of literary translations. More often than not the reviewer will gloss over the fundamental issue of whether a replacement of the SL material by equivalent textual material in TL took place. Lexical analysis may appear in some limited form if the translator happened to make a few outrageous errors. This type of reviewing may be due to the limited space in journals, but also, which is not an uncommon event, unfamiliarity of the reviewer with the language of the original. Generally, texts in this category take their origins in emotional rather than rational attitudes of their authors.

The technical texts often present themselves as more or less detailed taxonomies of the procedures the translator must follow to arrive at a successful end. Titles such as "Twenty-Three Restricted Rules of Translation" (Newmark, 1973), "The Principles of Translation" (Savory, 1968), or "The Lively Conventions of Translation" (Arrowsmith, 1961) abound here. Chapters on translation through the ages are usually included, together with some paradoxes that result from juxtaposition of the views on translation expressed by different authors at different times. The best sample of it the reader can find in Savory (1968:50). The authors often provide ample bibliographies and discuss views of other authors writing in the same way. They do not try to build or fortify the existent *mystique* of the translation of poetry, for example. On the contrary, they tend to admit that an act of translation is only secondary to a genuine creative effort of a writer's mind. Nevertheless, they can hardly put up with an idea that translating may be regarded as a field of systematic scholarly analysis: Cary (1965): "C'est qu'il n'existe pas de traduction dans l'abstrait"; or Newmark (1973), shedding the traditional moderation of a British subject: "purely theoretical treatises on translation are even less profitable than most purely theoretical treatises," and later on: "in spite of the claims of Nida and the Leipzig translation school . . . *there is no such thing as a science of translation, and never will be* [italics mine]." A number of works in this category raise the issue of untranslatability, although this problem is actually dealt with more extensively in the theoretical category. Jakobson's contention that whatever is expressible in one language can be translated into another, or in other words, the entire body of human knowledge may be expressed in any language, is not shared by many authors (cf. Werner Winter's "Impossibilities of Translation" in Arrowsmith, 1961). W. V. O. Quine was skeptical, only a year after Jakobson's article, maintaining that if anyone tried to translate "Neutrinos lack mass" into jungle language, he would have to coin words or distort the usage of old ones: "We may expect him to plead in extenuation that the natives lack the requisite concepts; also that they know too little physics. And he is right, except for the hint of there being some free-floating, linguistically neutral meaning which we capture, in 'Neutrinos lack mass', and the native cannot" Quine (1960:76).

It seems that Jakobson's assumption is valid if we recognize that interlingual translations are divided into different groups each of which has its own criteria of accuracy, quality, and style. If the purpose of a translation is, for example, to give the reader a good idea about some referents that are nonexistent in the TL, without the need to care about stylistic effects of the translator's work, then certainly the coining and distorting of terms will take place for the purpose of approximating the concepts expressed in the SL. The category of theoretical studies on translation is as diversified as its composition. The number of works entirely devoted to theoretical aspects of translation is small. Nida (1964) and Nida and Taber (1969) are the first and foremost publications arguing strongly in favor of systematic studies on translation processes. Catford (1965) applies the Firth-Halliday linguistics to translation, yet on a closer look it appears to be divorced from reality, at least some categories and taxonomies proposed by the author are bound to remain as Catford's idiosyncratic inventions. Of the most recent major works, we should again mention Steiner (1975), which, long as it is and overburdened with verbiage to boot, brings hardly anything new into the theoretical area of translation. If anything, Steiner seems to have a rather gloomy vision of the possibilities of translation.

The problem of untranslatability accounts for the diversity of the category. The quantity of articles, chapters, sub-chapters, and the like concerned with the impossibilities in the field is enormous, much too big even to begin listing them in the present paper. Writers from a very broad spectrum of disciplines continue to discourage any hopes for translatability. For example, Quine (1960) brings in his thesis of the indeterminacy of translation, or Wierzbicka (1975) informs the reader that there is more to the understanding of the process of translation than many a simple mind can imagine, maintaining that a sentence such as "She has only one parent" does not necessarily correspond to "She has only one mother or father" but rather to something worded in the following way: ("She has only one) parent" equals ("There is only one person who can be thought of as a grown-up member of a group one member of which is someone who is not grown-up, another member of which is this someone's father or mother"). It is a comforting observation, however, to see publications that argue with the 'untranslatability' attitude, like, for instance, Darmstadter (1967).

Generally speaking, texts falling into this category either evade or treat very superficially the practical matters (not necessarily because by definition they are not concerned with them but because many of the writers are not familiar enough with the kind of work the translator or interpreter is doing, and, applying the principle *pars pro toto* they question the validity of the entire endeavor). In the view of this author, the statement made by Searle (1969:11) is the one to be adopted by anyone elaborating on translation processes:

> As a native speaker of English I know that "oculist" is exactly synonymous with "eye doctor," that "bank" has (at least) two meanings, that "cat" is a noun, that "oxygen" is unambiguous, that "Shakespeare was a better playwright than poet" is meaningful, that "the slithy toves did gyre" is nonsensical, that "The cat is on the mat" is a sentence, etc. Yet I have no operational criteria for synonymy, ambiguity, nounhood, meaningfulness, or sentencehood. Furthermore, any criterion for any one of these concepts has to be consistent with my (our) knowledge or must be abandoned as inadequate. . . . one knows such facts about language independently of any ability to provide criteria of the preferred kinds of such knowledge.

Searle speaks only of language. Yet, it may be worth examining how much of what he says pertains to other sign systems that we know as native 'users' and 'makers' of a given culture. Some are more, others are less, familiar, so classificatory work will be inescapable (like, for example, the application of the six species of signs, as described by Sebeok, 1975). Perhaps the six species will appear insufficient for our purposes. A future theory of translation will have a semiotic framework embracing not only language but other anthropo- and zoosemiotic systems, although the priority will no doubt rest with language. In order to work out such a framework, which would unify the presently dispersed and individualistic approaches to translation, interdisciplinary cooperation is necessary.

The 'semiotic' category of writings on translation has been limited so far to only two works: Jakobson (1959) and Ludskanov (1975). Jakobson's remarks concerning intersemiotic processes were not treated extensively in his article because its main thrust was of linguistic nature, yet it makes him the originator of the semiotic approach to translation. Ludskanov's was the first explicit statement in favor of regarding the field of translation as an integral part of semiotic studies, although he points out that the theory of semiotics does not account for 'semiotic transformations' though "such transformations certainly exist." To remedy the situation a definition of semiotic transformations is offered: "Semiotic transformations (T^s) are replacements of the signs encoding a message by signs of another code, preserving (so far as possible in the face of entropy) invariant information with respect to a given system of reference." It clearly indicates Ludskanov's greater preoccupation with the theory of information than with that of semiotics, in fact, but in the course of time narrower and more adequate definitions will be worked out. A great merit of Ludskanov's paper is the stress put on the existence of a number of relatively new types of translation work that cannot rely on the traditional approaches: film and television dubbing or subtitles, interpreting conferences, artificial computer languages (why he should consider translation of children's books as a new field for translators is not explained!).

Fig. 1 is the matrix covering practically all anthroposemiotic systems as used in the interpersonal or intersocietal exchange of messages. It certainly offers a good start toward the ultimate: a semiotic theory of translation, even though it is clear that Ludskanov's starting point for his

$$L \quad \overset{\cdot}{\rightarrow} \quad L'$$

....

$$L^B \quad \overset{\cdot}{\rightarrow} \quad L^{B\prime} \qquad L^V \quad \overset{\cdot}{\rightarrow} \quad L^{V\prime} \qquad L^B \quad \overset{\cdot}{\leftrightarrow} \quad L^V$$

....

$$L^A \quad \overset{\cdot}{\rightarrow} \quad L^{A\prime} \qquad L^N \quad \overset{\cdot}{\rightarrow} \quad L^{N\prime} \qquad L^A \quad \overset{\cdot}{\leftrightarrow} \quad L^N$$

$$L_S^N \quad \overset{\cdot}{\rightarrow} \quad L_S^{N\prime}$$

....

$$L_{SP}^N \quad \overset{\cdot}{\rightarrow} \quad L_{SP}^{N\prime} \qquad L_{SG}^N \quad \overset{\cdot}{\rightarrow} \quad L_{SG}^{N\prime} \qquad L_{SP}^N \quad \overset{\cdot}{\leftrightarrow} \quad L_{SG}^N$$

KEY:

L	The most general notion of code.
L^B	The class of non-verbal codes.
L^V	The class of verbal codes, natural or artificial.
L^A	The class of artificial languages (e.g., programming, logic, math).
L^N	The class of natural languages.
L_S^N	The class of stylistic subcodes of L^N.
L_G^N	The class of graphic realizations of L^N.
L_P^N	The class of phonetic (oral) realizations of L^N.

From Ludskanov (1975:7)

Fig. 1

semiotic approach is information theory. That it may not necessarily be the best direction for us to follow (information theory, that is) is evidenced by failure of computers to prove themselves to be of greater value to a human translator than just a group of sophisticated and fast-working electronic devices usable only as aids (cf. Rubenstein, 1974: 2712). As we have mentioned earlier, the problem may actually be due more to man's failure to provide appropriate software, so it may develop in time that a semiotic framework for translation could bring the computer back into the game.

One aspect of Ludskanov's matrix, however, seems to qualify it as a 'semiolinguistic' rather than 'semiotic' (the notion of 'semiolinguistic' exchange of messages is discussed further in this paper).

The interpreter works in ways distinctly different from those of the translator. The latter, as was mentioned earlier, usually works without haste, and he is not pressed by the situation to complete his task in one fell swoop. He may do it in a discontinuous way, shelving the text for a while and returning to it at will. Works of literary art sometimes call for years of effort (the Polish version of Joyce's *Ulysses* took the translator more than ten years to complete).

The interpreter, on the other hand, has "less time than no time at all," as a Thurberian character would say. There are two basic techniques of interpreting: *consecutive* and *simultaneous*. Mixed techniques are used also in *ad hoc* situations. Detailed descriptions of each technique can be found in Seleskovitch (1968), but for our present purposes let us outline them in very broad terms.

In the course of the consecutive process the interpreter becomes a link between the parties involved, that is, speakers of at least two mutually unintelligible languages who intend to exchange oral messages. The interpreter listens to a message, or a fragment of it, in the SL, and when the speaker stops his delivery the interpreter renders the message in the TL. The length of text that the interpreter takes in at a time depends on his skill, primarily on the efficiency of his memory. The longer his memory span the fewer the intervals in the exchange of messages. The famed interpreters of the former League of Nations are described as being able to take in up to thirty minutes or more of text at one time. Since individuals with such unique memories are not numerous, a special notation for consecutive interpreters came into use.

The interpreters' notation is designed to register the order of ideas in a given passage of the message. The actual wording is much less important; therefore shorthand systems are not used extensively although some elements of shorthand constitute a part of the interpreter's notation. Abbreviation, acronyms, and *ideographic* signs are combined into one. Examples of such notations are given by Rozan (1965), Hoof (1963), Min'iar-Beloruchev (1969). The Russian system, as given by Beloruchev, relies to a large extent on signs or modification of signs used in topographical cartography: ✗ battle, fighting, war; ⌐ factory, industry, etc.; ◐ a bilateral conference; ♂ riots, revolution, etc., to give only a small sample; ↤ marks the past; ↦ the future, and ⊥ stands for now, present time. By recording a string of abbreviations, acronyms, and ideographic signs the interpreter helps his memory to recreate the message in the TL keeping the same "train of thought," so to speak. His command of the two languages involved should provide him the comfort of doing without the recording of the actual words used by the speaker. It must be stressed that since spoken messages are wrapped in a bundle of accompanying non-verbal messages, the interpreter has a difficult decision to make each time he does his job: how much of the non-verbal message should he convey? Ideally, of course, he should be as neutral or nonpartisan as possible since his sole preoccupation should be to provide the closest possible equivalent of the SL material without unnecessary embellishments or reductions. This is simply not feasible because as a human being he utters his text enveloped in what has come to be known as 'paralinguistic' or 'prosodic' features, and his face, for example, may convey certain quite unintended signals. Should he identify himself with the speaker and his style of delivery? Should he perform with as much detachment as possible? Such problems pertain to non-verbal codes more than to anything else. Admittedly, interpreters working even at the highest political levels are no more than human devices for accomplishing the necessary exchange of messages. Quite often, if not regularly, they hide behind the personalities they are working for at the moment, so that a picture of two heads of state, for instance, may show the two politicians smiling broadly at each other and giving the impression that their contact is as personal as can be. Aspects of such situations have received a very interesting treatment by Goffman (1966).

It is the work of the consecutive interpreter and the notation serving him as a mnemonic device that deserve an extensive semiotic analysis. A study of the existent notations and the working out of a single international system of ideographic notation offer an excellent opportunity for a monographic paper at least.

The work of a simultaneous interpreter is considerably different. He has no contact with the orator other than through a set of earphones. He has a very limited possibility of influencing the delivery of a given speech. More often than not, if the conference hall is equipped properly, the speakers do not even know and cannot see the interpreters in their booths. In some cases the interpreter can see the speaker only via closed-circuit television, and the speaker does not monitor the translation, so that while addressing his audience he assumes that his text is being interpreted. The simultaneous technique is relatively new in the field; it is made possible largely through the latest developments in electronics, such as miniaturization by the introduction of integrated circuits. Not only is the number of interpreters capable of performing this way limited but also many speakers at conferences provided with simultaneous interpreting do not quite understand the specificity of the technique. If an American whose training includes courses in public speaking, which invariably tell one to begin an address with a joke to set the mood on a positive if not friendly note, happens to be the first speaker of the day, when neither the audience nor the interpreters have yet "tuned in" properly, the poor orator is more often than not astonished at the listeners' different sense of humor, which forbids them to appreciate his well-chosen specimen.

The name of the technique is, of course, a nice simplification. It is hard to imagine two individuals generating simultaneously two sets of signs that would bear very·similar messages. The interpreter *implicite* follows the delivery in the SL. Now it is true that many public statements are filled with clichés or have stereotyped constructions that may help the interpreter guess what forthcoming portions of the message will contain, but he cannot always be totally sure of that. Even if typed or written texts are provided by the speaker as the graphic versions of his address the interpreter may not rely entirely on the speaker's word; during some extended public speeches the speaker may mistakenly miss a page or two of the pre-edited text, and, consequently, the interpreter who does not notice the omission in time will depart from the SL version considerably. An experienced interpreter can mend the situation, but this is not of immediate significance to the present topic.

Some features of the simultaneous technique deserve a closer semiotic look. The speaker and the listener are totally aware at the outset that their communication is accomplished through a third, invisible and often multipersonal, party. With the passing of time during a given speech, however, it is up to the interpreter to develop in the mind of the listener a notion of directness—that he is listening to the speaker himself. Though it is difficult to imagine it is nonetheless performed by some of the more gifted interpreters, and then, of course, a situation appears that is essential to all translation: If a written code, a TL code, that is, may impress itself on the reader's mind to the point that he stops thinking in terms of the SL and TL codes and only considers the TL while reading a given message, it is actually much easier for the interpreter to impress the listener in the same way since he has at his disposal the entire apparatus of vocal devices and features, which carry perhaps more emotional than cognitive values but which, nevertheless, are regarded highly as identifiers of belonging to the same culture, subculture, social subgroup, family, etc. An act of communication between the speaker and the listener(s) is accomplished by a human being (or several of them acting in a sequence) who uses electronic gadgetry, such as microphones, earphones, amplifiers, loudspeakers, batteries of pushbuttons, etc., to perform his function as a go-between for two parties using different languages. On account of his reliance on the electronic devices we may say that the ratio of masking noise, which impedes straightforward comprehension of both the SL and the TL messages, may be regarded as a more formidable obstacle than, for example, garbled handwriting or typescript.

As we have already pointed out, the time factor in this type of translation is of the utmost importance. In fact, potential interpreters unable to operate under such difficult conditions do not qualify for the job, as Johansson (1975) indirectly suggests in his concise paper: "a measure of a subject's ability to receive messages under masking noise is a good indication of overall proficiency, and . . . it might be possible to define a subject's proficiency by reference to a signal-to-noise ratio, i.e. the maximum noise level at which a subject can function efficiently." We mentioned above that several interpreters can act sequentially, translating different sections of the SL material. Instances of this type are most easily encountered at large international conferences where a single speaker, who happens to be a prominent politician, may continue single-handedly for several hours. This raises a minor but valid question: how does the switching of interpreters affect the communication? In addition, a word must be added about the practice, which is not openly discussed in the interpreters' milieu as it is regarded as a sort of disgrace, of interpreting via a "relay" system: an exotic, so to speak, language used at a conference in Europe may first be interpreted into one that is a standard conference language and then retranslated into other languages used at the given event. Such practices are certainly not supported by the statutes and policies of the International Association of Conference Interpreters (A.I.I.C., Paris) but everyday life situations often invalidate statutes. The loss of information in the course of such a "relay" process is also an interesting area for investigation. The fact that interpreters working at international conferences routinely switch every 30 to 45 minutes and that the listener is simply forced to combine his visual observations of the speaker with the vocal impressions of one or more hidden interpreters is another field for psycholinguistic and semiotic analyses. The disconnection between the originator of a sound message and his (or her) image while speaking is a standard device in literary, folk, and religious tales. The absence of the visual image combined with usually pathetic tone of the pronouncement builds a special communicational effect. Is it present in interpreting at conferences? The speakers of a given language have certain stereotype linkages built into their communicational circuitry. How does this factor affect the exchange of messages in simultaneous interpreting? This and related problems deserve systematic investigations if we want to account for the multiple aspects of translation as practiced today.

The matter of the proper combination with visual images of voice set, speech rate, and other paralinguistic or prosodic features is fundamentally important in the area of translation for the film industry. Two techniques are used with different effectiveness. The first one is that of providing frames with subtitles in the TL, leaving the entire SL phonic substance as is. This particular technique has only one interesting, from our point of view, communicational aspect. The frame makes it imperative for the translator to limit his text to a prescribed length, for where there are long passages of spoken text in the original dialogue a rendition of the complete text might cover the entire frame. The translator must decide what parts of such long utterances can be left out without hurting the verbal substance of the film.

A more complicated and hybridic operation occurs during dubbing, another technique of translating the original dialogue of the film into a TL. The peculiarity of the process lies in the need to synchronize with the lip movement of the film heroes, who, in most cases, speak their native tongues, although the film-making of the '60s and '70s introduced additional authenticity to certain sequences involving speakers of other languages (cf. scenes with German, Japanese, or Russian soldiers and officers in movies about the Second World War, to give only one example). In such instances the English version of the film is provided with appropriate subtitles. The authors of the dubbed text take into account a peculiar feature of communication: the viewer wants to see compatibility between sounds and lip movement, otherwise he immediately detects "foreignness" in the dialogue, which in turn leads to his distraction, discomfiture, and what have you, consequently ruining the job of the director. It is worth noting at this point, however, that certain categories of films tend to have a very fixed vocal–visual image, often because of the profusion of the kind: the Western, with its cowboys, mountains, colts, etc., is so strongly linked with American English that dubbing in the German "Fräulein Brown" for "Miss Brown," for example, would make the viewer feel very much ill-at-ease. This author circulated a questionnaire among a number of Polish students at Warsaw University in an attempt to determine whether dubbing was a favored technique.

Most of the answers were to the contrary: most of them stressed the "incompatibility," as the respondents called it, of scenes filmed in the American Southwest, where cowboys, Indians, and lone hunters played major roles, with dialogues in Polish; or of takes of the streets of Paris with Jean Gabin swearing in Warsaw Cockney! The students agreed, on the other hand, that films composed largely of close-ups of the actors or that rely heavily on facial gestures (e.g., *Twelve Angry Men* with Henry Fonda) do call for dubbing. In most cases they recognized the detrimental effect subtitles have on the reception of the visual signs of these movies, but they still preferred that hard way, seeing in it more authenticity and more directness. It is true also that some countries dub every film they import, but their reasons may be different, illiteracy of their audiences being only one of them, perhaps. A British translator writes about the dubbing of films in a way that certainly deserves a quotation:

> In film jargon, the Damoclean banc of the dubbing writer . . . is called *synch*. It is his insensate task to cause phonetically dissimilar dialogue to appear visually similar while still preserving the semantic and stylistic parallel between the original and the dubbed lines, the whole to form a dramatically vigorous and playable text. . . . The process is often one of trying to make the round vowels of one language look like square diphthongs of another. *The activity is a bastard offshoot of phonetics and has nothing to do with translation, except that in dubbing writing it is indissolubly linked to it, the wedding of the phonetic beast to the literary beauty* [italics mine; Rowe, 1960:117].

Another type of interpreting that presents specific difficulties is the simultaneous oral delivery of the already translated text. Jean Ure (1964) says that in such cases the interpreter must be a particularly alert person since the laughter or the applause must come to the same signal, and he quotes translations of plays read aloud by interpreters and relayed to the audience through earphones, as, for example, in the Jewish theater in Bucharest (using Yiddish). To the best knowledge of the present author, similar techniques are used in the Jewish theater in Warsaw. Ure mentions also that the Chinese theaters and opera houses project a written translation by means of a magic lantern onto a screen beside the stage, which makes it a part of the subtitling category, but technically different from that of the film industry.

There are also such rarely practiced forms of interpreting as the whispered simultaneous or consecutive, or the press agency teletype-room translation/interpreting (a fast teletyped text in the SL is immediately translated orally to a typist, who produces the typewritten TL version), and others. It was not my basic objective to discuss in detail all practiced forms of translation and interpreting, consequently, the reader interested in technicalities is referred to a diversity of papers scattered throughout the volumes of *Babel*.

An anecdotal interlude is perhaps in order here. A few years ago I was asked during a class if I saw any resemblance between Sir Alec Guinness, the actor, and a horse. Since no teacher likes to be made a fool of in front of his students I dragged on with a direct answer while forcing my mind to work furiously in search of all possible associations between a man and a horse. As well-worn phrases indicate, man likes to involve animals or their features when talking about other men. Entire populations will ascribe animalistic tendencies or characteristics to their neighbors or even to peoples from far away. With all respect to our British friends I must say that the Poles tend to see the lower jaw-bones of some Englishmen as much more pronounced than their own and, therefore, may refer to the innocent British subjects as people with 'a horse's jaw' (*końska szczęka*). I thought that the odd question stemmed from such an attitude but I found out later that it was a case of a poor translation of a film title. A Joyce Cary novel (*The Horse's Mouth*) and a film based on it had identical titles. The Polish version of the novel had a proper idiomatic translation of the title (*Z pierwszej ręki*) but the film appeared as *Koński Pysk* (A Horse's Mouth), which made many a movie-goer in Poland wonder how much equine beauty the leading man had.

Can we translate messages in Van Gogh's pictures, violin concertos, or Navajo rug designs? First, let us not confuse the relatively narrow concept of 'intersemiotic' processes introduced by Jakobson (1959) with the much broader framework of semiotics known to us today. He indicated the interaction between non-verbal signs and language in a particular way. Things such as traffic signs, for example, carry conventional messages adopted by members of a given community but if a sign turns out to be easily interpretable in more than one way attempts are made to replace it with a univocal, as it were, message. Therefore even though formally such signs are not verbal they are strictly an offshoot of language. In our understanding, the Jakobsonian 'intersemiotic' processes are not really intersemiotic since they automatically involve language. They are, for want of a better term, 'semio-linguistic' processes, as is the case with all instances when non-verbal messages are processed into verbal, regardless of whether it means vocal or graphic externalization or what we know as 'inner speech'.

A process closer to the intersemiotic exchange should embrace direct interaction of non-verbal elements, without the go-between of language. Music is perhaps the best example here. The highly subjective personal reception and internal interpretation of music does not require verbalization in any form (although one may indulge in such an activity trying to prove, for instance, that indeed there are dozens of shepherds in *The Pastoral Symphony*). The fact that music signals may by-pass the language channel and go through directly to our inner emotive and cognitive circuits makes them possess the fundamental feature of what we propose to call 'the semiotic processing', rather than 'intersemiotic' translation, transmutation, etc. Certainly we cannot 'translate' Van Gogh's powerful messages, but at the same time, while receiving them visually, we 'process' them in a number of ways, one of which can, of course, be a verbal externalization of our personal impressions and emotional reactions or an extension of our cognitive capabilities.

The semiotic framework for translation theory proposed in this paper assumed that man and animals are immersed in a sea of signals. The processing of signals starts at birth and ends with death while going on simultaneously at many levels, some of which we are familiar with and others which still escape our grasp. Semiotics offers an opportunity to work out tenets of an approach that could be accommodated interdisciplinarily. This is particularly clear in the field of translation, where so far randomness, subjectivity, and parochialism dominate.

The inevitable shortcomings of the presentation derive primarily from the absence of opinion of others working in the field. The views expressed here are no more than a brief attempt at stimulating interest in one of the fundamental activities of man and animals: the exchange of messages.

REFERENCES

Arrowsmith, William, and Shattuck, Roger, eds. 1961. *The Craft and Context of Translation*. Austin: University of Texas Press.

Cary, E. 1956. *La Traduction dans le monde moderne*. Geneva: Georg et Cie.

Catford, J. C. 1965. *A Linguistic Theory of Translation*. London: Oxford University Press.

Darmstadter, H. M. 1967. *W. V. O. Quine on Translation*. Ph.D. diss., Princeton University. Ann Arbor, Mich.: University Microfilms, Inc.

Goffman, E. 1963. *Behavior in Public Places*. Glencoe, Ill.: Free Press.

Herbert, J. 1965. *Manuel de l'Interprète*. Geneva: Georg et Cie.

van Hoof, H. 1963. *Théorie et pratique de l'interprétation*. Munich.

Jakobson, R. 1959. In *On Translation*, R. A. Brower, ed. Cambridge: Harvard University Press, pp.232–39.

Johansson, S. 1975. "Testing Listening Comprehension by Variable Speech Control (VSC). A Research Proposal." Lund University.

Lieberman, W. 1975. *On the Origins of Speech*. Chicago: Chicago University Press.

Ludskanov, A. 1975. "A Semiotic Approach to the Theory of Translation." *Language Sciences* 35 (April):5–8.

Marshack, J. 1972. *The Roots of Civilization: The Cognitive Beginnings of Man's First Art, Symbol, and Notation*. New York: McGraw-Hill.

Min'iar-Beloruchev, R. K. 1969. *Posobije po ustnomu p'erevodu*. Moscow.

Newmark, P. 1973. "Twenty-Three Restricted Rules of Translation." *The Incorporated Linguist* 12 (1):9–15.

Nida, E. 1964. *Toward a Science of Translating*. Leiden: Brill.

Nida, E., and Taber, Charles. 1969. *The Theory and Practice of Translation*. Leiden: Brill.

Quine, W. V. O. 1960. *Word and Object*. Cambridge: M.I.T. Press.

Rowe, T. L. 1960. "The English Dubbing Text." *Babel* VI (3):116–20.

Rozan, F. 1965. *La Prise de notes en interprétation consécutive*. Geneva: Georg et Cie.

Rubenstein, H. 1974. "Computer Applications." In *Current Trends in Linguistics*, vol. 12, part IV, T. A. Sebeok, ed. The Hague: Mouton.

Savory, T. 1957. *The Art of Translation*. London: Jonathan Cape.

Searle, J. R. 1969. *Speech Acts*. Cambridge: Cambridge University Press.

Sebeok, T. A. 1975. "Six Species of Signs: Some Propositions and Strictures." *Semiotica* 13 (3):233–60.

Seleskovitch, D. 1968. *L'Interprète dans les conférences internationales*. Paris: Minard.

Steiner, G. 1975. *After Babel*. London: Oxford University Press.

Ure, Jean. 1964. "Types of Translation and Translatability." *Babel* X (1):5–11.

Wierzbicka, A. 1975. "Translatability and Semantic Primitives." Paper presented at "Meaning in Anthropology and Linguistics" seminar, Australian National University. A reference to the paper is made in *Language Sciences* 40 (April 1976):25.

Winter, W. 1961. "The Impossibilities of Translation." In *The Craft and Context of Translation*, William Arrowsmith and Roger Shattuck, eds. Austin: University of Texas Press.

INDEX OF NAMES

Geertz, Clifford 201, 213, 218, 221, 222, 226, 227, 230, 234, 235, 236, 242, 243
Gelb, Jay J. 75
Glenville, John J. 30
Goffman, Erving viii, 137, 154, 275, 282
Going, Meridith 127, 154
Goldin-Meadow, Susan 168, 169, 171
Goldstein, Alvin G. 127, 153
Gombrich, Ernst H. 73, 75
Gomperz, Theodor 40
Goodenough, William H. 206, 213, 226
Goodman, Nelson 73, 75
Goodman, Richard M. 139, 154
Goody, Jack 233, 243, 260
Gorlin, Robert J. 139, 154
Goudge, Thomas A. 68
Grant, Ewan C. 152, 154
Gray, Thomas 61
Green, Steven 113, 116, 123
Greenberg, Joseph H. 228, 230
Greenlee, Douglas 3, 28, 171
Greimas, Algirdas J. 230, 246, 256
Griffin, Donald R. 113, 114, 123
Guinness, Sir Alec 280
Gumperz, John J. 230
Guthrie, R. Dale 151, 154
Guzzo, Augusto 28

Habermas, Jurgen 228
Hale, Kenneth L. 230
Hall, Edward T. 74, 75
Halliday, Michael 270
Hamilton, Sir William 60, 65, 67, 69
Hardwick, Charles S. 32, 63, 68
Harlow, Harry F. 16, 17, 28
Harman, Gilbert G. 228
Harris, Edith D. 69
Harris, Paul 200
Harris, Richard M. 156
Harris, William T. 69
Hartshorne, Charles 30, 32, 59
Haviland, Jeannette M. 138, 149, 154
Hayes, Alfred S. 226
Hayes, Catherine 170
Hayes, Keith 170
Head, Henry 179
Hedge, Levi 61
Hegel, Georg Wilhelm Friedrich 66, 95
Heidegger, Martin 105
Heider, Carl 141, 151
Henderson, Thomas S.T. 165, 171
Herbert, Jean 268, 282
Herculano de Carvalho, José G. 3, 19, 23, 25, 29
Hess, Eckhard H. 123, 137, 143, 154

Hewes, Gordon W. 169, 171
Hilgard, Julius E. 66
Hinde, Robert A. 123
Hippocrates 75
Hiż, Henry viii
Hitchcock, Alfred viii
Hjelmslev, Louis 81, 103, 109
Hobbes, Thomas 10, 57, 63
Hochberg, Julian E. 132, 154
Hockett, Charles 2, 18, 29
Hoijer, Harry 230
Hollenhorst, G. Donald 30
Holmes, Sherlock 219, 220
Holt, Emmet L., Jr. 189, 190, 200
Hoof, Henri van 274, 282
Hopkins, Thomas J. 239, 240, 243
Huber, Ernst 129, 154
Hume, David 10, 62, 84
Humphries, David A. 152
Husserl, Edmund 73
Huxley, Julian S. 16, 29
Huxley, Thomas 227
Hymes, Dell 215, 226, 230

Iliffe, Alan H. 135, 154
Inkeles, Alex 190, 191, 194, 200
Izard, Carroll E. 151, 154

Jakobson, Roman viii, ix, 19, 29, 74, 76, 81, 82, 90, 92, 95, 97, 99, 103, 110, 210, 212, 213, 215, 219, 222, 223, 225, 230, 267, 270, 272, 280, 282
James, William 49, 50, 54, 57, 70, 221, 224
Jewell, Peter A. 123
Johansson, Stig 277, 282
John of St. Thomas 29
Johnson, Harold G. 152, 154
Jordan, I. King 170
Jordan, Pascual 104, 110
Jordan, Roy U. 131, 154
Joseph, Michael 138, 154
Jourdain, Philip E.B. 55
Joyce, James 87, 274

Kant, Immanuel 10, 24, 34, 65
Kaplan, Bernard 227
Karp, Ivan 244, 256, 257
Katz, Martin M. 153
Katz, Steven 153, 200
Kavanagh, James F. 172
Keesing, Roger M. 226
Kehler, James H. 49
Kempe, Alfred B. 44, 45